Peace

MORE THAN AN THAN AN END TO WAR

Peace

MORE THAN AN END TO WAR

*Selections from the writings of
Bahá'u'lláh, the Báb,
'Abdu'l-Bahá,
Shoghi Effendi,
and the
Universal House of Justice*

compiled by
TERRILL G. HAYES
RICHARD A. HILL
ANNE MARIE SCHEFFER
ANNE G. ATKINSON
BETTY J. FISHER

BAHÁ'Í PUBLISHING TRUST
WILMETTE, ILLINOIS

Bahá'í Publishing Trust, Wilmette, Illinois 60091

Library of Congress Cataloging-in-Publication Data

Peace—more than an end to war.

    Bibliography: p.
    Includes index.
    1. Peace—Religious aspects—Bahai Faith.
2. Bahai Faith—Doctrines.   I. Hayes, Terrill G.,
1948-   II. Bahá'í Publishing Trust.
BP370.P43   1986   297'.8917873   86-3354
ISBN 0-87743-203-1
ISBN 0-87743-204-X (pbk.)

The publisher gratefully acknowledges the work of Anne Marie
Scheffer, whose research in many volumes of the Bahá'í writings on
numerous aspects of peace provided the basis for the compilation; of
Terrill Hayes and Richard Hill, who devoted many selfless hours to
shaping the manuscript for publication; of Dr. Betty J. Fisher, Anne
Atkinson, and Larry Bucknell, who lent their critical talents as a
sounding board; of the Research Department of the Universal House of
Justice for answering numerous questions; of Dr. John Walbridge and
Dr. Manouchehr Derakhshani, who resolved questions about Persian
and Arabic terms; of Dr. Peter Khan, who took time from a hectic
schedule to provide an eloquent foreword; of Diane Iverson and Kim
Meilicke, who devoted many hours to keyboarding the manuscript; and
of Frances Worthington, who patiently indexed the book. Dr. Firuz
Kazemzadeh's essay on the Bahá'í Faith is reprinted with permission
from *Encyclopædia Britannica,* 15th edition, © 1983 by Encyclopædia
Britannica, Inc. House style for the transliteration of Persian and Arabic
words has been used.

Design by John Solarz

Contents

FOREWORD / **ix**

Part One
A FRAMEWORK FOR PEACE

1 THE PROMISE OF WORLD PEACE / **3**

Preamble / **3**
Part I / **6**
Part II / **10**
Part III / **15**
Part IV / **19**

Part Two
THE PROMISE AND THE CHALLENGE

2 FROM ADOLESCENCE TO ADULTHOOD: CIVILIZATION COMES OF AGE / **25**

Understanding the Condition of Today's World / **25**
   The Roots of War and Strife / **25**
   The Pernicious Effects of a Material Civilization / **31**
Beyond Selfishness and Aggression: Releasing Forces for Social Reconstruction / **36**
Establishing a Single Social Order: The Goal of Human Evolution / **41**

3 IDENTIFYING THE SPIRITUAL ROOTS OF PEACE / **50**

The Unique Endowments of the Human Spirit / **50**
   The Source of Civilization and Prosperity / **50**
   The Inclination toward Transcendence / **54**
Understanding the Vital Role of Religion / **57**

*The Founders of Religion: Instruments for Galvanizing
Humanity's Spiritual and Social Progress* / **57**
*Religion: The Greatest Means for Ensuring
Morality and Order* / **62**
Irreligion: The Source of Selfishness and Aggression / **67**
Recognizing the Roots of Irreligion / **73**
    Conflicting Interpretations of Religious Leaders / **73**
    Artificial Barriers between Religion, Reason, and Science / **76**
    Human Imagination and Misunderstanding / **81**
Viewing the Founders of Religion as Agents of
One Civilizing Process / **86**
Abandoning Obsolete Doctrines through an Unbiased
Search for Truth / **93**

4 PREPARING THE PATH TO WORLD ORDER / **98**
Inducing the Will to Act / **98**
Eliminating Barriers to Peace / **102**
    Racism / **102**
    Extremes of Wealth and Poverty / **109**
        Preventing Economic Disparity / **109**
        Fostering Altruism and Philanthropy / **114**
    Unbridled Nationalism / **118**
    Religious Strife / **122**
    Denial of the Equality of Men and Women / **130**
    Ignorance and Lack of Education / **139**
    Multiplicity of Languages / **148**
Evoking Moral Attitudes Conducive to Enduring Peace / **151**
    *Material Achievements and Spiritual Perfections:
    Two Wings of Progress* / **151**
    The Power of a Moral Character / **157**

5 CONSTRUCTING A PEACEFUL AND GLOBAL
CIVILIZATION / **161**
Recognizing the Oneness of Humanity:
The Fundamental Prerequisite / **161**
Abandoning All Forms of Prejudice / **168**
Reducing the World's Armaments / **174**

Convoking an Assembly to Establish a Global
Union of Nations / **180**
Governing the Affairs of Humanity / **186**
  The Standard of Justice / **186**
  The Qualities of Statesmanship / **191**
  The Process of Consultation / **194**
  A System of World Government / **199**

6 SECURING THE BASIS OF HUMAN HAPPINESS / **207**

Achieving the Ultimate Goal: Humanity's Intrinsic Oneness / **207**
  Acknowledging the Spiritual Foundation of Unity / **207**
  Forging Enduring Bonds of Unity / **212**
Studying a Working Model of Unity and Diversity / **216**
  Aspects of Bahá'í Character / **216**
  Ideal Characteristics of the Bahá'í Community / **221**
Acknowledging the God-Given Capacity for
Human Progress / **226**
  Humanity's Potential for Spiritual Excellence / **226**
  *Knowing and Loving God: The Foundation of
  Human Well-Being and Development* / **229**
  Qualities That Will Advance Civilization / **233**
Transforming Civilization through the Power
of Divine Sovereignty / **237**
  The Revelation of Bahá'u'lláh / **237**
  The Sacrifice of Bahá'u'lláh for Establishing Peace / **242**
  The Promise of Peace / **247**

Part Three
PRAYERS FOR ACHIEVING PEACE

7 PRAYERS FOR PEACE / **255**

APPENDIX: *THE BAHÁ'Í FAITH* / **265**
GLOSSARY / **275**
REFERENCES / **279**
BIBLIOGRAPHY / **285**
INDEX / **289**

Foreword

IN THE midst of the chaos of our time a passionate desire for peace is growing throughout the world. Not only are nations yearning for peace and working to avert the destruction that world conflict would bring, but people are searching for the means to achieve harmonious relationships among the diverse and dissonant elements of society—racial, religious, cultural, and ideological. Moreover, individuals are attempting to establish cohesive family relationships and to prepare for enduring, fulfilling marriages, both of which are further signs of the quest for peace and stability.

Conditions for making world peace possible do, in fact, now exist. Humankind has the ability to transmit information efficiently over long distances, enabling widely scattered peoples to interact with increasing frequency and accessibility. Scientific accomplishments in agriculture, automation, and electronics allow individuals to have more time to enrich their spiritual lives and develop their social relationships. Advances in the understanding of human psychology provide greater insights into how to make such relationships healthy. But despite the achievements benefiting present-day society, people still find it difficult to behave in ways that are indispensable to an enduring peace.

Now the Universal House of Justice, the supreme governing and legislative body of the Bahá'í Faith, has addressed to the peoples of the world a statement inviting them to view the abolition of war as more than the banning of weapons and the signing of protocols and treaties and to consider that a new world order can be fostered by all peoples' seeing themselves as members of one universal family. The statement further asks them to put aside their belief that conflict and aggression

are intrinsic to human nature, to overcome the paralysis of
will that prevents them from finding solutions to the problems
facing them, and to support the convocation of an international assemblage of nations to determine "such ways and means
as will lay the foundations of the world's Great Peace." This
statement forms part one of the present volume. Part two
elaborates on the themes in the statement, drawing exclusively upon Bahá'í texts in order to make this relatively unknown
body of material available to a wider public. Part three contains a selection of Bahá'í prayers for achieving world peace.

The worldwide Bahá'í community, represented in over
one hundred thousand cities, towns, and villages around the
planet, demonstrates the capacity of Bahá'í principles to create
a dynamic unity among peoples who were hitherto alienated
or antagonistic. Following the principles laid down in the
Bahá'í writings, Bahá'ís attach great importance to consultative decision making and cooperative action and assign orga-
nizational responsibility to Assemblies, local and national,
which are elected by universal suffrage and secret ballot.
Whether serving as Assembly members or in other capacities,
Bahá'ís can practice interacting harmoniously and creatively
with people of all ages, cultures, races, and socioeconomic
and educational backgrounds. They encourage open-minded
attitudes toward modern scientific discoveries and a commitment to innovation—characteristics antithetical to those embraced by religious institutions over much of recorded history.
The distinction of the Bahá'ís is illustrated by their whole-
hearted endorsement of the principle of the equality of the
sexes enunciated by Bahá'u'lláh, the Founder of the Bahá'í
Faith, in the middle of the nineteenth century. This principle
is reflected in the composition of Bahá'í social institutions; in
the emphasis placed on the education of females and their full
participation in sciences, arts, and industry; and in the pre-
scription of means for strengthening marriage and the family.
Bahá'ís see a direct connection between the emancipation of
women and the achievement of world peace and envisage that
"when women participate fully and equally in the affairs of

the world, when they enter confidently and capably the great arena of laws and politics, war will cease; for woman will be the obstacle and hindrance to it."

Bahá'ís see human life as evolutionary and perceive the rise and fall of civilizations as part of an overall progression from families and tribes to city-states and nations. They see the turbulence of our time as evidence of a transition from sovereign national states to a world commonwealth that will establish and preserve peace, while safeguarding personal freedom and individual initiative. World peace, Bahá'ís believe, is inevitable, and they are confident that people of vision and motivation will guide mankind to its glorious destiny.

The Bahá'í approach to the achievement of peace calls for fundamental changes in all aspects of behavior—individual, interpersonal, corporate, and international—based upon the belief that human beings have an innate capacity for harmony and cooperation, which, unfortunately, has been suppressed by religious fanaticism and the spread of divisive ideologies. The Bahá'í teachings prescribe education for world citizenship, the fostering of effective communication, and the eradication of prejudice. They advocate social reconstruction and administration based on the principle of the oneness of mankind. Each of these behavioral changes supports the others, and all are bases for the Bahá'í commitment to encouraging the convocation of an international meeting of nations. According to 'Abdu'l-Bahá, the son and appointed successor of Bahá'u'lláh, such a meeting "must conclude a binding treaty" in which "the limits and frontiers of each and every nation should be clearly fixed, the principles underlying the relations of governments towards one another definitely laid down, and all international agreements and obligations ascertained."

The bulk of *Peace: More Than an End to War* is composed of authoritative statements from the successive heads of the Bahá'í Faith who preceded the Universal House of Justice—Bahá'u'lláh, 'Abdu'l-Bahá, and Shoghi Effendi. Although these statements differ markedly in style, the fundamental principles are the same, thus producing a unity of theme.

Several of the passages written by Bahá'u'lláh are taken from a series of letters He wrote between 1867 and 1873 to the rulers of the principal nations of Europe and the Middle East and to the world's religious leaders. These documents are remarkable in their anticipation of conditions that would evolve in the twentieth century and for the clear delineation of the means for world peace and unity.

In many instances the statements of 'Abdu'l-Bahá are taken from talks He delivered during an arduous lecture tour of Europe and North America between August 1911 and June 1913, during which time He warned of imminent world war and the forces of social dislocation that such a conflict would unleash and elaborated Bahá'u'lláh's principles of global concord. The extracts from the writings of Shoghi Effendi are taken mainly from a series of essays written to the Bahá'ís in the Western world on the theme of world order. In these writings he analyzed social conditions and trends and elucidated the means by which the Bahá'í teachings remove the barriers to unity.

The Universal House of Justice issued its statement on world peace at the beginning of a year the United Nations has designated as the International Year of Peace. But the call embodied in the statement of the House of Justice transcends a single year, or even a single decade. It reaches out to a future time, beyond the attainment of the political unification of the world, when the diverse elements of mankind will become unified in one universal family and will liberate the human spirit to produce a world civilization of dazzling splendor. The goal toward which Bahá'ís are laboring surpasses disarmament and the pacification of hitherto discordant peoples; rather, it is a creative fellowship designed to help produce a social order in which all humankind will find fulfillment and self-expression.

At this transitional period in history there can surely be no more fitting goal that people of goodwill can pursue.

PETER KHAN

Part One

A
FRAMEWORK
FOR
PEACE

Chapter 1
The Promise of World Peace

*A Statement of the Universal
House of Justice*   October 1985

To the Peoples of the World:

THE Great Peace towards which people of
goodwill throughout the centuries have inclined their hearts,
of which seers and poets for countless generations have expressed their vision, and for which from age to age the sacred
scriptures of mankind have constantly held the promise, is
now at long last within the reach of the nations. For the first
time in history it is possible for everyone to view the entire
planet, with all its myriad diversified peoples, in one perspective. World peace is not only possible but inevitable. It is the
next stage in the evolution of this planet—in the words of one
great thinker, "the planetization of mankind."

Whether peace is to be reached only after unimaginable
horrors precipitated by humanity's stubborn clinging to old
patterns of behavior, or is to be embraced now by an act of
consultative will, is the choice before all who inhabit the
earth. At this critical juncture when the intractable problems
confronting nations have been fused into one common concern for the whole world, failure to stem the tide of conflict
and disorder would be unconscionably irresponsible.

Among the favorable signs are the steadily growing
strength of the steps towards world order taken initially near
the beginning of this century in the creation of the League of
Nations, succeeded by the more broadly based United Nations
Organization; the achievement since the Second World War of
independence by the majority of all the nations on earth,
indicating the completion of the process of nation building,
and the involvement of these fledgling nations with older ones
in matters of mutual concern; the consequent vast increase in
cooperation among hitherto isolated and antagonistic peoples

and groups in international undertakings in the scientific, educational, legal, economic and cultural fields; the rise in recent decades of an unprecedented number of international humanitarian organizations; the spread of women's and youth movements calling for an end to war; and the spontaneous spawning of widening networks of ordinary people seeking understanding through personal communication.

The scientific and technological advances occurring in this unusually blessed century portend a great surge forward in the social evolution of the planet, and indicate the means by which the practical problems of humanity may be solved. They provide, indeed, the very means for the administration of the complex life of a united world. Yet barriers persist. Doubts, misconceptions, prejudices, suspicions and narrow self-interest beset nations and peoples in their relations one to another.

It is out of a deep sense of spiritual and moral duty that we are impelled at this opportune moment to invite your attention to the penetrating insights first communicated to the rulers of mankind more than a century ago by Bahá'u'lláh, Founder of the Bahá'í Faith, of which we are the Trustees.

"The winds of despair," Bahá'u'lláh wrote, "are, alas, blowing from every direction, and the strife that divides and afflicts the human race is daily increasing. The signs of impending convulsions and chaos can now be discerned, inasmuch as the prevailing order appears to be lamentably defective." This prophetic judgment has been amply confirmed by the common experience of humanity. Flaws in the prevailing order are conspicuous in the inability of sovereign states organized as United Nations to exorcise the specter of war, the threatened collapse of the international economic order, the spread of anarchy and terrorism, and the intense suffering which these and other afflictions are causing to increasing millions. Indeed, so much have aggression and conflict come to characterize our social, economic and religious systems, that many have succumbed to the view that such behavior is intrinsic to human nature and therefore ineradicable.

With the entrenchment of this view, a paralyzing contradiction has developed in human affairs. On the one hand, people of all nations proclaim not only their readiness but their longing for peace and harmony, for an end to the harrowing apprehensions tormenting their daily lives. On the other, uncritical assent is given to the proposition that human beings are incorrigibly selfish and aggressive and thus incapable of erecting a social system at once progressive and peaceful, dynamic and harmonious, a system giving free play to individual creativity and initiative but based on cooperation and reciprocity.

As the need for peace becomes more urgent, this fundamental contradiction, which hinders its realization, demands a reassessment of the assumptions upon which the commonly held view of mankind's historical predicament is based. Dispassionately examined, the evidence reveals that such conduct, far from expressing man's true self, represents a distortion of the human spirit. Satisfaction on this point will enable all people to set in motion constructive social forces which, because they are consistent with human nature, will encourage harmony and cooperation instead of war and conflict.

To choose such a course is not to deny humanity's past but to understand it. The Bahá'í Faith regards the current world confusion and calamitous condition in human affairs as a natural phase in an organic process leading ultimately and irresistibly to the unification of the human race in a single social order whose boundaries are those of the planet. The human race, as a distinct, organic unit, has passed through evolutionary stages analogous to the stages of infancy and childhood in the lives of its individual members, and is now in the culminating period of its turbulent adolescence approaching its long-awaited coming of age.

A candid acknowledgment that prejudice, war and exploitation have been the expression of immature stages in a vast historical process and that the human race is today experiencing the unavoidable tumult which marks its collective coming of age is not a reason for despair but a prerequisite to undertaking the stupendous enterprise of building a peaceful world. That such an enterprise is possible, that the necessary constructive forces do exist, that unifying social structures can be erected, is the theme we urge you to examine.

Whatever suffering and turmoil the years immediately ahead may hold, however dark the immediate circumstances, the Bahá'í community believes that humanity can confront this supreme trial with confidence in its ultimate outcome. Far from signalizing the end of civilization, the convulsive changes towards which humanity is being ever more rapidly impelled will serve to release the "potentialities inherent in the station of man" and reveal "the full measure of his destiny on earth, the innate excellence of his reality."

I

THE endowments which distinguish the human race from all other forms of life are summed up in what is known as the human spirit; the mind is its essential quality. These endowments have enabled humanity to build civilizations and to prosper materially. But such accomplishments alone have never satisfied the human spirit, whose mysterious nature inclines it towards transcendence, a reaching towards an invisible realm, towards the ultimate reality, that unknowable essence of essences called God. The religions brought to mankind by a succession of spiritual luminaries have been the primary link between humanity and that ultimate reality, and have galvanized and refined mankind's capacity to achieve spiritual success together with social progress.

No serious attempt to set human affairs aright, to achieve world peace, can ignore religion. Man's perception and practice of it are largely the stuff of history. An eminent historian described religion as a "faculty of human nature." That the perversion of this faculty has contributed to much of the confusion in society and the conflicts in and between individuals can hardly be denied. But neither can any fair-minded observer discount the preponderating influence exerted by religion on the vital expressions of civilization. Furthermore, its indispensability to social order has repeatedly been demonstrated by its direct effect on laws and morality.

Writing of religion as a social force, Bahá'u'lláh said: "Religion is the greatest of all means for the establishment of order in the world and for the peaceful contentment of all that dwell therein." Referring to the eclipse or corruption of religion, he wrote: "Should the lamp of religion be obscured, chaos and confusion will ensue, and the lights of fairness, of justice, of tranquillity and peace cease to shine." In an enumeration of such consequences the Bahá'í writings point out that the "perversion of human nature, the degradation of human conduct, the corruption and dissolution of human institutions, reveal themselves, under such circumstances, in their worst and most revolting aspects. Human character is debased, confidence is shaken, the nerves of discipline are relaxed, the voice of human conscience is stilled, the sense of decency and shame is obscured, conceptions of duty, of solidarity, of reciprocity and loyalty are distorted, and the very feeling of peacefulness, of joy and of hope is gradually extinguished."

If, therefore, humanity has come to a point of paralyzing conflict it must look to itself, to its own negligence, to the siren voices to which it has listened, for the source of the misunderstandings and confusion perpetrated in the name of religion. Those who have held blindly and selfishly to their particular orthodoxies, who have imposed on their votaries erroneous and conflicting interpretations of the pronouncements of the Prophets of God, bear heavy responsibility for this confusion—a confusion compounded by the artificial barriers erected between faith and reason, science and religion. For from a fair-minded examination of the actual utterances of the Founders of the great religions, and of the social milieus in which they were obliged to carry out their missions, there is nothing to support the contentions and prejudices deranging the religious communities of mankind and therefore all human affairs.

The teaching that we should treat others as we ourselves would wish to be treated, an ethic variously repeated in all the great religions, lends force to this latter observation in two particular respects: it sums up the moral attitude, the peace-inducing aspect, extending through these religions irrespective of their place or time of origin; it also signifies an aspect of unity which is their essential virtue, a virtue mankind in its disjointed view of history has failed to appreciate.

Had humanity seen the Educators of its collective childhood in their true character, as agents of one civilizing process, it would no doubt have reaped incalculably greater benefits from the cumulative effects of their successive missions. This, alas, it failed to do.

The resurgence of fanatical religious fervor occurring in many lands cannot be regarded as more than a dying convulsion. The very nature of the violent and disruptive phenomena associated with it testifies to the spiritual bankruptcy it represents. Indeed, one of the strangest and saddest features of the current outbreak of religious fanaticism is the extent to which, in each case, it is undermining not only the spiritual values which are conducive to the unity of mankind but also those unique moral victories won by the particular religion it purports to serve.

However vital a force religion has been in the history of mankind, and however dramatic the current resurgence of militant religious fanaticism, religion and religious institutions have, for many decades, been viewed by increasing numbers of people as irrelevant to the major concerns of the modern world. In its place they have turned either to the hedonistic pursuit of material satisfactions or to the following of man-made ideologies designed to rescue society from the evident evils under which it groans. All too many of these ideologies, alas, instead of embracing the concept of the oneness of mankind and promoting the increase of concord among different peoples, have tended to deify the state, to subordinate the rest of mankind to one nation, race or class, to attempt to suppress all discussion and interchange of ideas, or to callously abandon starving millions to the operations of a market system that all too clearly is aggravating the plight of the majority of mankind, while enabling small sections to live in a condition of affluence scarcely dreamed of by our forebears.

How tragic is the record of the substitute faiths that the worldly wise of our age have created. In the massive disillusionment of entire populations who have been taught to worship at their altars can be read history's irreversible verdict on their value. The fruits these doctrines have produced after decades of an increasingly unrestrained exercise of power by those who owe their ascendancy in human affairs to them, are the social and economic ills that blight every region of our world in the closing years of the twentieth century. Underlying all these outward afflictions is the spiritual damage reflected in the apathy that has gripped the mass of the peoples of all nations and by the extinction of hope in the hearts of deprived and anguished millions.

The time has come when those who preach the dogmas of materialism, whether of the east or the west, whether of capitalism or socialism, must give account of the moral stewardship they have presumed to exercise. Where is the "new world" promised by these ideologies? Where is the international peace to whose ideals they proclaim their devotion? Where are the breakthroughs into new realms of cultural achievement produced by the aggrandizement of this race, of that nation or of a particular class? Why is the vast majority of the world's peoples sinking ever deeper into hunger and wretchedness when wealth on a scale undreamed of by the Pharaohs, the Caesars, or even the imperialist powers of the nineteenth century is at the disposal of the present arbiters of human affairs?

Most particularly, it is in the glorification of material pursuits, at once the progenitor and common feature of all such ideologies, that we find the roots which nourish the falsehood that human beings are incorrigibly selfish and aggressive. It is here that the ground must be cleared for the building of a new world fit for our descendants.

That materialistic ideals have, in the light of experience, failed to satisfy the needs of mankind calls for an honest acknowledgment that a fresh effort must now be made to find the solutions to the agonizing problems of the planet. The intolerable conditions pervading society bespeak a common failure of all, a circumstance which tends to incite rather than relieve the entrenchment on every side. Clearly, a common remedial effort is urgently required. It is primarily a matter of attitude. Will humanity continue in its waywardness, holding to outworn concepts and unworkable assumptions? Or will its leaders, regardless of ideology, step forth and, with a resolute will, consult together in a united search for appropriate solutions?

Those who care for the future of the human race may well ponder this advice. "If long-cherished ideals and time-honored institutions, if certain social assumptions and religious formulae have ceased to promote the welfare of the generality of mankind, if they no longer minister to the needs of a continually evolving humanity, let them be swept away and relegated to the limbo of obsolescent and forgotten doctrines. Why should these, in a world subject to the immutable law of change and decay, be exempt from the deterioration that must needs overtake every human institution? For legal standards, political and economic theories are solely designed to safeguard the interests of humanity as a whole, and not humanity to be crucified for the preservation of the integrity of any particular law or doctrine."

II

BANNING nuclear weapons, prohibiting the use of poison gases, or outlawing germ warfare will not remove the root causes of war. However important such practical measures obviously are as elements of the peace process, they are in themselves too superficial to exert enduring influence. Peoples are ingenious enough to invent yet other forms of warfare, and to use food, raw materials, finance, industrial power, ideology, and terrorism to subvert one another in an endless quest for su-

premacy and dominion. Nor can the present massive dislocation in the affairs of humanity be resolved through the settle-
ment of specific conflicts or disagreements among nations. A
genuine universal framework must be adopted.

Certainly, there is no lack of recognition by national
leaders of the worldwide character of the problem, which is
self-evident in the mounting issues that confront them daily.
And there are the accumulating studies and solutions proposed by many concerned and enlightened groups as well as
by agencies of the United Nations, to remove any possibility
of ignorance as to the challenging requirements to be met.
There is, however, a paralysis of will; and it is this that must
be carefully examined and resolutely dealt with. This paralysis
is rooted, as we have stated, in a deep-seated conviction of the
inevitable quarrelsomeness of mankind, which has led to the
reluctance to entertain the possibility of subordinating national self-interest to the requirements of world order, and in an
unwillingness to face courageously the far-reaching implications of establishing a united world authority. It is also trace-
able to the incapacity of largely ignorant and subjugated masses to articulate their desire for a new order in which they can
live in peace, harmony and prosperity with all humanity.

The tentative steps towards world order, especially since
World War II, give hopeful signs. The increasing tendency of
groups of nations to formalize relationships which enable them
to cooperate in matters of mutual interest suggests that eventually all nations could overcome this paralysis. The Association of South East Asian Nations, the Caribbean Community
and Common Market, the Central American Common Market,
the Council for Mutual Economic Assistance, the European
Communities, the League of Arab States, the Organization of
African Unity, the Organization of American States, the South
Pacific Forum—all the joint endeavors represented by such
organizations prepare the path to world order.

The increasing attention being focused on some of the
most deep-rooted problems of the planet is yet another hopeful sign. Despite the obvious shortcomings of the United Na-

tions, the more than two score declarations and conventions adopted by that organization, even where governments have not been enthusiastic in their commitment, have given ordinary people a sense of a new lease on life. The Universal Declaration of Human Rights, the Convention on the Prevention and Punishment of the Crime of Genocide, and the similar measures concerned with eliminating all forms of discrimination based on race, sex or religious belief; upholding the rights of the child; protecting all persons against being subjected to torture; eradicating hunger and malnutrition; using scientific and technological progress in the interest of peace and the benefit of mankind—all such measures, if courageously enforced and expanded, will advance the day when the specter of war will have lost its power to dominate international relations. There is no need to stress the significance of the issues addressed by these declarations and conventions. However, a few such issues, because of their immediate relevance to establishing world peace, deserve additional comment.

Racism, one of the most baneful and persistent evils, is a major barrier to peace. Its practice perpetrates too outrageous a violation of the dignity of human beings to be countenanced under any pretext. Racism retards the unfoldment of the boundless potentialities of its victims, corrupts its perpetrators, and blights human progress. Recognition of the oneness of mankind, implemented by appropriate legal measures, must be universally upheld if this problem is to be overcome.

The inordinate disparity between rich and poor, a source of acute suffering, keeps the world in a state of instability, virtually on the brink of war. Few societies have dealt effectively with this situation. The solution calls for the combined application of spiritual, moral and practical approaches. A fresh look at the problem is required, entailing consultation with experts from a wide spectrum of disciplines, devoid of economic and ideological polemics, and involving the people directly affected in the decisions that must urgently be made. It is an issue that is bound up not only with the necessity for eliminating extremes of wealth and poverty but also with those spiritual verities the understanding of which can produce a new universal attitude. Fostering such an attitude is itself a major part of the solution.

Unbridled nationalism, as distinguished from a sane and legitimate patriotism, must give way to a wider loyalty, to the love of humanity as a whole. Bahá'u'lláh's statement is: "The earth is but one country, and mankind its citizens." The concept of world citizenship is a direct result of the contraction of the world into a single neighborhood through scientific advances and of the indisputable interdependence of nations. Love of all the world's peoples does not exclude love of one's country. The advantage of the part in a world society is best served by promoting the advantage of the whole. Current international activities in various fields which nurture mutual affection and a sense of solidarity among peoples need greatly to be increased.

Religious strife, throughout history, has been the cause of innumerable wars and conflicts, a major blight to progress, and is increasingly abhorrent to the people of all faiths and no faith. Followers of all religions must be willing to face the basic questions which this strife raises, and to arrive at clear answers. How are the differences between them to be resolved, both in theory and in practice? The challenge facing the religious leaders of mankind is to contemplate, with hearts filled with the spirit of compassion and a desire for truth, the plight of humanity, and to ask themselves whether they cannot, in humility before their Almighty Creator, submerge their theological differences in a great spirit of mutual forbearance that will enable them to work together for the advancement of human understanding and peace.

The emancipation of women, the achievement of full equality between the sexes, is one of the most important, though less acknowledged prerequisites of peace. The denial of such equality perpetrates an injustice against one half of the world's population and promotes in men harmful attitudes and habits that are carried from the family to the workplace, to political life, and ultimately to international relations. There are no grounds, moral, practical, or biological, upon which such denial can be justified. Only as women are welcomed into full partnership in all fields of human endeavor will the moral and psychological climate be created in which international peace can emerge.

The cause of universal education, which has already enlisted in its service an army of dedicated people from every faith and nation, deserves the utmost support that the governments of the world can lend it. For ignorance is indisputably the principal reason for the decline and fall of peoples and the perpetuation of prejudice. No nation can achieve success unless education is accorded all its citizens. Lack of resources limits the ability of many nations to fulfill this necessity, imposing a certain ordering of priorities. The decision-making agencies involved would do well to consider giving first priority to the education of women and girls, since it is through educated mothers that the benefits of knowledge can be most effectively and rapidly diffused throughout society. In keeping with the requirements of the times, consideration should also be given to teaching the concept of world citizenship as part of the standard education of every child.

A fundamental lack of communication between peoples seriously undermines efforts towards world peace. Adopting an international auxiliary language would go far to resolving this problem and necessitates the most urgent attention.

Two points bear emphasizing in all these issues. One is that the abolition of war is not simply a matter of signing treaties and protocols; it is a complex task requiring a new level of commitment to resolving issues not customarily associated with the pursuit of peace. Based on political agreements alone, the idea of collective security is a chimera. The other point is that the primary challenge in dealing with issues of peace is to raise the context to the level of principle, as distinct from pure pragmatism. For, in essence, peace stems from an inner state supported by a spiritual or moral attitude, and it is chiefly in evoking this attitude that the possibility of enduring solutions can be found.

There are spiritual principles, or what some call human values, by which solutions can be found for every social problem. Any well-intentioned group can in a general sense devise practical solutions to its problems, but good intentions and practical knowledge are usually not enough. The essential merit of spiritual principle is that it not only presents a perspective which harmonizes with that which is immanent in human nature, it also induces an attitude, a dynamic, a will, an aspiration, which facilitate the discovery and implementation of practical measures. Leaders of governments and all in authority would be well served in their efforts to solve problems if they would first seek to identify the principles involved and then be guided by them.

III

THE primary question to be resolved is how the present world, with its entrenched pattern of conflict, can change to a world in which harmony and cooperation will prevail.

World order can be founded only on an unshakable consciousness of the oneness of mankind, a spiritual truth which all the human sciences confirm. Anthropology, physiology, psychology, recognize only one human species, albeit infinitely varied in the secondary aspects of life. Recognition of this truth requires abandonment of prejudice—prejudice of every kind—race, class, color, creed, nation, sex, degree of material civilization, everything which enables people to consider themselves superior to others.

Acceptance of the oneness of mankind is the first fundamental prerequisite for reorganization and administration of the world as one country, the home of humankind. Universal acceptance of this spiritual principle is essential to any successful attempt to establish world peace. It should therefore be universally proclaimed, taught in schools, and constantly asserted in every nation as preparation for the organic change in the structure of society which it implies.

In the Bahá'í view, recognition of the oneness of mankind "calls for no less than the reconstruction and the demilitarization of the whole civilized world—a world organically unified in all the essential aspects of its life, its political machinery, its spiritual aspiration, its trade and finance, its script and language, and yet infinite in the diversity of the national characteristics of its federated units."

Elaborating the implications of this pivotal principle, Shoghi Effendi, the Guardian of the Bahá'í Faith, commented in 1931 that: "Far from aiming at the subversion of the existing foundations of society, it seeks to broaden its basis, to remold its institutions in a manner consonant with the needs of an ever-changing world. It can conflict with no legitimate allegiances, nor can it undermine essential loyalties. Its purpose is neither to stifle the flame of a sane and intelligent patriotism in men's hearts, nor to abolish the system of national autonomy so essential if the evils of excessive centralization are to be avoided. It does not ignore, nor does it attempt to suppress, the diversity of ethnical origins, of climate, of history, of language and tradition, of thought and habit, that differentiate the peoples and nations of the world. It calls for a wider loyalty, for a larger aspiration than any that has animated the human race. It insists upon the subordination of national impulses and interests to the imperative claims of a unified world. It repudiates excessive centralization on one hand, and disclaims all attempts at uniformity on the other. Its watchword is unity in diversity. . . ."

The achievement of such ends requires several stages in the adjustment of national political attitudes, which now verge on anarchy in the absence of clearly defined laws or universally accepted and enforceable principles regulating the relationships between nations. The League of Nations, the United Nations, and the many organizations and agreements produced by them have unquestionably been helpful in attenuating some of the negative effects of international conflicts, but they have shown themselves incapable of preventing war. Indeed, there have been scores of wars since the end of the Second World War; many are yet raging.

The predominant aspects of this problem had already emerged in the nineteenth century when Bahá'u'lláh first advanced his proposals for the establishment of world peace. The principle of collective security was propounded by him in statements addressed to the rulers of the world. Shoghi Effendi commented on his meaning: "What else could these weighty words signify," he wrote, "if they did not point to the inevitable curtailment of unfettered national sovereignty as an indispensable preliminary to the formation of the future Commonwealth of all the nations of the world? Some form of a world superstate must needs be evolved, in whose favor all the nations of the world will have willingly ceded every claim to make war, certain rights to impose taxation and all rights to maintain armaments, except for purposes of maintaining internal order within their respective dominions. Such a state will have to include within its orbit an International Executive adequate to enforce supreme and unchallengeable authority on every recalcitrant member of the commonwealth; a World Parliament whose members shall be elected by the people in their respective countries and whose election shall be confirmed by their respective governments; and a Supreme Tribunal whose judgment will have a binding effect even in such cases where the parties concerned did not voluntarily agree to submit their case to its consideration.

"A world community in which all economic barriers will have been permanently demolished and the interdependence of capital and labor definitely recognized; in which the clamor of religious fanaticism and strife will have been forever stilled; in which the flame of racial animosity will have been finally extinguished; in which a single code of international law—the product of the considered judgment of the world's federated representatives—shall have as its sanction the instant and coercive intervention of the combined forces of the federated units; and finally a world community in which the fury of a capricious and militant nationalism will have been transmuted into an abiding consciousness of world citizenship—such indeed, appears, in its broadest outline, the Order anticipated by Bahá'u'lláh, an Order that shall come to be regarded as the fairest fruit of a slowly maturing age."

The implementation of these far-reaching measures was indicated by Bahá'u'lláh: "The time must come when the imperative necessity for the holding of a vast, an all-embracing assemblage of men will be universally realized. The rulers and kings of the earth must needs attend it, and, participating in its deliberations, must consider such ways and means as will lay the foundations of the world's Great Peace amongst men."

The courage, the resolution, the pure motive, the selfless love of one people for another—all the spiritual and moral qualities required for effecting this momentous step towards peace are focused on the will to act. And it is towards arousing the necessary volition that earnest consideration must be given to the reality of man, namely, his thought. To understand the relevance of this potent reality is also to appreciate the social necessity of actualizing its unique value through candid, dispassionate and cordial consultation, and of acting upon the results of this process. Bahá'u'lláh insistently drew attention to the virtues and indispensability of consultation for ordering human affairs. He said: "Consultation bestows greater awareness and transmutes conjecture into certitude. It is a shining light which, in a dark world, leads the way and guides. For everything there is and will continue to be a station of perfection and maturity. The maturity of the gift of understanding is made manifest through consultation." The very attempt to achieve peace through the consultative action he proposed can release such a salutary spirit among the peoples of the earth that no power could resist the final, triumphal outcome.

Concerning the proceedings for this world gathering, 'Abdu'l-Bahá, the son of Bahá'u'lláh and authorized interpreter of his teachings, offered these insights: "They must make the Cause of Peace the object of general consultation, and seek by every means in their power to establish a Union of the nations of the world. They must conclude a binding treaty and establish a covenant, the provisions of which shall be sound, inviolable and definite. They must proclaim it to all the world and obtain for it the sanction of all the human race. This supreme and noble undertaking—the real source of the peace and well-being of all the world—should be regarded as sacred by all that dwell on earth. All the forces of humanity must be mobilized to ensure the stability and permanence of this Most Great Covenant. In this all-embracing Pact the limits and frontiers of each and every nation should be clearly fixed, the principles underlying the relations of governments towards one another definitely laid down, and all international agreements and obligations ascertained. In like manner, the size of the armaments of every government should be strictly limited, for if the preparations for war and the military forces of any nation should be allowed to increase, they will arouse the suspicion of others. The fundamental principle underlying this solemn Pact should be so fixed that if any government later violate any one of its provisions, all the governments on earth should arise to reduce it to utter submission, nay the human race as a whole should resolve, with every power at its disposal, to destroy that government. Should this greatest of all remedies be applied to the sick body of the world, it will assuredly recover from its ills and will remain eternally safe and secure.''

The holding of this mighty convocation is long overdue.

With all the ardor of our hearts, we appeal to the leaders of all nations to seize this opportune moment and take irreversible steps to convoke this world meeting. All the forces of history impel the human race towards this act which will mark for all time the dawn of its long-awaited maturity.

Will not the United Nations, with the full support of its membership, rise to the high purposes of such a crowning event?

Let men and women, youth and children everywhere recognize the eternal merit of this imperative action for all peoples and lift up their voices in willing assent. Indeed, let it be this generation that inaugurates this glorious stage in the evolution of social life on the planet.

IV

THE source of the optimism we feel is a vision transcending the cessation of war and the creation of agencies of international cooperation. Permanent peace among nations is an essential stage, but not, Bahá'u'lláh asserts, the ultimate goal of the social development of humanity. Beyond the initial armistice forced upon the world by the fear of nuclear holocaust, beyond the political peace reluctantly entered into by suspicious rival nations, beyond pragmatic arrangements for security and coexistence, beyond even the many experiments in cooperation which these steps will make possible lies the crowning goal: the unification of all the peoples of the world in one universal family.

Disunity is a danger that the nations and peoples of the earth can no longer endure; the consequences are too terrible to contemplate, too obvious to require any demonstration. "The well-being of mankind," Bahá'u'lláh wrote more than a century ago, "its peace and security, are unattainable unless and until its unity is firmly established." In observing that "mankind is groaning, is dying to be led to unity, and to terminate its agelong martyrdom," Shoghi Effendi further commented that: "Unification of the whole of mankind is the hallmark of the stage which human society is now approaching. Unity of family, of tribe, of city-state, and nation have been successively attempted and fully established. World unity is the goal towards which a harassed humanity is striving. Nation-building has come to an end. The anarchy inherent in state sovereignty is moving towards a climax. A world, growing to maturity, must abandon this fetish, recognize the oneness and wholeness of human relationships, and establish once for all the machinery that can best incarnate this fundamental principle of its life."

All contemporary forces of change validate this view. The proofs can be discerned in the many examples already cited of the favorable signs towards world peace in current international movements and developments. The army of men and women, drawn from virtually every culture, race and nation on earth, who serve the multifarious agencies of the United Nations, represent a planetary "civil service" whose impressive accomplishments are indicative of the degree of cooperation that can be attained even under discouraging conditions. An urge towards unity, like a spiritual springtime, struggles to express itself through countless international congresses that bring together people from a vast array of disciplines. It motivates appeals for international projects involving children and youth. Indeed, it is the real source of the remarkable movement towards ecumenism by which members of historically antagonistic religions and sects seem irresistibly drawn towards one another. Together with the opposing tendency to warfare and self-aggrandizement against which it ceaselessly struggles, the drive towards world unity is one of the dominant, pervasive features of life on the planet during the closing years of the twentieth century.

The experience of the Bahá'í community may be seen as an example of this enlarging unity. It is a community of some three to four million people drawn from many nations, cultures, classes and creeds, engaged in a wide range of activities serving the spiritual, social and economic needs of the peoples of many lands. It is a single social organism, representative of the diversity of the human family, conducting its affairs through a system of commonly accepted consultative principles, and cherishing equally all the great outpourings of divine guidance in human history. Its existence is yet another convincing proof of the practicality of its Founder's vision of a united world, another evidence that humanity can live as one global society, equal to whatever challenges its coming of age may entail. If the Bahá'í experience can contribute in whatever measure to reinforcing hope in the unity of the human race, we are happy to offer it as a model for study.

In contemplating the supreme importance of the task now challenging the entire world, we bow our heads in humility before the awesome majesty of the divine Creator, Who out of His infinite love has created all humanity from the same stock; exalted the gemlike reality of man; honored it with intellect and wisdom, nobility and immortality; and conferred upon man the "unique distinction and capacity to know Him and to love Him," a capacity that "must needs be regarded as the generating impulse and the primary purpose underlying the whole of creation."

We hold firmly the conviction that all human beings have been created "to carry forward an ever-advancing civilization"; that "to act like the beasts of the field is unworthy of man"; that the virtues that befit human dignity are trustworthiness, forbearance, mercy, compassion and loving kindness towards all peoples. We reaffirm the belief that the "potentialities inherent in the station of man, the full measure of his destiny on earth, the innate excellence of his reality, must all be manifested in this promised Day of God." These are the motivations for our unshakable faith that unity and peace are the attainable goal towards which humanity is striving.

At this writing, the expectant voices of Bahá'ís can be heard despite the persecution they still endure in the land in which their Faith was born. By their example of steadfast hope, they bear witness to the belief that the imminent realization of this age-old dream of peace is now, by virtue of the transforming effects of Bahá'u'lláh's revelation, invested with the force of divine authority. Thus we convey to you not only a vision in words: we summon the power of deeds of faith and sacrifice; we convey the anxious plea of our coreligionists everywhere for peace and unity. We join with all who are the victims of aggression, all who yearn for an end to conflict and contention, all whose devotion to principles of peace and world order promotes the ennobling purposes for which humanity was called into being by an all-loving Creator.

In the earnestness of our desire to impart to you the fervor of our hope and the depth of our confidence, we cite the emphatic promise of Bahá'u'lláh: "These fruitless strifes, these ruinous wars shall pass away, and the 'Most Great Peace' shall come."　　　　　*—The Universal House of Justice*　**1**

Part Two

THE PROMISE AND THE CHALLENGE

From Adolescence to Adulthood: Civilization Comes of Age

Understanding the Condition of Today's World

The Roots of War and Strife

BEHOLD the disturbances which, for many a long year, have afflicted the earth, and the perturbation that hath seized its peoples. It hath either been ravaged by war, or tormented by sudden and unforeseen calamities. Though the world is encompassed with misery and distress, yet no man hath paused to reflect what the cause or source of that may be. . . . No two men can be found who may be said to be outwardly and inwardly united. The evidences of discord and malice are apparent everywhere, though all were made for harmony and union. —*Bahá'u'lláh* **1**

The world is wrapped in the thick darkness of open revolt and swept by a whirlwind of hate. It is the fires of malevolence that have cast up their flames to the clouds of heaven, it is a blood-drenched flood that rolleth across the plains and down the hills, and no one on the face of the earth can find any peace. —*'Abdu'l-Bahá* **2**

The world is at war and the human race is in travail and mortal combat. The dark night of hate hath taken over, and the light of good faith is blotted out. The peoples and kindreds of the earth have sharpened their claws, and are hurling themselves one against the other. It is the very foundation of the human race that is being destroyed. It is thousands of households that are vagrant and dispossessed, and every year seeth thousands upon thousands of human beings weltering in their lifeblood on dusty battlefields. The tents of life and joy are down. The generals practice their generalship, boasting of the blood they shed, competing one with the next in inciting to violence. "With this sword," saith one of them, "I beheaded a people!" And another: "I toppled a nation to the ground!" And yet another: "I brought a government down!" On such things do men pride themselves, in such do they glory! Love—righteousness—these are everywhere censured, while despised are harmony, and devotion to the truth.   —'Abdu'l-Bahá **3**

Today no state in the world is in a condition of peace or tranquillity, for security and trust have vanished from among the people. Both the governed and the governors are alike in danger.   —'Abdu'l-Bahá **4**

I wonder at the human savagery that still exists in the world! How is it possible for men to fight from morning until evening, killing each other, shedding the blood of their fellowmen: And for what object? To gain possession of a part of the earth! Even the animals, when they fight, have an immediate and more reasonable cause for their attacks! How terrible it is that men, who are of the higher kingdom, can descend to slaying and bringing misery to their fellow beings, for the possession of a tract of land!

The highest of created beings fighting to obtain the lowest form of matter, earth! Land belongs not to one people, but to all people. This earth is not man's home, but his tomb. It is for their tombs these men are fighting. There is nothing so horrible in this world as the tomb, the abode of the decaying bodies of men.

However great the conqueror, however many countries he may reduce to slavery, he is unable to retain any part of these devastated lands but one tiny portion—his tomb! If more land is required for the improvement of the condition of the people, for the spread of civilization (for the substitution of just laws for brutal customs)—surely it would be possible to acquire peaceably the necessary extension of territory.

But war is made for the satisfaction of men's ambition;

for the sake of worldly gain to the few, terrible misery is brought to numberless homes, breaking the hearts of hundreds of men and women!

How many widows mourn their husbands, how many stories of savage cruelty do we hear! How many little orphaned children are crying for their dead fathers, how many women are weeping for their slain sons!

There is nothing so heartbreaking and terrible as an outburst of human savagery!   — 'Abdu'l-Bahá **5**

For centuries and cycles humanity has been engaged in war and conflict. At one time the pretext for war has been religion, at another time patriotism, racial prejudice, national politics, territorial conquest or commercial expansion; in brief, humanity has never been at peace during the period of known history. What blood has been shed! How many fathers have mourned the loss of sons; how many sons have wept for fathers, and mothers for dear ones! Human beings have been the food and targets of the battlefield, and everywhere warfare and strife have been the theme and burden of history. Ferocity has characterized men even more than animals. The lion, tiger, bear and wolf are ferocious because of their needs. Unless they are fierce, cruel and unrelenting, they will die of starvation. The lion cannot graze; its teeth are fitted only for food of flesh. This is also true of other wild animals. Ferocity is natural to them as their means of subsistence; but human ferocity proceeds from selfishness, greed and oppression. It springs from no natural necessity. Man needlessly kills a thousand fellow creatures, becomes a hero and is glorified through centuries of posterity. A great city is destroyed in one day by a commanding general. How ignorant, how inconsistent is humankind! If a man slays another man, we brand him as a murderer and criminal and sentence him to capital punishment, but if he kills one hundred thousand men, he is a military genius, a great celebrity, a Napoleon idolized by his nation. If a man steals one dollar, he is called a thief and put into prison; if he rapes and pillages an innocent country by military invasion, he is crowned a hero. How ignorant is humankind! Ferocity does not belong to the kingdom of man. It is the province of man to confer life, not death. It behooves him to be the cause of human welfare, but inasmuch as he glories in the savagery of animalism, it is an evidence that divine civilization has not been established in human society.

— *'Abdu'l-Bahá* 6

Beset on every side by the cumulative evidences of disintegration, of turmoil and of bankruptcy, serious-minded men and women, in almost every walk of life, are beginning to doubt whether society, as it is now organized, can, through its unaided efforts, extricate itself from the slough into which it is steadily sinking. Every system, short of the unification of the human race, has been tried, repeatedly tried, and been found wanting. Wars again and again have been fought, and conferences without number have met and deliberated. Treaties, pacts and covenants have been painstakingly negotiated, concluded and revised. Systems of government have been patiently tested, have been continually recast and superseded. Economic plans of reconstruction have been carefully devised, and meticulously executed. And yet crisis has succeeded crisis, and the rapidity with which a perilously unstable world is declining has been correspondingly accelerated. A yawning gulf threatens to involve in one common disaster both the satisfied and dissatisfied nations, democracies and dictatorships, capitalists and wage-earners, Europeans and Asiatics, Jew and Gentile, white and colored. An angry Providence, the cynic might well observe, has abandoned a hapless planet to its fate, and fixed irrevocably its doom.   — *Shoghi Effendi* 7

Is it not a fact . . . that the fundamental cause of this world unrest is attributable . . . to the failure of those into whose hands the immediate destinies of peoples and nations have been committed, to adjust their system of economic and political institutions to the imperative needs of a rapidly evolving age? Are not these intermittent crises that convulse present-day society due primarily to the lamentable inability of the world's recognized leaders to read aright the signs of the times, to rid themselves once for all of their preconceived ideas and fettering creeds, and to reshape the machinery of their respective governments according to those standards that are implicit in Bahá'u'lláh's supreme declaration of the Oneness of Mankind—the chief and distinguishing feature of the Faith He proclaimed? —*Shoghi Effendi* **8**

Please God, the peoples of the world may be led, as the result of the high endeavors exerted by their rulers and the wise and learned amongst men, to recognize their best interests. How long will humanity persist in its waywardness? How long will injustice continue? How long is chaos and confusion to reign amongst men? How long will discord agitate the face of society? . . . The winds of despair are, alas, blowing from every direction, and the strife that dividenth and afflicteth the human race is daily increasing. The signs of impending convulsions and chaos can now be discerned, inasmuch as the prevailing order appeareth to be lamentably defective. I beseech God, exalted be His glory, that He may graciously awaken the peoples of the earth, may grant that the end of their conduct may be profitable unto them, and aid them to accomplish that which beseemeth their station. —*Bahá'u'lláh* **9**

We have created you from one tree and have caused you to be as the leaves and fruit of the same tree, that haply ye may become a source of comfort to one another. Regard ye not others save as ye regard your own selves, that no feeling of aversion may prevail amongst you. . . . It behooveth you all to be one indivisible people. . . . —*The Báb* **10**

Today there is no greater glory for man than that of service in the cause of the Most Great Peace. Peace is light, whereas war is darkness. Peace is life; war is death. Peace is guidance; war is error. Peace is the foundation of God; war is a satanic institution. Peace is the illumination of the world of humanity; war is the destroyer of human foundations. When we consider outcomes in the world of existence, we find that peace and fellowship are factors of upbuilding and betterment, whereas war and strife are the causes of destruction and disintegration. All created things are expressions of the affinity and cohesion of elementary substances, and nonexistence is the absence of their attraction and agreement. Various elements unite harmoniously in composition, but when these elements become discordant, repelling each other, decomposition and nonexistence result. Everything partakes of this nature and is subject to this principle, for the creative foundation in all its degrees and kingdoms is an expression or outcome of love. Consider the restlessness and agitation of the human world today because of war. Peace is health and construction; war is disease and dissolution. When the banner of truth is raised, peace becomes the cause of the welfare and advancement of the human world. In all cycles and ages war has been a factor of derangement and discomfort, whereas peace and brotherhood have brought security and consideration of human interests. This distinction is especially pronounced in the present world conditions, for warfare in former centuries had not attained the degree of savagery and destructiveness which now characterizes it. If two nations were at war in olden times, ten or twenty thousand would be sacrificed, but in this century the destruction of one hundred thousand lives in a day is quite possible. So perfected has the science of killing become and so efficient the means and instruments of its accomplishment that a whole nation can be obliterated in a short time. Therefore, comparison with the methods and results of ancient warfare is out of the question.

According to an intrinsic law all phenomena of being attain to a summit and degree of consummation, after which a new order and condition is established. As the instruments and science of war have reached the degree of thoroughness and proficiency, it is hoped that the transformation of the human world is at hand and that in the coming centuries all the energies and inventions of man will be utilized in promoting the interests of peace and brotherhood.

—'Abdu'l-Bahá 11

O ye individuals of humanity, find ye means for the stoppage of this wholesale murder and bloodshed. Now is the appointed time! Now is the opportune time! Arise ye, show ye an effort, put ye forth an extraordinary force, and unfurl ye the Flag of Universal Peace and dam the irresistible fury of this raging torrent which is wreaking havoc and ruin everywhere.

—'Abdu'l-Bahá **12**

The Pernicious Effects of a Material Civilization

THE civilization, so often vaunted by the learned exponents of arts and sciences, will, if allowed to overleap the bounds of moderation, bring great evil upon men. Thus warneth you He Who is the All-Knowing. If carried to excess, civilization will prove as prolific a source of evil as it had been of goodness when kept within the restraints of moderation.

—Bahá'u'lláh **13**

Consider the civilization of the West, how it hath agitated and alarmed the peoples of the world. An infernal engine hath been devised, and hath proved so cruel a weapon of destruction that its like none hath ever witnessed or heard. The purging of such deeply rooted and overwhelming corruptions cannot be effected unless the peoples of the world unite in pursuit of one common aim and embrace one universal faith. Incline your ears unto the Call of this Wronged One and adhere firmly to the Lesser Peace.

Strange and astonishing things exist in the earth but they are hidden from the minds and the understanding of men. These things are capable of changing the whole atmosphere of the earth and their contamination would prove lethal.

—Bahá'u'lláh **14**

Consider: What is this material civilization of the day giving forth? Has it not produced the instruments of warfare and destruction? In olden times the weapon of war was the sword; today it is the smokeless gun. Warships a century ago were sailing vessels; now we have dreadnoughts. Instruments and means of human destruction have enormously multiplied in this era of material civilization. But if material civilization shall become organized in conjunction with divine civilization, if the man of moral integrity and intellectual acumen shall unite for human betterment and uplift with the man of spiritual capacity, the happiness and progress of the human race will be assured. All the nations of the world will then be closely related and companionable, and the religions will merge into one, for the divine reality within them all is one reality. Abraham proclaimed this reality; Jesus promulgated it; all the Prophets who have appeared in the world have founded Their teachings upon it. Therefore, the people of the world have this one true, unchangeable basis for peace and agreement, and war, which has raged for thousands of years, will pass away. —'Abdu'l-Bahá 15

No matter how far the material world advances, it cannot establish the happiness of mankind. Only when material and spiritual civilization are linked and coordinated will happiness be assured. Then material civilization will not contribute its energies to the forces of evil in destroying the oneness of humanity, for in material civilization good and evil advance together and maintain the same pace. For example, consider the material progress of man in the last decade.* Schools and colleges, hospitals, philanthropic institutions, scientific academies and temples of philosophy have been founded, but hand in hand with these evidences of development, the invention and production of means and weapons for human destruction have correspondingly increased.
. . . If the moral precepts and foundations of divine civilization become united with the material advancement of man, there is no doubt that the happiness of the human world will be attained and that from every direction the glad tidings of peace upon earth will be announced. —'Abdu'l-Bahá 16

---

*This talk was delivered in Pittsburgh, Pennsylvania, on 7 May 1912.

Since my arrival in this country* I find that material civilization has progressed greatly, that commerce has attained the utmost degree of expansion; arts, agriculture and all details of material civilization have reached the highest stage of perfection, but spiritual civilization has been left behind. Material civilization is like unto the lamp, while spiritual civilization is the light in that lamp. If the material and spiritual civilization become united, then we will have the light and the lamp together, and the outcome will be perfect. For material civilization is like unto a beautiful body, and spiritual civilization is like unto the spirit of life. If that wondrous spirit of life enters this beautiful body, the body will become a channel for the distribution and development of the perfections of humanity.   —'Abdu'l-Bahá **17**

For man two wings are necessary. One wing is physical power and material civilization; the other is spiritual power and divine civilization. With one wing only, flight is impossible. Two wings are essential. Therefore, no matter how much material civilization advances, it cannot attain to perfection except through the uplift of spiritual civilization.
                                   —'Abdu'l-Bahá **18**

Two calls to success and prosperity are being raised from the heights of the happiness of mankind. . . .
The one is the call of civilization, of the progress of the material world. This pertaineth to the world of phenomena, promoteth the principles of material achievement, and is the trainer for the physical accomplishments of mankind. It compriseth the laws, regulations, arts and sciences through which the world of humanity hath developed; laws and regulations which are the outcome of lofty ideals and the result of sound minds, and which have stepped forth into the arena of existence through the efforts of the wise and cultured in past and

---

*The United States. 'Abdu'l-Bahá began an eight-month tour of the United States and Canada on 11 April 1912.

subsequent ages. The propagator and executive power of this call is just government.

The other is the soul-stirring call of God, Whose spiritual teachings are safeguards of the everlasting glory, the eternal happiness and illumination of the world of humanity, and cause attributes of mercy to be revealed in the human world and the life beyond.

This second call is founded upon the instructions and exhortations of the Lord and the admonitions and altruistic emotions belonging to the realm of morality which, like unto a brilliant light, brighten and illumine the lamp of the realities of mankind. Its penetrative power is the Word of God.

However, until material achievements, physical accomplishments and human virtues are reinforced by spiritual perfections, luminous qualities and characteristics of mercy, no fruit or result shall issue therefrom, nor will the happiness of the world of humanity, which is the ultimate aim, be attained. For although, on the one hand, material achievements and the development of the physical world produce prosperity, which exquisitely manifests its intended aims, on the other hand dangers, severe calamities and violent afflictions are imminent.

Consequently, when thou lookest at the orderly pattern of kingdoms, cities and villages, with the attractiveness of their adornments, the freshness of their natural resources, the refinement of their appliances, the ease of their means of travel, the extent of knowledge available about the world of nature, the great inventions, the colossal enterprises, the noble discoveries and scientific researches, thou wouldst conclude that civilization conduceth to the happiness and the progress of the human world. Yet shouldst thou turn thine eye to the discovery of destructive and infernal machines, to the development of forces of demolition and the invention of fiery implements, which uproot the tree of life, it would become evident and manifest unto thee that civilization is conjoined with barbarism. Progress and barbarism go hand in hand, unless material civilization be confirmed by Divine Guidance, by the revelations of the All-Merciful and by godly virtues, and be reinforced by spiritual conduct, by the ideals of the Kingdom and by the outpourings of the Realm of Might.

—*'Abdu'l-Bahá* **19**

The chief reason for the evils now rampant in society is the lack of spirituality. The materialistic civilization of our age has so much absorbed the energy and interest of mankind that people in general do no longer feel the necessity of raising themselves above the forces and conditions of their daily material existence. There is not sufficient demand for things that we should call spiritual to differentiate them from the needs and requirements of our physical existence.

The universal crisis affecting mankind is, therefore, essentially spiritual in its causes. The spirit of the age, taken on the whole, is irreligious. Man's outlook on life is too crude and materialistic to enable him to elevate himself into the higher realms of the spirit. —*Shoghi Effendi* **20**

Sore-tried and disillusioned, humanity has no doubt lost its orientation, and would seem to have lost as well its faith and hope. It is hovering, unshepherded and visionless, on the brink of disaster. A sense of fatality seems to pervade it. An ever-deepening gloom is settling on its fortunes as she recedes further and further from the outer fringes of the darkest zone of its agitated life and penetrates its very heart.

—*Shoghi Effendi* **21**

The process of disintegration must inexorably continue, and its corrosive influence must penetrate deeper and deeper into the very core of a crumbling age. Much suffering will still be required ere the contending nations, creeds, classes and races of mankind are fused in the crucible of universal affliction, and are forged by the fires of a fierce ordeal into one organic commonwealth, one vast, unified, and harmoniously functioning system. Adversities unimaginably appalling, undreamed of crises and upheavals, war, famine, and pestilence, might well combine to engrave in the soul of an unheeding generation those truths and principles which it has disdained to recognize and follow. A paralysis more painful than any it has yet experienced must creep over and further afflict the fabric of a broken society ere it can be rebuilt and regenerated.

—Shoghi Effendi **22**

The body of the human world is sick. Its remedy and healing will be the oneness of the kingdom of humanity. Its life is the Most Great Peace. Its illumination and quickening is love. Its happiness is the attainment of spiritual perfections. It is my wish and hope that in the bounties and favors of the Blessed Perfection* we may find a new life, acquire a new power and attain to a wonderful and supreme source of energy so that the Most Great Peace of divine intention shall be established upon the foundations of the unity of the world of men with God.   *—'Abdu'l-Bahá* **23**

Beyond Selfishness and Aggression: Releasing Forces for Social Reconstruction

IN MAN there are two natures; his spiritual or higher nature and his material or lower nature. In one he approaches God, in the other he lives for the world alone. Signs of both these natures are to be found in men. In his material aspect he expresses untruth, cruelty and injustice; all these are the outcome of his lower nature. The attributes of his Divine nature are shown forth in love, mercy, kindness, truth and justice, one and all being expressions of his higher nature. Every good habit, every noble quality belongs to man's spiritual nature, whereas all his imperfections and sinful actions are born of his material nature. If a man's Divine nature dominates his human nature, we have a saint.

Man has the power both to do good and to do evil; if his

---

*Bahá'u'lláh, the Prophet-Founder of the Bahá'í Faith. See the appendix for details on His life.

power for good predominates and his inclinations to do wrong are conquered, then man in truth may be called a saint. But if, on the contrary, he rejects the things of God and allows his evil passions to conquer him, then he is no better than a mere animal.   —'Abdu'l-Bahá 24

Indeed the actions of man himself breed a profusion of satanic power. For were men to abide by and observe the divine teachings, every trace of evil would be banished from the face of the earth. However, the widespread differences that exist among mankind and the prevalence of sedition, contention, conflict and the like are the primary factors which provoke the appearance of the satanic spirit. . . . A world in which naught can be perceived save strife, quarrels and corruption is bound to become the seat of the throne, the very metropolis, of Satan.   —Bahá'u'lláh 25

The evil spirit, Satan or whatever is interpreted as evil, refers to the lower nature in man. This baser nature is symbolized in various ways. In man there are two expressions: One is the expression of nature; the other, the expression of the spiritual realm. The world of nature is defective. Look at it clearly, casting aside all superstition and imagination. If you should leave a man uneducated and barbarous in the wilds of Africa, would there be any doubt about his remaining ignorant? God has never created an evil spirit; all such ideas and nomenclature are symbols expressing the mere human or earthly nature of man.   —'Abdu'l-Bahá 26

The Almighty hath not created in man the claws and teeth of ferocious animals, nay rather hath the human form been fashioned and set with the most comely attributes and adorned with the most perfect virtues. The honor of this creation and the worthiness of this garment therefore require man to have love and affinity for his own kind, nay rather, to act towards all living creatures with justice and equity.

Similarly, consider how the cause of the welfare, happiness, joy and comfort of humankind are amity and union, whereas dissension and discord are most conducive to hardship, humiliation, agitation and failure.

But a thousand times alas, that man is negligent and unaware of these facts, and daily doth he strut abroad with the characteristics of a wild beast. Lo! At one moment he turneth into a ferocious tiger; at the next he becometh a creeping, venomous viper! But the sublime achievements of man reside in those qualities and attributes that exclusively pertain to the angels of the Supreme Concourse. Therefore, when praiseworthy qualities and high morals emanate from man, he becometh a heavenly being, an angel of the Kingdom, a divine reality and a celestial effulgence. On the other hand, when he engageth in warfare, quarreling and bloodshed, he becometh viler than the most fierce of savage creatures, for if a bloodthirsty wolf devoureth a lamb in a single night, man slaughtereth a hundred thousand in the field of battle, strewing the ground with their corpses and kneading the earth with their blood.

In short, man is endowed with two natures: one tendeth towards moral sublimity and intellectual perfection, while the other turneth to bestial degradation and carnal imperfections. If ye travel the countries of the globe ye shall observe on one side the remains of ruin and destruction, while on the other ye shall see the signs of civilization and development. Such desolation and ruin are the result of war, strife and quarreling, while all development and progress are fruits of the lights of virtue, cooperation and concord.   —'Abdu'l-Bahá 27

Man is in the highest degree of materiality, and at the beginning of spirituality—that is to say, he is the end of imperfection and the beginning of perfection. He is at the last degree of darkness, and at the beginning of light; that is why it has been said that the condition of man is the end of the night and the beginning of day, meaning that he is the sum of all the degrees of imperfection, and that he possesses the degrees of perfection. He has the animal side as well as the angelic side, and the aim of an educator is to so train human souls that their angelic aspect may overcome their animal side. Then if the divine power in man, which is his essential perfection, overcomes the satanic power, which is absolute imperfection, he becomes the most excellent among the creatures; but if the satanic power overcomes the divine power, he becomes the lowest of the creatures. That is why he is the end of imperfection and the beginning of perfection. Not in any other of the species in the world of existence is there such a difference, contrast, contradiction and opposition as in the species of man.

. . . knowledge is a quality of man, and so is ignorance; truthfulness is a quality of man; so is falsehood; trustworthiness and treachery, justice and injustice, are qualities of man, and so forth. Briefly, all the perfections and virtues, and all the vices, are qualities of man.   —'Abdu'l-Bahá **28**

It is clear from what has already been said that man's glory and greatness do not consist in his being avid for blood and sharp of claw, in tearing down cities and spreading havoc, in butchering armed forces and civilians. What would mean a bright future for him would be his reputation for justice, his kindness to the entire population whether high or low, his building up countries and cities, villages and districts, his making life easy, peaceful and happy for his fellow beings, his laying down fundamental principles for progress, his raising the standards and increasing the wealth of the entire population.   —'Abdu'l-Bahá **29**

Man must sever himself from the influences of the world of matter, from the world of nature and its laws; for the material world is the world of corruption and death. It is the world of evil and darkness, of animalism and ferocity, bloodthirstiness, ambition and avarice, of self-worship, egotism and passion; it is the world of nature. Man must strip himself of all these imperfections, must sacrifice these tendencies which are peculiar to the outer and material world of existence.

On the other hand, man must acquire heavenly qualities and attain divine attributes. He must become the image and likeness of God. He must seek the bounty of the eternal,

become the manifestor of the love of God, the light of guidance, the tree of life and the depository of the bounties of
God. That is to say, man must sacrifice the qualities and attributes of the world of nature for the qualities and attributes of
the world of God.   —*'Abdu'l-Bahá* **30**

How long shall we drift on the wings of passion and vain
desire; how long shall we spend our days like barbarians in
the depths of ignorance and abomination? God has given us
eyes, that we may look about us at the world, and lay hold of
whatsoever will further civilization and the arts of living. He
has given us ears, that we may hear and profit by the wisdom
of scholars and philosophers and arise to promote and practice
it. Senses and faculties have been bestowed upon us, to be
devoted to the service of the general good; so that we, distinguished above all other forms of life for perceptiveness and
reason, should labor at all times and along all lines, whether
the occasion be great or small, ordinary or extraordinary, until
all mankind are safely gathered into the impregnable stronghold of knowledge. We should continually be establishing
new bases for human happiness and creating and promoting
new instrumentalities toward this end. How excellent, how
honorable is man if he arises to fulfill his responsibilities; how
wretched and contemptible, if he shuts his eyes to the welfare
of society and wastes his precious life in pursuing his own
selfish interests and personal advantages. Supreme happiness
is man's, and he beholds the signs of God in the world and in
the human soul, if he urges on the steed of high endeavor in
the arena of civilization and justice. . . .

And this is man's uttermost wretchedness: that he should
live inert, apathetic, dull, involved only with his own base appetites. When he is thus, he has his being in the deepest ignorance and savagery, sinking lower than the brute beasts. . . .

We must now highly resolve to arise and lay hold of all
those instrumentalities that promote the peace and well-being
and happiness, the knowledge, culture and industry, the dignity, value and station, of the entire human race. Thus, through
the restoring waters of pure intention and unselfish effort, the

earth of human potentialities will blossom with its own latent excellence and flower into praiseworthy qualities, and bear and flourish until it comes to rival that rose garden of knowledge which belonged to our forefathers. —'Abdu'l-Bahá **31**

Great is the station of man. Great must also be his endeavors for the rehabilitation of the world and the well-being of nations. I beseech the One true God to graciously confirm thee in that which beseemeth man's station. —Bahá'u'lláh **32**

Establishing a Single Social Order: The Goal of Human Evolution

THE whole earth is now in a state of pregnancy. The day is approaching when it will have yielded its noblest fruits, when from it will have sprung forth the loftiest trees, the most enchanting blossoms, the most heavenly blessings.

—Bahá'u'lláh **33**

Soon will the present-day order be rolled up, and a new one spread out in its stead. Verily, thy Lord speaketh the truth, and is the Knower of things unseen. —Bahá'u'lláh **34**

This is the Day in which God's most excellent favors have been poured out upon men, the Day in which His most mighty grace hath been infused into all created things. It is incumbent upon all the peoples of the world to reconcile their differences, and, with perfect unity and peace, abide beneath the shadow of the Tree of His care and loving kindness. It behooveth them to cleave to whatsoever will, in this Day, be conducive to the exaltation of their stations, and to the promotion of their best interests. —Bahá'u'lláh **35**

The potentialities inherent in the station of man, the full measure of his destiny on earth, the innate excellence of his reality, must all be manifested in this promised Day of God.

—Bahá'u'lláh **36**

Consider how discord and dissension have prevailed in this great human family for thousands of years. Its members have ever been engaged in war and bloodshed. Up to the present time in history the world of humanity has neither attained nor enjoyed any measure of peace, owing to incessant conditions of hostility and strife. History is a continuous and consecutive record of warfare brought about by religious, sectarian, racial, patriotic and political causes. The world of humanity has found no rest. Mankind has always been in conflict, engaged in destroying the foundations, pillaging the properties and possessing the lands and territory of each other, especially in the earlier periods of savagery and barbarism where whole races and peoples were carried away captive by their conquerors. Who shall measure or estimate the tremendous destruction of human life resulting from this hostility and strife? What human powers and forces have been employed in the prosecution of war and applied to inhuman purposes of battle and bloodshed? In this most radiant century it has become necessary to divert these energies and utilize them in other directions, to seek the new path of fellowship and unity, to unlearn the science of war and devote supreme human forces to the blessed arts of peace. After long trial and experience we are convinced of the harmful and satanic outcomes of dissension; now we must seek after means by which the benefits of agreement and concord may be enjoyed. When such means are found, we must give them a trial.

—'Abdu'l-Bahá 37

In this great century the most important accomplishment is the unity of mankind. Although in former centuries and times this subject received some measure of mention and consideration, it has now become the paramount issue and question in the religious and political conditions of the world. History shows that throughout the past there has been continual warfare and strife among the various nations, peoples and sects; but now—praise be to God!—in this century of illumination, hearts are inclined toward agreement and fellowship, and minds are thoughtful upon the question of the unification

of mankind. There is an emanation of the universal consciousness today which clearly indicates the dawn of a great unity.
— 'Abdu'l-Bahá **38**

Praise be to God, throughout succeeding centuries and
ages the call of civilization hath been raised, the world of
humanity hath been advancing and progressing day by day,
various countries have been developing by leaps and bounds,
and material improvements have increased, until the world of
existence obtained universal capacity to receive the spiritual
teachings and to hearken to the Divine Call. The suckling
babe passeth through various physical stages, growing and
developing at every stage, until its body reacheth the age of
maturity. Having arrived at this stage it acquireth the capacity
to manifest spiritual and intellectual perfections. The lights of
comprehension, intelligence and knowledge become percep-
tible in it and the powers of its soul unfold. Similarly, in the
contingent world, the human species hath undergone progressive physical changes and, by a slow process, hath scaled the
ladder of civilization, realizing in itself the wonders, excellen-
cies and gifts of humanity in their most glorious form, until it
gained the capacity to express the splendors of spiritual perfections and divine ideals and became capable of hearkening
to the call of God. Then at last the call of the Kingdom was
raised, the spiritual virtues and perfections were revealed, the
Sun of Reality dawned, and the teachings of the Most Great
Peace, of the oneness of the world of humanity and of the
universality of men, were promoted. We hope that the effulgence of these rays shall become more and more intense, and
the ideal virtues more resplendent, so that the goal of this
universal human process will be attained and the love of God
will appear in the utmost grace and beauty and bedazzle all
hearts.   — 'Abdu'l-Bahá **39**

All created things have their degree or stage of maturity.
The period of maturity in the life of a tree is the time of its
fruit-bearing. . . . The animal attains a stage of full growth and
completeness, and in the human kingdom man reaches his

maturity when the light of his intelligence attains its greatest power and development. . . . Similarly there are periods and stages in the collective life of humanity. At one time it was passing through its stage of childhood, at another its period of youth, but now it has entered its long-predicted phase of maturity, the evidences of which are everywhere apparent. . . . That which was applicable to human needs during the early history of the race can neither meet nor satisfy the demands of this day, this period of newness and consummation. Humanity has emerged from its former state of limitation and preliminary training. Man must now become imbued with new virtues and powers, new moral standards, new capacities. New bounties, perfect bestowals, are awaiting and already descending upon him. The gifts and blessings of the period of youth, although timely and sufficient during the adolescence of mankind, are now incapable of meeting the requirements of its maturity.   —*'Abdu'l-Bahá* **40**

In cycles gone by, though harmony was established, yet, owing to the absence of means, the unity of all mankind could not have been achieved. Continents remained widely divided, nay even among the peoples of one and the same continent association and interchange of thought were well-nigh impossible. Consequently intercourse, understanding and unity amongst all the peoples and kindreds of the earth were unattainable. In this day, however, means of communication have multiplied, and the five continents of the earth have virtually merged into one. And for everyone it is now easy to travel to any land, to associate and exchange views with its peoples, and to become familiar, through publications, with the conditions, the religious beliefs and the thoughts of all men. In like manner all the members of the human family, whether peoples or governments, cities or villages, have become increasingly interdependent. For none is self-sufficiency any longer possible, inasmuch as political ties unite all peoples and nations, and the bonds of trade and industry, of agriculture and education, are being strengthened every day. Hence the unity of all mankind can in this day be achieved. Verily this is none other but one of the wonders of this wondrous age, this glorious century. Of this past ages have been deprived, for this century—the century of light—hath been endowed with unique and unprecedented glory, power and illumination. Hence the miraculous unfolding of a fresh marvel every day. Eventually it will be seen how bright its candles will burn in the assemblage of man.

Behold how its light is now dawning upon the world's darkened horizon. The first candle is unity in the political realm, the early glimmerings of which can now be discerned. The second candle is unity of thought in world undertakings, the consummation of which will erelong be witnessed. The third candle is unity in freedom which will surely come to pass. The fourth candle is unity in religion which is the cornerstone of the foundation itself, and which, by the power of God, will be revealed in all its splendor. The fifth candle is the unity of nations—a unity which in this century will be securely established, causing all the peoples of the world to regard themselves as citizens of one common fatherland. The sixth candle is unity of races, making of all that dwell on earth peoples and kindreds of one race. The seventh candle is unity of language, i.e., the choice of a universal tongue in which all peoples will be instructed and converse. Each and every one of these will inevitably come to pass, inasmuch as the power of the Kingdom of God will aid and assist in their realization.

—'Abdu'l-Bahá 41

The world is, in truth, moving on towards its destiny. The interdependence of the peoples and nations of the earth, whatever the leaders of the divisive forces of the world may say or do, is already an accomplished fact. Its unity in the economic sphere is now understood and recognized. The welfare of the part means the welfare of the whole, and the distress of the part brings distress to the whole. The Revelation of Bahá'u'lláh has, in His own words, "lent a fresh impulse and set a new direction" to this vast process now operating in the world. The fires lit by this great ordeal are the consequences of men's failure to recognize it. They are, moreover, hastening its consummation. Adversity, prolonged, worldwide, afflictive, allied to chaos and universal destruction, must needs convulse the nations, stir the conscience of the world, disillusion the masses, precipitate a radical change in the very conception of society, and coalesce ultimately the disjointed, the bleeding limbs of mankind into one body, single, organically united, and indivisible.   —*Shoghi Effendi* 42

The flames which His* Divine justice have kindled cleanse an unregenerate humanity, and fuse its discordant, its warring elements as no other agency can cleanse or fuse them. It is not only a retributory and destructive fire, but a disciplinary and creative process, whose aim is the salvation, through unification, of the entire planet. Mysteriously, slowly, and resistlessly God accomplishes His design, though the sight that meets our eyes in this day be the spectacle of a world hopelessly entangled in its own meshes, utterly careless of the Voice which, for a century, has been calling it to God, and miserably subservient to the siren voices which are attempting to lure it into the vast abyss.

God's purpose is none other than to usher in, in ways He alone can bring about, and the full significance of which He alone can fathom, the Great, the Golden Age of a long-divided, a long-afflicted humanity. Its present state, indeed even its immediate future, is dark, distressingly dark. Its distant future, however, is radiant, gloriously radiant—so radiant that no eye can visualize it.   —*Shoghi Effendi* 43

What we witness at the present time, during "this gravest crisis in the history of civilization," recalling such times in which "religions have perished and are born," is the adolescent stage in the slow and painful evolution of humanity, preparatory to the attainment of the stage of manhood, the stage of maturity, the promise of which is embedded in the teachings, and enshrined in the prophecies, of Bahá'u'lláh.

---

*God's.

The tumult of this age of transition is characteristic of the impetuosity and irrational instincts of youth, its follies, its prodigality, its pride, its self-assurance, its rebelliousness, and contempt of discipline.

The ages of its infancy and childhood are past, never again to return, while the Great Age, the consummation of all ages, which must signalize the coming of age of the entire human race, is yet to come. The convulsions of this transitional and most turbulent period in the annals of humanity are the essential prerequisites, and herald the inevitable approach, of that Age of Ages, "the time of the end," in which the folly and tumult of strife that has, since the dawn of history, blackened the annals of mankind, will have been finally transmuted into the wisdom and the tranquillity of an undisturbed, a universal, and lasting peace, in which the discord and separation of the children of men will have given way to the worldwide reconcilation, and the complete unification of the divers elements that constitute human society.

This will indeed be the fitting climax of that process of integration which, starting with the family, the smallest unit in the scale of human organization, must, after having called successively into being the tribe, the city-state, and the nation, continue to operate until it culminates in the unification of the whole world, the final object and the crowning glory of human evolution on this planet. It is this stage which humanity, willingly or unwillingly, is resistlessly approaching. It is for this stage that this vast, this fiery ordeal which humanity is experiencing is mysteriously paving the way.   —*Shoghi Effendi* **44**

In the great outcry raised by postwar nationalism* in blindly defending and upholding the unfettered supremacy of its own sovereignty, and in repudiating unreservedly the conception of a world superstate, can we not discern the reenactment only on a larger scale of the dramatic struggles that heralded the birth of the reconstructed and unified nations of

---

*World War I.

the West? Has not authentic history clearly revealed in the case of these nations the painful yet inevitable merging of rival, particularistic and independent cities and principalities into one unified national entity, the evolving of a crude and narrow creed into a nobler and wider conception? Is not a parallel struggle being now manifested on the world stage of ever-advancing humanity? Can it lead to any other result than that which shall reaffirm the truth of humanity's onward march towards an ever-widening conception, and the ever-brightening glory of its destiny? Reverses and setbacks, such as we have already witnessed, no doubt will retard the ripening of the choicest fruit on the tree of human development. Yet the fierceness of controversy, the weight of argument advanced in its disfavor, cannot but contribute to the broadening of the basis and the consolidation of the foundations upon which the stately edifice of unified mankind must ultimately rest.

—Shoghi Effendi **45**

The powers of earth cannot withstand the privileges and bestowals which God has ordained for this great and glorious century. It is a need and exigency of the time. Man can withstand anything except that which is divinely intended and indicated for the age and its requirements. Now—praise be to God!—in all countries of the world, lovers of peace are to be found, and these principles are being spread among mankind, especially in this country.* Praise be to God! This thought is prevailing, and souls are continually arising as defenders of the oneness of humanity, endeavoring to assist and establish international peace. There is no doubt that this wonderful democracy will be able to realize it, and the banner of international agreement will be unfurled here to spread onward and outward among all the nations of the world. I give thanks to God that I find you imbued with such susceptibilities and lofty aspirations, and I hope that you will be the means of spreading this light to all men. Thus may the Sun of Reality

---

*The United States.

shine upon the East and West. The enveloping clouds shall pass away, and the heat of the divine rays will dispel the mist. The reality of man shall develop and come forth as the image of God, his Creator. The thoughts of man shall take such upward flight that former accomplishments shall appear as the play of children, for the ideas and beliefs of the past and the prejudices regarding race and religion have ever lowered and been destructive to human evolution. I am most hopeful that in this century these lofty thoughts shall be conducive to human welfare. Let this century be the sun of previous centuries, the effulgences of which shall last forever, so that in times to come they shall glorify the twentieth century, saying the twentieth century was the century of lights, the twentieth century was the century of life, the twentieth century was the century of international peace, the twentieth century was the century of divine bestowals, and the twentieth century has left traces which shall last forever. —*'Abdu'l-Bahá* **46**

Lofty is the station of man! Not long ago this exalted Word streamed forth from the treasury of Our Pen of Glory: Great and blessed is this Day—the Day in which all that lay latent in man hath been and will be made manifest. —*Bahá'u'lláh* **47**

Identifying the Spiritual Roots of Peace

The Unique Endowments of the Human Spirit

The Source of Civilization and Prosperity

KNOW thou that, according to what thy Lord, the Lord of all men, hath decreed in His Book, the favors vouchsafed by Him unto mankind have been, and will ever remain, limitless in their range. First and foremost among these favors, which the Almighty hath conferred upon man, is the gift of understanding. His purpose in conferring such a gift is none other except to enable His creature to know and recognize the one true God—exalted be His glory. This gift giveth man the power to discern the truth in all things, leadeth him to that which is right, and helpeth him to discover the secrets of creation. —*Bahá'u'lláh* **1**

The station of man is great, very great. God has created man after His own image and likeness. He has endowed him with a mighty power which is capable of discovering the mysteries of phenomena. Through its use man is able to arrive at ideal conclusions instead of being restricted to the mere plane of sense impressions. As he possesses sense endowment in common with the animals, it is evident that he is distinguished above them by his conscious power of penetrating abstract realities. He acquires divine wisdom; he searches out the mysteries of creation; he witnesses the radiance of omnipotence; he attains the second birth—that is to say, he is born out of the material world just as he is born of the mother; he attains to everlasting life; he draws nearer to God; his heart is replete with the love of God. This is the foundation of the

world of humanity; this is the image and likeness of God; this
is the reality of man. . . .   —'Abdu'l-Bahá 2

God's greatest gift to man is that of intellect, or understanding.

The understanding is the power by which man acquires
his knowledge of the several kingdoms of creation, and of
various stages of existence, as well as of much which is invisible.

Possessing this gift, he is, in himself, the sum of earlier
creations—he is able to get into touch with those kingdoms;
and by this gift, he can frequently, through his scientific knowledge, reach out with prophetic vision.

Intellect is, in truth, the most precious gift bestowed
upon man by the Divine Bounty. Man alone, among created
beings, has this wonderful power.

All creation, preceding Man, is bound by the stern law of
nature. The great sun, the multitudes of stars, the oceans and
seas, the mountains, the rivers, the trees, and all animals, great
or small—none is able to evade obedience to nature's law.

Man alone has freedom, and, by his understanding or
intellect, has been able to gain control of and adapt some of
those natural laws to his own needs. By the power of his
intellect he has discovered means by which he not only trav-
erses great continents in express trains and crosses vast oceans
in ships, but, like the fish he travels under water in subma-
rines, and, imitating the birds, he flies through the air in
airships.

Man has succeeded in using electricity in several ways—
for light, for motive power, for sending messages from one
end of the earth to the other—and by electricity he can even
hear a voice many miles away!

By this gift of understanding or intellect he has also been
able to use the rays of the sun to picture people and things,
and even to capture the form of distant heavenly bodies.

We perceive in what numerous ways man has been able
to bend the powers of nature to his will.

How grievous it is to see how man has used his God-given gift to frame instruments of war, for breaking the Commandment of God "Thou shalt not kill," and for defying Christ's injunction to "Love one another."

God gave this power to man that it might be used for the advancement of civilization, for the good of humanity, to increase love and concord and peace. But man prefers to use this gift to destroy instead of to build, for injustice and oppression, for hatred and discord and devastation, for the destruction of his fellow creatures, whom Christ has commanded that he should love as himself!

I hope that you will use *your* understanding to promote the unity and tranquillity of mankind, to give enlightenment and civilization to the people, to produce love in all around you, and to bring about the universal peace.

Study the sciences,* acquire more and more knowledge. Assuredly one may learn to the end of one's life! Use your knowledge always for the benefit of others; so may war cease on the face of this beautiful earth, and a glorious edifice of peace and concord be raised.   — *'Abdu'l-Bahá* **3**

The virtues of humanity are many, but science is the most noble of them all. The distinction which man enjoys above and beyond the station of the animal is due to this paramount virtue. It is a bestowal of God; it is not material; it is divine. Science is an effulgence of the Sun of Reality, the power of investigating and discovering the verities of the universe, the means by which man finds a pathway to God. All the powers and attributes of man are human and hereditary in origin— outcomes of nature's processes—except the intellect, which is supernatural. Through intellectual and intelligent inquiry science is the discoverer of all things. It unites present and past,

---

*The word for *sciences* in Persian, the language in which 'Abdu'l-Bahá delivered the talk, has the broader meaning of organized bodies of knowledge, including both the humanities and sciences.

reveals the history of bygone nations and events, and confers upon man today the essence of all human knowledge and attainment throughout the ages. By intellectual processes and logical deductions of reason this superpower in man can penetrate the mysteries of the future and anticipate its happenings. . . .

. . . The man of science is perceiving and endowed with vision, whereas he who is ignorant and neglectful of this development is blind. The investigating mind is attentive, alive; the callous and indifferent mind is deaf and dead. A scientific man is a true index and representative of humanity, for through processes of inductive reasoning and research he is informed of all that appertains to humanity, its status, conditions and happenings. He studies the human body politic, understands social problems and weaves the web and texture of civilization. In fact, science may be likened to a mirror wherein the infinite forms and images of existing things are revealed and reflected. It is the very foundation of all individual and national development. Without this basis of investigation, development is impossible. Therefore, seek with diligent endeavor the knowledge and attainment of all that lies within the power of this wonderful bestowal. . . .

How shall we utilize these gifts and expend these bounties? By directing our efforts toward the unification of the human race. We must use these powers in establishing the oneness of the world of humanity, appreciate these virtues by accomplishing the unity of whites and blacks, devote this divine intelligence to the perfecting of amity and accord among all branches of the human family so that under the protection and providence of God the East and West may hold each other's hands and become as lovers. Then will mankind be as one nation, one race and kind—as waves of one ocean.

—'Abdu'l-Bahá 4

Consider carefully: all these highly varied phenomena, these concepts, this knowledge, these technical procedures and philosophical systems, these sciences, arts, industries and inventions—all are emanations of the human mind. Whatever people has ventured deeper into this shoreless sea, has come to excel the rest. The happiness and pride of a nation consist in this, that it should shine out like the sun in the high heaven of knowledge. . . . And the honor and distinction of the individual consist in this, that he among all the world's multitudes should become a source of social good. Is any larger bounty conceivable than this, that an individual, looking within himself, should find that by the confirming grace of God he has become the cause of peace and well-being, of happiness and advantage to his fellow men? No, by the one true God, there is no greater bliss, no more complete delight.   —*'Abdu'l-Bahá*   5

The source of crafts, sciences and arts is the power of reflection. Make ye every effort that out of this ideal mine there may gleam forth such pearls of wisdom and utterance as will promote the well-being and harmony of all the kindreds of the earth.   —*Bahá'u'lláh*   6

The Inclination toward Transcendence

THE soul is a sign of God, a heavenly gem whose reality the most learned of men hath failed to grasp, and whose mystery no mind, however acute, can ever hope to unravel. It is the first among all created things to declare the excellence of its Creator, the first to recognize His glory, to cleave to His truth, and to bow down in adoration before Him. If it be faithful to God, it will reflect His light, and will, eventually, return unto Him. If it fail, however, in its allegiance to its Creator, it will become a victim to self and passion, and will, in the end, sink in their depths.   —*Bahá'u'lláh*   7

O friend, the heart is the dwelling of eternal mysteries, make it not the home of fleeting fancies; waste not the treasure of thy precious life in employment with this swiftly passing world. Thou comest from the world of holiness—bind not thine heart to the earth; thou art a dweller in the court of nearness—choose not the homeland of the dust.

—*Bahá'u'lláh*   **8**

God has created all earthly things under a law of progression in material degrees, but He has created man and endowed him with powers of advancement toward spiritual and transcendental kingdoms. He has not created material phenomena after His own image and likeness, but He has created man after that image and with potential power to attain that likeness. He has distinguished man above all other created things. All created things except man are captives of nature and the sense world, but in man there has been created an ideal power by which he may perceive intellectual or spiritual realities. He has brought forth everything necessary for the life of this world, but man is a creation intended for the reflection of divine virtues. . . . God has opened the doors of ideal virtues and attainments before the face of man. He has created in his being the mysteries of the divine Kingdom. He has bestowed upon him the power of intellect so that through the attribute of reason, when fortified by the Holy Spirit, he may penetrate and discover ideal realities and become informed of the mysteries of the world of significances. As this power to penetrate the ideal knowledges is superhuman, supernatural, man becomes the collective center of spiritual as well as material forces so that the divine spirit may manifest itself in his being, the effulgences of the Kingdom shine within the sanctuary of his heart, the signs of the attributes and perfections of God reveal themselves in a newness of life, the everlasting glory and eternal existence be attained, the knowledge of God illumine, and the mysteries of the realm of might be unsealed.

—*'Abdu'l-Bahá*   **9**

Nature is inert; man is progressive. Nature has no consciousness; man is endowed with it. Nature is without volition and acts perforce, whereas man possesses a mighty will. Nature is incapable of discovering mysteries or realities, whereas man is especially fitted to do so. Nature is not in touch with the realm of God; man is attuned to its evidences. Nature is uninformed of God; man is conscious of Him. Man acquires divine virtues; nature is denied them. Man can voluntarily discontinue vices; nature has no power to modify the influence of its instincts. Altogether it is evident that man is more noble and superior, that in him there is an ideal power surpassing nature. He has consciousness, volition, memory, intelligent power, divine attributes and virtues of which nature is completely deprived and bereft; therefore, man is higher and nobler by reason of the ideal and heavenly force latent and manifest in him.   —'Abdu'l-Bahá **10**

Spiritual perfections . . . are man's birthright and belong to him alone of all creation. Man is, in reality, a spiritual being, and only when he lives in the spirit is he truly happy. This spiritual longing and perception belongs to all men alike. . . .
                                        —'Abdu'l-Bahá **11**

Man must be lofty in endeavor. He must seek to become heavenly and spiritual, to find the pathway to the threshold of God and become acceptable in the sight of God. This is eternal glory—to be near to God. This is eternal sovereignty—to be imbued with the virtues of the human world. This is boundless blessing—to be entirely sanctified and holy above every stain and dross.

Consider the human world. See how nations have come and gone. They have been of all minds and purposes. Some were mere captives of self and desire, engulfed in the passions of the lower nature. They attained to wealth, to the comforts of life, to fame. And what was the final outcome? Utter evanescence and oblivion. Reflect upon this. Look upon it with the eye of admonition. No trace of them remains, no fruit, no result, no benefit; they have gone utterly—complete effacement.   —'Abdu'l-Bahá **12**

God . . . has created for us both material blessings and spiritual bestowals. He has given us material gifts and spiritual graces, outer sight to view the lights of the sun and inner vision by which we may perceive the glory of God. He has designed the outer ear to enjoy the melodies of sound and the inner hearing wherewith we may hear the voice of our Creator. We must strive with energies of heart, soul and mind to develop and manifest the perfections and virtues latent within the realities of the phenomenal world. . . . Through education and culture these virtues deposited by the loving God will become apparent in the human reality. . . .   —'Abdu'l-Bahá **13**

Let us endeavor to attain capacity, susceptibility and worthiness that we may hear the call of the glad tidings of the Kingdom, become revivified by the breaths of the Holy Spirit, hoist the standard of the oneness of humanity, establish human brotherhood, and under the protection of divine grace attain the everlasting and eternal life.   —'Abdu'l-Bahá **14**

O Son of Being! Thou art My lamp and My light is in thee. Get thou from it thy radiance and seek none other than Me. For I have created thee rich and have bountifully shed My favor upon thee.   —Bahá'u'lláh **15**

Understanding the Vital Role of Religion

The Founders of Religion: Instruments for Galvanizing Humanity's Spiritual and Social Progress

THE source of all learning is the knowledge of God, exalted be His Glory, and this cannot be attained save through the knowledge of His Divine Manifestation.   —Bahá'u'lláh **16**

The one true God hath, in His all-highest and transcendent station, ever been, and will everlastingly continue to be, exalted above the praise and conception of all else but Him. His creation hath ever existed, and the Manifestations of His Divine glory and the Daysprings of eternal holiness have been sent down from time immemorial, and been commissioned to summon mankind to the one true God.   —*Bahá'u'lláh* **17**

He . . . hath ordained the knowledge of these sanctified Beings to be identical with the knowledge of His own Self. Whoso recognizeth them hath recognized God.

—*Bahá'u'lláh* **18**

These sanctified Mirrors, these Daysprings of ancient glory, are, one and all, the Exponents on earth of Him Who is the central Orb of the universe, its Essence and ultimate Purpose. From Him proceed their knowledge and power; from Him is derived their sovereignty. The beauty of their countenance is but a reflection of His image, and their revelation a sign of His deathless glory. They are the Treasuries of Divine knowledge, and the Repositories of celestial wisdom. Through them is transmitted a grace that is infinite, and by them is revealed the Light that can never fade. . . . These Tabernacles of Holiness, these Primal Mirrors which reflect the light of unfading glory, are but expressions of Him Who is the Invisible of the Invisibles. By the revelation of these Gems of Divine virtue all the names and attributes of God, such as knowledge and power, sovereignty and dominion, mercy and wisdom, glory, bounty, and grace, are made manifest.   —*Bahá'u'lláh* **19**

These mirrors are the Messengers of God Who tell the story of Divinity, just as the material mirror reflects the light and disc of the outer sun in the skies. In this way the image and effulgence of the Sun of Reality appear in the mirrors of the Manifestations of God. This is what Jesus Christ meant when He declared, "the father is in the son," the purpose being that the reality of that eternal Sun had become reflected in its glory in Christ Himself. It does not signify that the Sun of Reality had descended from its place in heaven or that its essential being had effected an entrance into the mirror, for there is neither entrance nor exit for the reality of Divinity; there is no ingress or egress; it is sanctified above all things and ever occupies its own holy station. Changes and transformations are not applicable to that eternal reality. Transformation from condition to condition is the attribute of contingent realities. — *'Abdu'l-Bahá* **20**

The Holy Manifestations of God . . . are the focal points where the signs, tokens and perfections of that sacred, pre-existent Reality appear in all their splendor. They are an eternal grace, a heavenly glory, and on Them dependeth the everlasting life of humankind. — *'Abdu'l-Bahá* **21**

Men at all times and under all conditions stand in need of one to exhort them, guide them, and to instruct and teach them. Therefore He hath sent forth His Messengers, His Prophets and chosen ones that they might acquaint the people with the divine purpose underlying the revelation of Books and the raising up of Messengers, and that everyone may become aware of the trust of God which is latent in the reality of every soul. —*Bahá'u'lláh* **22**

God's purpose in sending His Prophets unto men is two-fold. The first is to liberate the children of men from the darkness of ignorance, and guide them to the light of true understanding. The second is to ensure the peace and tranquillity of mankind, and provide all the means by which they can be established.

The Prophets of God should be regarded as physicians whose task is to foster the well-being of the world and its peoples, that, through the spirit of oneness, they may heal the sickness of a divided humanity. . . . every time the Prophets of God have illumined the world with the resplendent radiance of the Daystar of Divine knowledge, they have invariably summoned its peoples to embrace the light of God through such means as best befitted the exigencies of the age in which they appeared. They were thus able to scatter the darkness of ignorance, and to shed upon the world the glory of their own knowledge. It is towards the inmost essence of these Prophets, therefore, that the eye of every man of discernment must be directed, inasmuch as their one and only purpose hath always been to guide the erring, and give peace to the afflicted. . . . These are not days of prosperity and triumph. The whole of mankind is in the grip of manifold ills. Strive, therefore, to save its life through the wholesome medicine which the almighty hand of the unerring Physician hath prepared.   —*Bahá'u'lláh* **23**

These Essences of Detachment, these resplendent Realities are the channels of God's all-pervasive grace. Led by the light of unfailing guidance, and invested with supreme sovereignty, They are commissioned to use the inspiration of Their words, the effusions of Their infallible grace and the sanctifying breeze of Their Revelation for the cleansing of every longing heart and receptive spirit from the dross and dust of earthly cares and limitations. Then, and only then, will the Trust of God, latent in the reality of man, emerge, as resplendent as the rising Orb of Divine Revelation, from behind the veil of concealment, and implant the ensign of its revealed glory upon the summits of men's hearts.   —*Bahá'u'lláh* **24**

The purpose of the one true God in manifesting Himself is to summon all mankind to truthfulness and sincerity, to piety and trustworthiness, to resignation and submissiveness to the Will of God, to forbearance and kindliness, to uprightness and wisdom. His object is to array every man with the mantle of a saintly character, and to adorn him with the ornament of holy and goodly deeds.   —*Bahá'u'lláh* **25**

Man is said to be the greatest representative of God, and he is the Book of Creation because all the mysteries of beings exist in him. If he comes under the shadow of the True Educator and is rightly trained, he becomes the essence of essences, the light of lights, the spirit of spirits; he becomes the center of the divine appearances, the source of spiritual qualities, the rising-place of heavenly lights, and the receptacle of divine inspirations. If he is deprived of this education, he becomes the manifestation of satanic qualities, the sum of animal vices, and the source of all dark conditions.
                    —*'Abdu'l-Bahá* **26**

Through the rise of these Luminaries of God the world is made new, the waters of everlasting life stream forth, the billows of loving kindness surge, the clouds of grace are gathered, and the breeze of bounty bloweth upon all created things. It is the warmth that these Luminaries of God generate, and the undying fires they kindle, which cause the light of the love of God to burn fiercely in the heart of humanity. It is through the abundant grace of these Symbols of Detachment that the Spirit of life everlasting is breathed into the bodies of the dead.   —*Bahá'u'lláh* **27**

Through the Teachings of this Daystar of Truth every man will advance and develop until he attaineth the station at which he can manifest all the potential forces with which his inmost true self hath been endowed. It is for this very purpose that in every age and dispensation the Prophets of God and His chosen Ones have appeared amongst men, and have evinced such power as is born of God and such might as only the Eternal can reveal.   —*Bahá'u'lláh* **28**

When the holy, divine Manifestations or Prophets appear in the world, a cycle of radiance, an age of mercy dawns. Everything is renewed. Minds, hearts and all human forces are reformed, perfections are quickened, sciences, discoveries and investigations are stimulated afresh, and everything appertaining to the virtues of the human world is revitalized.
                                    —*'Abdu'l-Bahá* **29**

The mission of the Prophets, the revelation of the Holy Books, the manifestation of the heavenly Teachers and the purpose of divine philosophy all center in the training of the human realities so that they may become clear and pure as mirrors and reflect the light and love of the Sun of Reality. Therefore, I hope that—whether you be in the East or the West—you will strive with heart and soul in order that day by day the world of humanity may become glorified, more spiritual, more sanctified; and that the splendor of the Sun of Reality may be revealed fully in human hearts as in a mirror.

This is worthy of the world of mankind. This is the true evolution and progress of humanity. This is the supreme bestowal.
—*'Abdu'l-Bahá* **30**

Religion: The Greatest Means for Ensuring Morality and Order

THEY whom God hath endued with insight will readily recognize that the precepts laid down by God constitute the highest means for the maintenance of order in the world and the security of its peoples. He that turneth away from them, is accounted among the abject and foolish.   —*Bahá'u'lláh* **31**

The greatest bestowal of God in the world of humanity is religion, for assuredly the divine teachings of religion are above all other sources of instruction and development to man. Religion confers upon man eternal life and guides his footsteps in the world of morality. It opens the doors of unending happiness and bestows everlasting honor upon the human kingdom. It has been the basis of all civilization and progress in the history of mankind.   —*'Abdu'l-Bahá* **32**

The ordinances of God have been sent down from the heaven of His most august Revelation. All must diligently observe them. Man's supreme distinction, his real advancement, his final victory, have always depended, and will continue to depend, upon them. Whoso keepeth the commandments of God shall attain everlasting felicity.   —*Bahá'u'lláh* **33**

It is certain that man's highest distinction is to be lowly before and obedient to his God; that his greatest glory, his most exalted rank and honor, depend on his close observance of the Divine commands and prohibitions. Religion is the light of the world, and the progress, achievement, and happiness of man result from obedience to the laws set down in the holy Books. Briefly, it is demonstrable that in this life, both outwardly and inwardly the mightiest of structures, the most solidly established, the most enduring, standing guard over the world, assuring both the spiritual and the material perfections of mankind, and protecting the happiness and the civilization of society—is religion.

It is true that there are foolish individuals who have never properly examined the fundamentals of the Divine religions, who have taken as their criterion the behavior of a few religious hypocrites and measured all religious persons by that yardstick, and have on this account concluded that religions are an obstacle to progress, a divisive factor and a cause of malevolence and enmity among peoples. They have not even observed this much, that the principles of the Divine religions can hardly be evaluated by the acts of those who only claim to follow them. For every excellent thing, peerless though it may be, can still be diverted to the wrong ends. A lighted lamp in the hands of an ignorant child or of the blind will not dispel the surrounding darkness nor light up the house—it will set both the bearer and the house on fire. Can we, in such an instance, blame the lamp? No, by the Lord God! To the seeing, a lamp is a guide and will show him his path; but it is a disaster to the blind. . . .

It is certain that the greatest of instrumentalities for achieving the advancement and the glory of man, the supreme agency for the enlightenment and the redemption of the world, is love and fellowship and unity among all the members of the human race. Nothing can be effected in the world, not even conceivably, without unity and agreement, and the perfect means for engendering fellowship and union is true religion. "Hadst Thou spent all the riches of the earth, Thou couldst not have united their hearts; but God hath united them. . . ."*

With the advent of the Prophets of God, their power of creating a real union, one which is both external and of the heart, draws together malevolent peoples who have been

---

*Qur'án 8:64.

thirsting for one another's blood, into the one shelter of the
Word of God. Then a hundred thousand souls become as one
soul, and unnumbered individuals emerge as one body.

—*Bahá'u'lláh* **34**

The holy, divine Manifestations of God confer general
education upon humanity. They arise to bestow universal moral training. For example, Moses was a universal Teacher. He
trained and disciplined the people of Israel, enabled them to
rescue themselves from the lowest abyss of despair and ignorance and caused them to attain an advanced degree of knowledge and development. They were captives and in the bondage of slavery; through Him they became free. He led them
out of Egypt into the Holy Land and opened the doors of their
advancement into higher civilization. Through His training
this oppressed and downtrodden people, slaves and captives
of the Pharaohs, established the splendor of the Solomonic
sovereignty. This is an example of a universal Teacher, a universal Educator. Again, consider Christ: how that marvelous
expression of unity bestowed education and ethical training
upon the Roman, Greek, Egyptian, Syrian and Assyrian nations
and welded together a people from them in a permanent and
indissoluble bond. These nations were formerly at enmity and
in a state of continual hostility and strife. He cemented them
together, caused them to agree, conferred tranquillity upon
humanity and established the foundations of human welfare
throughout the world. Therefore, He was a real Educator, the
Instructor of reality.

When we review the conditions existing in the East prior
to the rise of the Prophet of Arabia, we find that throughout
the Arabian peninsula intense mental darkness and the utmost
ignorance prevailed among its inhabitants. Those tribal peoples were constantly engaged in war, killing and shedding
blood, burning and pillaging the homes of each other and
living in conditions of the utmost debasement and immorality.
They were lower and more brutal than the animals. Muḥammad appeared as a Prophet among such a people. He educated
these barbarous tribes, lifted them out of their ignorance and

savagery and put an end to the continuous strife and hatred which had existed among them. He established agreement and reconciliation among them, unified them and taught them to look upon each other as brothers. Through His training they advanced rapidly in prestige and civilization. They were formerly ignorant; they became wise. They were barbarous; they attained refinement and culture. They were debased and brutal; He uplifted and elevated them. They were humiliated and despised; their civilization and renown spread throughout the world. This is perfect proof that Muḥammad was an Educator and Teacher.   *—'Abdu'l-Bahá* **35**

These holy Manifestations of God are the Educators and Trainers of the world of existence, the Teachers of the world of humanity. They liberate man from the darkness of the world of nature, deliver him from despair, error, ignorance, imperfections and all evil qualities. They clothe him in the garment of perfections and exalted virtues. Men are ignorant; the Manifestations of God make them wise. They are animalistic; the Manifestations make them human. They are savage and cruel; the Manifestations lead them into kingdoms of light and love. They are unjust; the Manifestations cause them to become just. Man is selfish; They sever him from self and desire. Man is haughty; They make him meek, humble and friendly. He is earthly; They make him heavenly. Men are material; the Manifestations transform them into divine semblance. They are immature children; the Manifestations develop them into maturity. Man is poor; They endow him with wealth. Man is base, treacherous and mean; the Manifestations of God uplift him into dignity, nobility and loftiness.   *—'Abdu'l-Bahá* **36**

There are some who imagine that an innate sense of human dignity will prevent man from committing evil actions and ensure his spiritual and material perfection. That is, that an individual who is characterized with natural intelligence, high resolve, and a driving zeal, will, without any consideration for the severe punishments consequent on evil acts, or for the great rewards of righteousness, instinctively refrain from

inflicting harm on his fellowmen and will hunger and thirst to
do good. And yet, if we ponder the lessons of history it will
become evident that this very sense of honor and dignity is
itself one of the bounties deriving from the instructions of the
Prophets of God. We also observe in infants the signs of
aggression and lawlessness, and that if a child is deprived of a
teacher's instructions his undesirable qualities increase from
one moment to the next. It is therefore clear that the emer-
gence of this natural sense of human dignity and honor is the
result of education. Secondly, even if we grant for the sake of
the argument that instinctive intelligence and an innate moral
quality would prevent wrongdoing, it is obvious that individuals
so characterized are as rare as the philosopher's stone. An assumption of this sort cannot be validated by mere words, it must
be supported by the facts. Let us see what power in creation
impels the masses toward righteous aims and deeds! . . .

Universal benefits derive from the grace of the Divine
religions, for they lead their true followers to sincerity of
intent, to high purpose, to purity and spotless honor, to surpassing kindness and compassion, to the keeping of their
covenants when they have covenanted, to concern for the
rights of others, to liberality, to justice in every aspect of life,
to humanity and philanthropy, to valor and to unflagging efforts in the service of mankind. It is religion, to sum up, which
produces all human virtues, and it is these virtues which are
the bright candles of civilization. If a man is not characterized
by these excellent qualities, it is certain that he has never
attained to so much as a drop out of the fathomless river of the
waters of life that flows through the teachings of the Holy
Books, nor caught the faintest breath of the fragrant breezes
that blow from the gardens of God; for nothing on earth can
be demonstrated by words alone, and every level of existence
is known by its signs and symbols, and every degree in man's
development has its identifying mark.

The purpose of these statements is to make it abundantly
clear that the Divine religions, the holy precepts, the heavenly
teachings, are the unassailable basis of human happiness, and

that the peoples of the world can hope for no real relief or deliverance without this one great remedy. —*'Abdu'l-Bahá* **37**

It is self-evident that the unity of the human world and the Most Great Peace cannot be accomplished through material means. They cannot be established through political power, for the political interests of nations are various and the policies of peoples are divergent and conflicting. They cannot be founded through racial or patriotic power, for these are human powers, selfish and weak. The very nature of racial differences and patriotic prejudices prevents the realization of this unity and agreement. Therefore, it is evidenced that the promotion of the oneness of the kingdom of humanity, which is the essence of the teachings of all the Manifestations of God, is impossible except through the divine power and breaths of the Holy Spirit. Other powers are too weak and are incapable of accomplishing this. —*'Abdu'l-Bahá* **38**

Know thou that all the powers combined have not the power to establish universal peace, nor to withstand the overmastering dominion, at every time and season, of these endless wars. Erelong, however, shall the power of heaven, the dominion of the Holy Spirit, hoist on the high summits the banners of love and peace, and there above the castles of majesty and might shall those banners wave in the rushing winds that blow out of the tender mercy of God.

—*'Abdu'l-Bahá* **39**

Irreligion: The Source of Selfishness and Aggression

THE vitality of men's belief in God is dying out in every land. . . . The corrosion of ungodliness is eating into the vitals of human society. —*Bahá'u'lláh* **40**

The weakening of the pillars of religion hath strengthened the foolish and emboldened them and made them more arrogant. Verily I say: The greater the decline of religion, the more grievous the waywardness of the ungodly. This cannot but lead in the end to chaos and confusion. Hear Me, O men of insight, and be warned, ye who are endued with discernment!   *—Bahá'u'lláh* **41**

The face of the world hath altered. The way of God and the religion of God have ceased to be of any worth in the eyes of men.   *—Bahá'u'lláh* **42**

Religion is a mighty bulwark. If the edifice of religion shakes and totters, commotion and chaos will ensue and the order of things will be utterly upset, for in the world of mankind there are two safeguards that protect man from wrongdoing. One is the law which punishes the criminal; but the law prevents only the manifest crime and not the concealed sin; whereas the ideal safeguard, namely, the religion of God, prevents both the manifest and the concealed crime, trains man, educates morals, compels the adoption of virtues and is the all-inclusive power which guarantees the felicity of the world of mankind.   *—'Abdu'l-Bahá* **43**

If the spiritual qualities of the soul, open to the breath of the Divine Spirit, are never used, they become atrophied, enfeebled, and at last incapable; whilst the soul's material qualities alone being exercised, they become terribly powerful—and the unhappy, misguided man, becomes more savage, more unjust, more vile, more cruel, more malevolent than the lower animals themselves. All his aspirations and desires being strengthened by the lower side of the soul's nature, he becomes more and more brutal, until his whole being is in no way superior to that of the beasts that perish. Men such as this, plan to work evil, to hurt and to destroy; they are entirely without the spirit of Divine compassion, for the celestial quality of the soul has been dominated by that of the material. If, on the contrary, the spiritual nature of the soul has been so strengthened that it holds the material side in subjection, then does the man approach the Divine; his humanity becomes so glorified that the virtues of the Celestial Assembly are manifested in him; he radiates the Mercy of God, he stimulates the spiritual progress of mankind, for he becomes a lamp to show light on their path.   —'Abdu'l-Bahá   44

A Greek philosopher living in the days of the youth of Christianity . . . wrote thus: "It is my belief that religion is the very foundation of true civilization." For, unless the moral character of a nation is educated, as well as its brain and its talents, civilization has no sure basis.

As religion inculcates morality, it is therefore the truest philosophy, and on it is built the only lasting civilization. . . .

. . . Because man has stopped his ears to the Voice of Truth and shut his eyes to the Sacred Light, neglecting the Law of God, for this reason has the darkness of war and tumult, unrest and misery, desolated the earth.   —'Abdu'l-Bahá   45

Consider to what a remarkable extent the spirituality of people has been overcome by materialism so that spiritual susceptibility seems to have vanished, divine civilization become decadent, and guidance and knowledge of God no longer remain. All are submerged in the sea of materialism. Although some attend churches and temples of worship and devotion, it is in accordance with the traditions and imitations of their fathers and not for the investigation of reality.

                                                —'Abdu'l-Bahá   46

Man is submerged in the affairs of this world. His aims, objects and attainments are mortal, whereas God desires for him immortal accomplishments. In his heart there is no thought of God. He has sacrificed his portion and birthright of divine spirituality. Desire and passion, like two unmanageable horses, have wrested the rein of control from him and are galloping madly in the wilderness. This is the cause of the degradation of the world of humanity. This is the cause of its retrogression into the appetites and passions of the animal kingdom. Instead of divine advancement we find sensual captivity and debasement of heavenly virtues of the soul. By devotion to the carnal, mortal world human susceptibilities sink to the level of animalism.   —'Abdu'l-Bahá **47**

Day by day the power of the Kingdom in human hearts is weakened, and material forces gain the ascendancy. The divine signs are becoming less and less, and human evidences grow stronger. They have reached such a degree that materialists are advancing and aggressive while divine forces are waning and vanishing. Irreligion has conquered religion.
          —'Abdu'l-Bahá **48**

When, as a result of human perversity, the light of religion is quenched in men's hearts, and the divinely appointed Robe, designed to adorn the human temple, is deliberately discarded, a deplorable decline in the fortunes of humanity immediately sets in, bringing in its wake all the evils which a wayward soul is capable of revealing. The perversion of human nature, the degradation of human conduct, the corruption and dissolution of human institutions, reveal themselves, under such circumstances, in their worst and most revolting aspects. Human character is debased, confidence is shaken, the nerves of discipline are relaxed, the voice of human conscience is stilled, the sense of decency and shame is obscured, conceptions of duty, of solidarity, of reciprocity and loyalty are distorted, and the very feeling of peacefulness, of joy and of hope is gradually extinguished.
    Such, we might well admit, is the state which individuals and institutions alike are approaching.   —Shoghi Effendi **49**

In whichever direction we turn our gaze, no matter how cursory our observation of the doings and sayings of the present generation, we cannot fail to be struck by the evidences of moral decadence which, in their individual lives no less than in their collective capacity, men and women around us exhibit.

There can be no doubt that the decline of religion as a social force, of which the deterioration of religious institutions is but an external phenomenon, is chiefly responsible for so grave, so conspicuous an evil.   —*Shoghi Effendi* **50**

This vital force [religion] is dying out, this mighty agency has been scorned, this radiant light obscured, this impregnable stronghold abandoned, this beauteous robe discarded. God Himself has indeed been dethroned from the hearts of men, and an idolatrous world passionately and clamorously hails and worships the false gods which its own idle fancies have fatuously created, and its misguided hands so impiously exalted. The chief idols in the desecrated temple of mankind are none other than the triple gods of Nationalism, Racialism and Communism, at whose altars governments and peoples, whether democratic or totalitarian, at peace or at war, of the East or of the West, Christian or Islamic, are, in various forms and in different degrees, now worshiping. Their high priests are the politicians and the worldly wise, the so-called sages of the age; their sacrifice, the flesh and blood of the slaughtered multitudes; their incantations outworn shibboleths and insidious and irreverent formulas; their incense, the smoke of anguish that ascends from the lacerated hearts of the bereaved, the maimed, and the homeless.

The theories and policies, so unsound, so pernicious, which deify the state and exalt the nation above mankind, which seek to subordinate the sister races of the world to one single race, which discriminate between the black and the white, and which tolerate the dominance of one privileged class over all others—these are the dark, the false, and crooked doctrines for which any man or people who believes in them, or acts upon them, must, sooner or later, incur the wrath and chastisement of God. . . .

Not only must irreligion and its monstrous offspring, the triple curse that oppresses the soul of mankind in this day, be held responsible for the ills which are so tragically besetting it, but other evils and vices, which are, for the most part, the direct consequences of the "weakening of the pillars of religion," must also be regarded as contributory factors to the manifold guilt of which individuals and nations stand convicted. The signs of moral downfall, consequent to the dethronement of religion and the enthronement of these usurping idols, are too numerous and too patent for even a superficial observer of the state of present-day society to fail to notice. The spread of lawlessness, of drunkenness, of gambling, and of crime; the inordinate love of pleasure, of riches, and other earthly vanities; the laxity of morals, revealing itself in the irresponsible attitude towards marriage, in the weakening of parental control, in the rising tide of divorce, in the deterioration in the standard of literature and of the press, and in the advocacy of theories that are the very negation of purity, of morality and chastity—these evidences of moral decadence, invading both the East and the West, permeating every stratum of society, and instilling their poison in its members of both sexes, young and old alike, blacken still further the scroll upon which are inscribed the manifold transgressions of an unrepentant humanity.

Small wonder that Bahá'u'lláh, the Divine Physician, should have declared: "In this day the tastes of men have changed, and their power of perception hath altered. The contrary winds of the world, and its colors, have provoked a cold, and deprived men's nostrils of the sweet savors of Revelation."   —*Shoghi Effendi* **51**

Alas! we see on all sides how cruel, prejudiced and unjust is man, and how slow he is to believe in God and follow His commandments. . . .

Why is man so hard of heart? It is because he does not yet know God. If he had knowledge of God he could not act in direct opposition to His laws; if he were spiritually minded such a line of conduct would be impossible to him. If only the laws and precepts of the prophets of God had been believed, understood and followed, wars would no longer darken the face of the earth.   —*'Abdu'l-Bahá* **52**

In truth, religion is a radiant light and an impregnable stronghold for the protection and welfare of the peoples of the world, for the fear of God impelleth man to hold fast to that which is good, and shun all evil. Should the lamp of religion be obscured, chaos and confusion will ensue, and the lights of fairness and justice, of tranquillity and peace cease to shine. Unto this will bear witness every man of true understanding.

—Bahá'u'lláh **53**

Were men but to take heed they would readily appreciate that whatever hath streamed from and is set down by the Pen of Glory is even as the sun for the whole world and that therein lie the welfare, security and true interests of all men; otherwise the earth will be tormented by a fresh calamity every day and unprecedented commotions will break out. God grant that the people of the world may be graciously aided to preserve the light of His loving counsels within the globe of wisdom. We cherish the hope that everyone may be adorned with the vesture of true wisdom, the basis of the government of the world.   *—Bahá'u'lláh* **54**

Recognizing the Roots of Irreligion

Conflicting Interpretations of Religious Leaders

LEADERS of religion, in every age, have hindered their people from attaining the shores of eternal salvation, inasmuch as they held the reins of authority in their mighty grasp. Some for the lust of leadership, others through want of knowledge and understanding, have been the cause of the deprivation of the people. By their sanction and authority, every Prophet of God hath drunk from the chalice of sacrifice, and winged His flight unto the heights of glory. What unspeakable cruelties they that have occupied the seats of authority and learning have inflicted upon the true Monarchs of the world, those Gems of divine virtue!   *—Bahá'u'lláh* **55**

Consider the Dispensation of Jesus Christ. Behold, how all the learned men of that generation, though eagerly anticipating the coming of the Promised One, have nevertheless denied Him. Both Annas, the most learned among the divines of His day, and Caiaphas, the high priest, denounced Him and pronounced the sentence of His death.

In like manner, when Muḥammad, the Prophet of God—may all men be a sacrifice unto Him—appeared, the learned men of Mecca and Medina arose, in the early days of His Revelation, against Him and rejected His Message, while they who were destitute of all learning recognized and embraced His Faith.   —Bahá'u'lláh **56**

These leaders ["the divines of the age"], owing to their immersion in selfish desires, and their pursuit of transitory and sordid things, have regarded these divine Luminaries as being opposed to the standards of their knowledge and understanding, and the opponents of their ways and judgments. As they have literally interpreted the Word of God, and the sayings and traditions of the Letters of Unity, and expounded them according to their own deficient understanding, they have therefore deprived themselves and all their people of the bountiful showers of the grace and mercies of God.
                    —Bahá'u'lláh **57**

It is clear and evident that whenever the Manifestations of Holiness were revealed, the divines of their day have hindered the people from attaining unto the way of truth. To this testify the records of all the scriptures and heavenly books. Not one Prophet of God was made manifest Who did not fall a victim to the relentless hate, to the denunciation, denial, and execration of the clerics of His day!   —Bahá'u'lláh **58**

The chief cause ["of the unrest among nations"] is the misrepresentation of religion by the religious leaders and teachers. They teach their followers to believe that their own form of religion is the only one pleasing to God, and that followers of any other persuasion are condemned by the All-Loving Father and deprived of His Mercy and Grace. Hence arise among the peoples, disapproval, contempt, disputes and hatred. If these religious prejudices could be swept away, the nations would soon enjoy peace and concord.

—'Abdu'l-Bahá **59**

Consider history. What has brought unity to nations, morality to peoples and benefits to mankind? If we reflect upon it, we will find that establishing the divine religions has been the greatest means toward accomplishing the oneness of humanity. The foundation of divine reality in religion has done this, not imitations of ancestral religious forms. Imitations are opposed to each other and have ever been the cause of strife, enmity, jealousy and war.   —'Abdu'l-Bahá **60**

All the divine Manifestations have proclaimed the oneness of God and the unity of mankind. They have taught that men should love and mutually help each other in order that they might progress. Now if this conception of religion be true, its essential principle is the oneness of humanity. The fundamental truth of the Manifestations is peace. This underlies all religion, all justice. The divine purpose is that men should live in unity, concord and agreement and should love one another. Consider the virtues of the human world and realize that the oneness of humanity is the primary foundation of them all. Read the Gospel and the other Holy Books. You will find their fundamentals are one and the same. Therefore, unity is the essential truth of religion and, when so understood, embraces all the virtues of the human world. Praise be to God! This knowledge has been spread, eyes have been opened, and ears have become attentive. Therefore, we must endeavor to promulgate and practice the religion of God which has been founded by all the Prophets. And the religion of God is absolute love and unity.   —'Abdu'l-Bahá **61**

Artificial Barriers between Religion, Reason, and Science

ANOTHER cause of dissension and disagreement is the fact that religion has been pronounced at variance with science. Between scientists and the followers of religion there has always been controversy and strife for the reason that the latter have proclaimed religion superior in authority to science and considered scientific announcement opposed to the teachings of religion.   —*'Abdu'l-Bahá* **62**

There is no contradiction between true religion and science. When a religion is opposed to science it becomes mere superstition: that which is contrary to knowledge is ignorance.

How can a man believe to be a fact that which science has proved to be impossible? If he believes in spite of his reason, it is rather ignorant superstition than faith. The true principles of all religions are in conformity with the teachings of science.

The Unity of God is logical, and this idea is not antagonistic to the conclusions arrived at by scientific study.

All religions teach that we must do good, that we must be generous, sincere, truthful, law-abiding, and faithful; all this is reasonable, and logically the only way in which humanity can progress.

All religious laws conform to reason, and are suited to the people for whom they are framed, and for the age in which they are to be obeyed.

Religion has two main parts: (1) The Spiritual. (2) The Practical.

The spiritual part never changes. All the Manifestations of God and His Prophets have taught the same truths and given the same spiritual law. They all teach the one code of morality. There is no division in the truth. The Sun has sent forth many rays to illumine human intelligence, the light is always the same.

The practical part of religion deals with exterior forms

and ceremonies, and with modes of punishment for certain offenses. This is the material side of the law, and guides the customs and manners of the people.

. . . whilst the spiritual law never alters, the practical rules must change their application with the necessities of the time. The spiritual aspect of religion is the greater, the more important of the two, and this is the same for all time, it never changes! It is the same, yesterday, today, and for ever! "As it was in the beginning, is now, and ever shall be."

Now, all questions of morality contained in the spiritual, immutable law of every religion are logically right. If religion were contrary to logical reason then it would cease to be a religion and be merely a tradition. Religion and science are the two wings upon which man's intelligence can soar into the heights, with which the human soul can progress. It is not possible to fly with one wing alone! Should a man try to fly with the wing of religion alone he would quickly fall into the quagmire of superstition, whilst on the other hand, with the wing of science alone he would also make no progress, but fall into the despairing slough of materialism. All religions of the present day have fallen into superstitious practices, out of harmony alike with the true principles of the teaching they represent and with the scientific discoveries of the time. Many religious leaders have grown to think that the importance of religion lies mainly in the adherence to a collection of certain dogmas and the practice of rites and ceremonies! Those whose souls they profess to cure are taught to believe likewise, and these cling tenaciously to the outward forms, confusing them with the inward truth.

Now, these forms and rituals differ in the various churches and amongst the different sects, and even contradict one another; giving rise to discord, hatred, and disunion. The outcome of all this dissension is the belief of many cultured men that religion and science are contradictory terms, that religion needs no powers of reflection, and should in no wise be regulated by science, but must of necessity be opposed, the one to the other. The unfortunate effect of this is that science has drifted apart from religion, and religion has be-come a mere blind and more or less apathetic following of the precepts of certain religious teachers, who insist on their own favorite dogmas being accepted even when they are contrary to science. This is foolishness, for it is quite evident that science is the light, and, being so, religion *truly* so-called does not oppose knowledge.

We are familiar with the phrases "Light and Darkness," "Religion and Science." But the religion which does not walk hand in hand with science is itself in the darkness of superstition and ignorance.

Much of the discord and disunion of the world is created by these man-made oppositions and contradictions. If religion were in harmony with science and they walked together, much of the hatred and bitterness now bringing misery to the human race would be at an end.

Consider what it is that singles man out from among created beings, and makes of him a creature apart. Is it not his reasoning power, his intelligence? Shall he not make use of these in his study of religion? I say unto you: weigh carefully in the balance of reason and science everything that is presented to you as religion. If it passes this test, then accept it, for it is truth! If, however, it does not so conform, then reject it, for it is ignorance!   —'Abdu'l-Bahá **63**

If religious belief and doctrine is at variance with reason, it proceeds from the limited mind of man and not from God; therefore, it is unworthy of belief and not deserving of attention; the heart finds no rest in it, and real faith is impossible. How can man believe that which he knows to be opposed to reason? Is this possible? Can the heart accept that which reason denies? Reason is the first faculty of man, and the religion of God is in harmony with it.   —'Abdu'l-Bahá **64**

God has bestowed the gift of mind upon man in order that he may weigh every fact or truth presented to him and adjudge whether it be reasonable. That which conforms to his reason he may accept as true, while that which reason and science cannot sanction may be discarded as imagination and superstition, as a phantom and not reality.   —*'Abdu'l-Bahá* **65**

Look around and see how the world of today is drowned in superstition and outward forms!

Some worship the product of their own imagination: they make for themselves an imaginary God and adore this, when the creation of their finite minds cannot be the Infinite Mighty Maker of all things visible and invisible! Others worship the sun or trees, also stones! In past ages there were those who adored the sea, the clouds, and even clay!

Today, men have grown into such adoring attachment to outward forms and ceremonies that they dispute over this point of ritual or that particular practice, until one hears on all sides of wearisome arguments and unrest. There are individuals who have weak intellects and their powers of reasoning have not developed, but the strength and power of religion must not be doubted because of the incapacity of these persons to understand.

A small child cannot comprehend the laws that govern nature, but this is on account of the immature intellect of that child; when he is grown older and has been educated he too will understand the everlasting truths. A child does not grasp the fact that the earth revolves round the sun, but, when his intelligence is awakened, the fact is clear and plain to him.

It is impossible for religion to be contrary to science, even though some intellects are too weak or too immature to understand truth.

God made religion and science to be the measure, as it were, of our understanding. Take heed that you neglect not such a wonderful power. Weigh all things in this balance.

—*'Abdu'l-Bahá* **66**

True science is reason and reality, and religion is essentially reality and pure reason; therefore, the two must correspond. Religious teaching which is at variance with science and reason is human invention and imagination unworthy of acceptance, for the antithesis and opposite of knowledge is superstition born of the ignorance of man. If we say religion is opposed to science, we lack knowledge of either true science or true religion, for both are founded upon the premises and conclusions of reason, and both must bear its test.

—'Abdu'l-Bahá **67**

Inasmuch as the blind imitations or dogmatic interpretations current among men do not coincide with the postulates of reason, and the mind and scientific investigation cannot acquiesce thereto, many souls in the human world today shun and deny religion. That is to say, imitations, when weighed in the scales of reason, will not conform to its standard and requirement. Therefore, these souls deny religion and become irreligious, whereas if the reality of the divine religions becomes manifest to them and the foundation of the heavenly teachings is revealed coinciding with facts and evident truths, reconciling with scientific knowledge and reasonable proof, all may acknowledge them, and irreligion will cease to exist. In this way all mankind may be brought to the foundation of religion, for reality is true reason and science, while all that is not conformable thereto is mere superstition. —'Abdu'l-Bahá **68**

While the religion of God is the promoter of truth, the founder of science and knowledge, it is full of goodwill for learned men; it is the civilizer of mankind, the discoverer of the secrets of nature, and the enlightener of the horizons of the world. Consequently, how can it be said to oppose knowledge? God forbid! Nay, for God, knowledge is the most glorious gift of man and the most noble of human pefections. To oppose knowledge is ignorant, and he who detests knowledge and science is not a man, but rather an animal without intelligence. For knowledge is light, life, felicity, perfection, beauty and the means of approaching the Threshold of Unity. It is the honor and glory of the world of humanity, and the greatest bounty of God. Knowledge is identical with guidance, and ignorance is real error.

Happy are those who spend their days in gaining knowledge, in discovering the secrets of nature, and in penetrating the subtleties of pure truth! Woe to those who are contented with ignorance, whose hearts are gladdened by thoughtless imitation, who have fallen into the lowest depths of ignorance and foolishness, and who have wasted their lives!

—'Abdu'l-Bahá **69**

Put all your beliefs into harmony with science; there can be no opposition, for truth is one. When religion, shorn of its superstitions, traditions, and unintelligent dogmas, shows its conformity with science, then will there be a great unifying, cleansing force in the world which will sweep before it all wars, disagreements, discords and struggles—and then will mankind be united in the power of the Love of God.

—'Abdu'l-Bahá **70**

Human Imagination and Misunderstanding

PONDER awhile. What is it that prompted, in every Dispensation, the peoples of the earth to shun the Manifestation of the All-Merciful? What could have impelled them to turn away from Him and to challenge His authority? . . . It is the veil of idle imaginations which, in the days of the Manifestations of the Unity of God and the Daysprings of His everlasting glory, hath intervened, and will continue to intervene, between them and the rest of mankind. For in those days, He Who is the Eternal Truth manifesteth Himself in conformity with that which He Himself hath purposed, and not according to the desires and expectations of men. *—Bahá'u'lláh* **71**

In every age, when a new Manifestation hath appeared and a fresh revelation of God's transcendent power was vouchsafed unto men, they that misbelieved in Him, deluded by the appearance of the peerless and everlasting Beauty in the garb of mortal men, have failed to recognize Him. They have erred from His path and eschewed His company—the company of Him Who is the Symbol of nearness to God. They have even arisen to decimate the ranks of the faithful and to exterminate such as believed in Him.   *—Bahá'u'lláh* 72

Consider how men for generations have been blindly imitating their fathers, and have been trained acccording to such ways and manners as have been laid down by the dictates of their Faith. Were these men, therefore, to discover suddenly that a Man, Who hath been living in their midst, Who, with respect to every human limitation hath been their equal, had risen to abolish every established principle imposed by their Faith—principles by which for centuries they have been disciplined, and every opposer and denier of which they have come to regard as infidel, profligate and wicked—they would of a certainty be veiled and hindered from acknowledging His truth. Such things are as "clouds" that veil the eyes of those whose inner being hath not tasted the Salsabíl of detachment, nor drunk from the Kawthar of the Knowledge of God.*
—Bahá'u'lláh 73

There can be no doubt whatever that had these Apostles† appeared, in bygone ages and cycles, in accordance with the vain imaginations which the hearts of men had devised, no one would have repudiated the truth of these sanctified Beings. Though such men have been, night and day, remembering the one true God, and have been devoutly engaged in the exercise of their devotions, yet they failed in the end to recognize, and partake of the grace of, the Daysprings of the signs of God and the Manifestations of His irrefutable evidences. To this the Scriptures bear witness. Thou hast, no doubt, heard about it.
—Bahá'u'lláh 74

The Divine Messengers have been sent down, and their Books were revealed, for the purpose of promoting the knowl-

---

Salsabíl is a fountain or river in Paradise. *Kawthar* is the river in Paradise from which all other rivers derive their source.
†Manifestations of God.

edge of God, and of furthering unity and fellowship amongst
men. But now behold, how they have made the Law of God a
cause and pretext for perversity and hatred. How pitiful, how
regrettable, that most men are cleaving fast to, and have busied
themselves with, the things they possess, and are unaware of,
and shut out as by a veil from, the things God possesseth!

—*Bahá'u'lláh* 75

One of the forms of prejudice which afflict the world of
mankind is religious bigotry and fanaticism. When this hatred
burns in human hearts, it becomes the cause of revolution,
destruction, abasement of humankind and deprivation of the
mercy of God. For the holy Manifestations and divine Founders of religion Themselves were completely unified in love
and agreement, whereas Their followers are characterized by
bitter antagonism and attitudes of hostility toward each other.
God has desired for mankind the effulgence of love, but
through blindness and misapprehension man has enveloped
himself in veils of discord, strife and hatred. The supreme
need of humanity is cooperation and reciprocity. The stronger
the ties of fellowship and solidarity amongst men, the greater
will be the power of constructiveness and accomplishment in
all the planes of human activity. Without cooperation and
reciprocal attitude the individual member of human society
remains self-centered, uninspired by altruistic purposes, limited and solitary in development. . . . God has destined and
intended religion to be the cause and means of cooperative
effort and accomplishment among mankind. To this end He
has sent the Prophets of God, the holy Manifestations of the
Word, in order that the fundamental reality and religion of
God may prove to be the bond of human unity, for the divine
religions revealed by these holy Messengers have one and the
same foundation. All will admit, therefore, that the divine
religions are intended to be the means of true human cooperation, that they are united in the purpose of making humanity
one family, for they rest upon the universal foundation of love,
and love is the first effulgence of Divinity.

Each one of the divine religions has established two kinds of ordinances: the essential and the accidental. The essential ordinances rest upon the firm, unchanging, eternal foundations of the Word itself. They concern spiritualities, seek to stabilize morals, awaken intuitive susceptibilities, reveal the knowledge of God and inculcate the love of all mankind. The accidental laws concern the administration of outer human actions and relations, establishing rules and regulations requisite for the world of bodies and their control. These are ever subject to change and supersedure according to exigencies of time, place and condition. . . . by adherence to these temporary laws, blindly following and imitating ancestral forms, difference and divergence have arisen among followers of the various religions, resulting in disunion, strife and hatred. Blind imitations and dogmatic observances are conducive to alienation and disagreement; they lead to bloodshed and destruction of the foundations of humanity. Therefore, the religionists of the world must lay aside these imitations and investigate the essential foundation or reality itself, which is not subject to change or transformation. This is the divine means of agreement and unification.

The purpose of all the divine religions is the establishment of the bonds of love and fellowship among men, and the heavenly phenomena of the revealed Word of God are intended to be a source of knowledge and illumination to humanity. So long as man persists in his adherence to ancestral forms and imitation of obsolete ceremonials, denying higher revelations of the divine light in the world, strife and contention will destroy the purpose of religion and make love and fellowship impossible. Each of the holy Manifestations announced the glad tidings of His successor, and each One confirmed the message of His predecessor. Therefore, inasmuch as They were agreed and united in purpose and teaching, it is incumbent upon Their followers to be likewise unified in love and spiritual fellowship. In no other way will discord and alienation disappear and the oneness of the world of humanity be established.   — 'Abdu'l-Bahá **76**

What a wonderful century this is! It is an age of universal reformation. Laws and statutes of civil and federal governments are in process of change and transformation. Sciences and arts are being molded anew. Thoughts are metamorphosed. The foundations of human society are changing and strengthening. Today sciences of the past are useless. The Ptolemaic system of astronomy and numberless other systems and theories of scientific and philosophical explanation are discarded, known to be false and worthless. Ethical precedents and principles cannot be applied to the needs of the modern world. Thoughts and theories of past ages are fruitless now. Thrones and governments are crumbling and falling. All conditions and requisites of the past unfitted and inadequate for the present time are undergoing radical reform. It is evident, therefore, that counterfeit and spurious religious teaching, antiquated forms of belief and ancestral imitations which are at variance with the foundations of divine reality must also pass away and be reformed. They must be abandoned and new conditions be recognized. The morals of humanity must undergo change. New remedies and solutions for human problems must be adopted. Human intellects themselves must change and be subject to the universal reformation. Just as the thoughts and hypotheses of past ages are fruitless today, likewise dogmas and codes of human invention are obsolete and barren of product in religion. Nay, it is true that they are the cause of enmity and conducive to strife in the world of humanity; war and bloodshed proceed from them, and the oneness of mankind finds no recognition in their observance. Therefore, it is our duty in this radiant century to investigate the essentials of divine religion, seek the realities underlying the oneness of the world of humanity and discover the source of fellowship and agreement which will unite mankind in the heavenly bond of love. This unity is the radiance of eternity, the divine spirituality, the effulgence of God and the bounty of the Kingdom. We must investigate the divine source of these heavenly bestowals and adhere unto them steadfastly. For if we remain fettered and restricted by human inventions and dogmas, day by day the world of mankind will be degraded, day by day warfare and strife will increase and satanic forces converge toward the destruction of the human race.

—*'Abdu'l-Bahá* **77**

Were men to meditate upon the lives of the Prophets of old, so easily would they come to know and understand the ways of these Prophets that they would cease to be veiled by such deeds and words as are contrary to their own worldly desires, and thus consume every intervening veil with the fire burning in the Bush of divine knowledge, and abide secure upon the throne of peace and certitude.   —*Bahá'u'lláh* **78**

Arise, O people, and, by the power of God's might, resolve to gain the victory over your own selves, that haply the whole earth may be freed and sanctified from its servitude to the gods of its idle fancies—gods that have inflicted such loss upon, and are responsible for the misery of their wretched worshipers. These idols form the obstacle that impedeth man in his efforts to advance in the path of perfection. We cherish the hope that the Hand of divine power may lend its assistance to mankind and deliver it from its state of grievous abasement.

—*Bahá'u'lláh* **79**

Viewing the Founders of Religion as Agents of One Civilizing Process

ALL the Prophets are the Temples of the Cause of God, Who have appeared clothed in divers attire. If thou wilt observe with discriminating eyes, thou wilt behold Them all abiding in the same tabernacle, soaring in the same heaven, seated upon the same throne, uttering the same speech, and proclaiming the same Faith. Such is the unity of those Essences of Being, those Luminaries of infinite and immeasurable splendor! Wherefore, should one of these Manifestations of Holiness proclaim saying: "I am the return of all the Prophets," He, verily, speaketh the truth. In like manner, in every subsequent Revelation, the return of the former Revelation is a fact, the truth of which is firmly established. . . .

—Bahá'u'lláh **80**

Know thou assuredly that the essence of all the Prophets of God is one and the same. Their unity is absolute. God, the Creator, saith: There is no distinction whatsoever among the Bearers of My Message. They all have but one purpose; their secret is the same secret. To prefer one in honor to another, to exalt certain ones above the rest, is in no wise to be permitted. Every true Prophet hath regarded His Message as fundamentally the same as the Revelation of every other Prophet gone before Him. If any man, therefore, should fail to comprehend this truth, and should consequently indulge in vain and unseemly language, no one whose sight is keen and whose understanding is enlightened would ever allow such idle talk to cause him to waver in his belief.

The measure of the revelation of the Prophets of God in this world, however, must differ. Each and every one of them hath been the Bearer of a distinct Message, and hath been commissioned to reveal Himself through specific acts. It is for this reason that they appear to vary in their greatness. Their Revelation may be likened unto the light of the moon that sheddeth its radiance upon the earth. Though every time it appeareth, it revealeth a fresh measure of its brightness, yet its inherent splendor can never diminish, nor can its light suffer extinction.

It is clear and evident, therefore, that any apparent variation in the intensity of their light is not inherent in the light itself, but should rather be attributed to the varying receptivity of an ever-changing world. Every Prophet Whom the Almighty and Peerless Creator hath purposed to send to the peoples of the earth hath been entrusted with a Message, and charged to act in a manner that would best meet the requirements of the age in which He appeared.   *—Bahá'u'lláh* **81**

Each Manifestation of God hath a distinct individuality, a definitely prescribed mission, a predestined revelation, and specially designated limitations. Each one of them is known by a different name, is characterized by a special attribute, fulfills a definite mission, and is entrusted with a particular Revelation. . . .

It is because of this difference in their station and mission that the words and utterances flowing from these wellsprings of Divine knowledge appear to diverge and differ. Otherwise, in the eyes of them that are initiated into the mysteries of Divine wisdom, all their utterances are, in reality, but the expressions of one Truth. As most of the people have failed to appreciate those stations to which We have referred, they, therefore, feel perplexed and dismayed at the varying utterances pronounced by Manifestations that are essentially one and the same.   *—Bahá'u'lláh* **82**

From the days of Adam until today, the religions of God have been made manifest, one following the other, and each one of them fulfilled its due function, revived mankind, and provided education and enlightenment. They freed the people from the darkness of the world of nature and ushered them into the brightness of the Kingdom. As each succeeding Faith and Law became revealed it remained for some centuries a richly fruitful tree and to it was committed the happiness of humankind. However, as the centuries rolled by, it aged, it flourished no more and put forth no fruit, wherefore was it then made young again.

The religion of God is one religion, but it must ever be renewed. Moses, for example, was sent forth to man and He established a Law, and the Children of Israel, through that Mosaic Law, were delivered out of their ignorance and came into the light; they were lifted up from their abjectness and attained to a glory that fadeth not. Still, as the long years wore on, that radiance passed by, that splendor set, that bright day turned to night; and once that night grew triply dark, the star of the Messiah dawned, so that again a glory lit the world.

Our meaning is this: the religion of God is one, and it is the educator of humankind, but still, it needs must be made new. When thou dost plant a tree, its height increaseth day by day. It putteth forth blossoms and leaves and luscious fruits. But after a long time, it doth grow old, yielding no fruitage anymore. Then doth the Husbandman of Truth take up the seed from that same tree, and plant it in a pure soil; and lo, there standeth the first tree, even as it was before.

Note thou carefully that in this world of being, all things must ever be made new. Look at the material world about thee, see how it hath now been renewed. The thoughts have changed, the ways of life have been revised, the sciences and arts show a new vigor, discoveries and inventions are new, perceptions are new. How then could such a vital power as religion—the guarantor of mankind's great advances, the very means of attaining everlasting life, the fosterer of infinite excellence, the light of both worlds—not be made new? This would be incompatible with the grace and loving kindness of the Lord.   —'Abdu'l-Bahá 83

Every divine Manifestation is the very life of the world, and the skilled physician of each ailing soul. The world of man is sick, and that competent Physician knoweth the cure, arising as He doth with teachings, counsels and admonishments that are the remedy for every pain, the healing balm to every wound. It is certain that the wise physician can diagnose his patient's needs at any season, and apply the cure. . . .

The treatment ordered by wise physicians of the past, and by those that follow after, is not one and the same, rather doth it depend on what aileth the patient; and although the remedy may change, the aim is always to bring the patient back to health.   —'Abdu'l-Bahá 84

The divine religions embody two kinds of ordinances. First, there are those which constitute essential, or spiritual, teachings of the Word of God. These are faith in God, the acquirement of the virtues which characterize perfect manhood, praiseworthy moralities, the acquisition of the bestowals and bounties emanating from the divine effulgences—in brief, the ordinances which concern the realm of morals and ethics. This is the fundamental aspect of the religion of God, and this is of the highest importance because knowledge of God is the fundamental requirement of man. Man must comprehend the oneness of Divinity. He must come to know and acknowledge the precepts of God and realize for a certainty that the ethical development of humanity is dependent upon religion. He must get rid of all defects and seek the attainment of heavenly virtues in order that he may prove to be the image and likeness of God. It is recorded in the Holy Bible that God said, "Let us make man in our image, after our likeness." It is self-evident that the image and likeness mentioned do not apply to the form and semblance of a human being because the reality of Divinity is not limited to any form or figure. Nay, rather, the attributes and characteristics of God are intended. Even as God is pronounced to be just, man must likewise be just. As God is loving and kind to all men, man must likewise manifest loving kindness to all humanity. As God is loyal and truthful, man must show forth the same attributes in the human world. Even as God exercises mercy toward all, man must prove himself to be the manifestation of mercy. In a word, the image and likeness of God constitute the virtues of God, and man is intended to become the recipient of the effulgences of divine attributes. This is the esssential foundation of all the divine religions, the reality itself, common to all. Abraham promulgated this; Moses proclaimed it. Christ and all the Prophets upheld this standard and aspect of divine religion.

Second, there are laws and ordinances which are temporary and nonessential. These concern human transactions and relations. They are accidental and subject to change according to the exigencies of time and place. These ordinances are neither permanent nor fundamental. For instance, during the time of Noah it was expedient that seafood be considered as lawful; therefore, God commanded Noah to partake of all marine animal life. During the time of Moses this was not in accordance with the exigencies of Israel's existence; therefore, a second command was revealed partly abrogating the law concerning marine foods. During the time of Abraham—upon Him be peace!—camel's milk was considered a lawful and acceptable food; likewise, the flesh of the camel; but during Jacob's time, because of a certain vow He made, this became unlawful. These are nonessential, temporary laws. In the Holy Bible there are certain commandments which according to those by-gone times constituted the very spirit of the age, the very light of that period. For example, according to the law of the Torah if a man committed theft of a certain amount, they cut off his hand. Is it practicable and reasonable in this present day to cut off a man's hand for the theft of a dollar? In the Torah there are ten ordinances concerning murder. Could these be made effective today? Unquestionably no; times have changed. According to the explicit text of the Bible if a man should change or break the law of the Sabbath or if he should touch fire on the Sabbath, he must be killed. Today such a law is abrogated. The Torah declares that if a man should speak a disrespectful word to his father, he should suffer the penalty of death. Is this possible of enforcement now? No; human conditions have undergone changes. Likewise, during the time of Christ certain minor ordinances conformable to that period were enforced.

It has been shown conclusively, therefore, that the foundation of the religion of God remains permanent and unchanging. It is that fixed foundation which ensures the progress and stability of the body politic and the illumination of humanity. It has ever been the cause of love and justice amongst men. It works for the true fellowship and unification of all mankind, for it never changes and is not subject to supersedure. The accidental, or nonessential, laws which regulate the transactions of the social body and everyday affairs of life are changeable and subject to abrogation.   — 'Abdu'l-Bahá **85**

The holy Manifestations Who have been the Sources or Founders of the various religious systems were united and agreed in purpose and teaching. Abraham, Moses, Zoroaster, Buddha, Jesus, Muhammad, the Báb and Bahá'u'lláh are one in spirit and reality. Moreover, each Prophet fulfilled the promise of the One Who came before Him and, likewise, Each announced the One Who would follow. Consider how Abraham foretold the coming of Moses, and Moses embodied the

Abrahamic statement. Moses prophesied the Messianic cycle, and Christ fulfilled the law of Moses. It is evident, therefore, that the Holy Manifestations Who founded the religious systems are united and agreed; there is no differentiation possible in Their mission and teachings; all are reflectors of reality, and all are promulgators of the religion of God. The divine religion is reality, and reality is not multiple; it is one. Therefore, the foundations of the religious systems are one because all proceed from the indivisible reality. . . .   —'Abdu'l-Bahá **86**

In brief, the sun is one sun, the light is one light which shines upon all phenomenal beings. Every creature has a portion thereof, but the pure mirror can reveal the story of its bounty more fully and completely. Therefore, we must adore the light of the Sun, no matter through what mirror it may be revealed. We must not entertain prejudice, for prejudice is an obstacle to realization. Inasmuch as the effulgence is one effulgence, the human realities must all become recipients of the same light, recognizing in it the compelling force that unites them in its illumination.   —'Abdu'l-Bahá **87**

I hope that the lights of the Sun of Reality will illumine the whole world so that no strife and warfare, no battles and bloodshed remain. May fanaticism and religious bigotry be unknown, all humanity enter the bond of brotherhood, souls consort in perfect agreement, the nations of earth at last hoist the banner of truth, and the religions of the world enter the divine temple of oneness, for the foundations of the heavenly religions are one reality. Reality is not divisible; it does not admit multiplicity. All the holy Manifestations of God have proclaimed and promulgated the same reality. They have summoned mankind to reality itself, and reality is one. The clouds and mists of imitations have obscured the Sun of Truth. We must forsake these imitations, dispel these clouds and mists and free the Sun from the darkness of superstition. Then will the Sun of Truth shine most gloriously; then all the inhabitants of the world will be united, the religions will be one, sects and denominations will reconcile, all nationalities will flow together in the recognition of one Fatherhood, and all degrees of humankind will gather in the shelter of the same tabernacle, under the same banner.   —*'Abdu'l-Bahá* **88**

Abandoning Obsolete Doctrines through an Unbiased Search for Truth

PEOPLE for the most part delight in superstitions. They regard a single drop of the sea of delusion as preferable to an ocean of certitude. By holding fast unto names they deprive themselves of the inner reality and by clinging to vain imaginings they are kept back from the Dayspring of heavenly signs. God grant you may be graciously aided under all conditions to shatter the idols of superstition and to tear away the veils of the imaginations of men.   —*Bahá'u'lláh* **89**

It is incumbent upon thee, by the permission of God, to cleanse the eye of thine heart from the things of the world, that thou mayest realize the infinitude of divine knowledge, and mayest behold Truth so clearly that thou wilt need no proof to demonstrate His reality, nor any evidence to bear witness unto His testimony.   —*Bahá'u'lláh* **90**

Equity is the most fundamental among human virtues. The evaluation of all things must needs depend upon it. . . .

Say: Observe equity in your judgment, ye men of understanding heart! He that is unjust in his judgment is destitute of the characteristics that distinguish man's station. . . .

We have forbidden men to walk after the imaginations of their hearts, that they may be enabled to recognize Him Who is the sovereign Source and Object of all knowledge, and may acknowledge whatsoever He may be pleased to reveal. Witness how they have entangled themselves with their idle fancies and vain imaginations. By My life! They are themselves the victims of what their own hearts have devised, and yet they perceive it not. Vain and profitless is the talk of their lips, and yet they understand not.

We beseech God that He may graciously vouchsafe His grace unto all men, and enable them to attain the knowledge of Him and of themselves.   *—Bahá'u'lláh* **91**

No man shall attain the shores of the ocean of true understanding except he be detached from all that is in heaven and on earth. Sanctify your souls, O ye peoples of the world, that haply ye may attain that station which God hath destined for you. . . .

The essence of these words is this: they that tread the path of faith, they that thirst for the wine of certitude, must cleanse themselves of all that is earthly—their ears from idle talk, their minds from vain imaginings, their hearts from worldly affections, their eyes from that which perisheth. They should put their trust in God, and, holding fast unto Him, follow in His way. Then will they be made worthy of the effulgent glories of the sun of divine knowledge and understanding, and become the recipients of a grace that is infinite and unseen, inasmuch as man can never hope to attain unto the knowledge of the All-Glorious, can never quaff from the stream of divine knowledge and wisdom, can never enter the abode of immortality, nor partake of the cup of divine nearness and favor, unless and until he ceases to regard the words and deeds of mortal men as a standard for the true understanding and recognition of God and His Prophets.   *—Bahá'u'lláh* **92**

God has given man the eye of investigation by which he may see and recognize truth. He has endowed man with ears that he may hear the message of reality and conferred upon him the gift of reason by which he may discover things for himself. This is his endowment and equipment for the investigation of reality. Man is not intended to see through the eyes of another, hear through another's ears nor comprehend with another's brain. Each human creature has individual endowment, power and responsibility in the creative plan of God. Therefore, depend upon your own reason and judgment and adhere to the outcome of your own investigation; otherwise, you will be utterly submerged in the sea of ignorance and deprived of all the bounties of God.   — *'Abdu'l-Bahá* **93**

Know ye that God has created in man the power of reason, whereby man is enabled to investigate reality. God has not intended man to imitate blindly his fathers and ancestors. He has endowed him with mind, or the faculty of reasoning, by the exercise of which he is to investigate and discover the truth, and that which he finds real and true he must accept. He must not be an imitator or blind follower of any soul. He must not rely implicitly upon the opinion of any man without investigation; nay, each soul must seek intelligently and independently, arriving at a real conclusion and bound only by that reality. The greatest cause of bereavement and disheartening in the world of humanity is ignorance based upon blind imitation. It is due to this that wars and battles prevail; from this cause hatred and animosity arise continually among mankind.
      — *'Abdu'l-Bahá* **94**

Man must seek reality himself, forsaking imitations and adherence to mere hereditary forms. As the nations of the world are following imitations in lieu of truth and as imitations are many and various, differences of belief have been productive of strife and warfare. So long as these imitations remain, the oneness of the world of humanity is impossible. Therefore, we must investigate reality in order that by its light the clouds and darkness may be dispelled. Reality is one reality; it does not admit multiplicity or division. If the nations of the world investigate reality, they will agree and become united.
      — *'Abdu'l-Bahá* **95**

Consider: Are the laws of past ages applicable to present human conditions? Evidently they are not. For example, the laws of former centuries sanctioned despotic forms of government. Are the laws of despotic control fitted for present-day conditions? How could they be applied to solve the questions surrounding modern nations? Similarly, we ask: Would the status of ancient thought, the crudeness of arts and crafts, the insufficiency of scientific attainment serve us today? Would the agricultural methods of the ancients suffice in the twentieth century? Transportation in the former ages was restricted to conveyance by animals. How would it provide for human needs today? If modes of transportation had not been reformed, the teeming millions now upon the earth would die of starvation. Without the railway and the fast-going steamship, the world of the present day would be as dead. How could great cities such as New York and London subsist if dependent upon ancient means of conveyance? It is also true of other things which have been reformed in proportion to the needs of the present time. Had they not been reformed, man could not find subsistence.

If these material tendencies are in such need of reformation, how much greater the need in the world of the human spirit, the world of human thought, perception, virtues and bounties! Is it possible that that need has remained stationary while the world has been advancing in every other condition and direction? It is impossible.

Therefore, we must invoke and supplicate God and strive with the utmost effort in order that the world of human existence in all its degrees may receive a mighty impulse, complete human happiness be attained and the resuscitation of all spirits and emanations be realized through the boundless favor of the mercy of God.   —'Abdu'l-Bahá **96**

The word of truth, no matter which tongue utters it, must be sanctioned. Absolute verities, no matter in what book they be recorded, must be accepted. If we harbor prejudice, it will be the cause of deprivation and ignorance. —'Abdu'l-Bahá **97**

Verily, the century of radiance has dawned, minds are advancing, perceptions are broadening, realizations of human possibilities are becoming universal, susceptibilities are developing, the discovery of realities is progressing. Therefore, it is necessary that we should cast aside all the prejudices of ignorance, discard superannuated beliefs in traditions of past ages and raise aloft the banner of international agreement. Let us cooperate in love and through spiritual reciprocity enjoy eternal happiness and peace. —'Abdu'l-Bahá 98

Chapter 4

Preparing the Path to
World Order

Inducing the Will to Act

ALL men have been created in the nature made
by God, the Guardian, the Self-Subsisting. Unto each one hath
been prescribed a preordained measure, as decreed in God's
mighty and guarded Tablets. All that which ye potentially
possess can, however, be manifested only as a result of your
own volition. Your own acts testify to this truth. Consider, for
instance, that which hath been forbidden . . . unto men. God
hath . . . by His behest, decreed as lawful whatsoever He hath
pleased to decree, and hath, through the power of His sovereign might, forbidden whatsoever He elected to forbid. . . .
Men, however, have wittingly broken His law. Is such a behavior to be attributed to God, or to their proper selves? Be fair in
your judgment. Every good thing is of God, and every evil thing
is from yourselves. Will ye not comprehend?   —*Bahá'u'lláh* 1

It is incumbent upon every man of insight and understanding to strive to translate that which hath been written
into reality and action. . . .   —*Bahá'u'lláh* 2

Mere knowledge of principles is not sufficient. We all
know and admit that justice is good, but there is need of
volition and action to carry out and manifest it. For example,
we might think it good to build a church, but simply thinking
of it as a good thing will not help its erection. The ways and
means must be provided; we must will to build it and then
proceed with the construction. All of us know that international peace is good, that it is conducive to human welfare and the
glory of man, but volition and action are necessary before it
can be established. Action is essential. Inasmuch as this cen-

tury is a century of light, capacity for action is assured to mankind. Necessarily the divine principles will be spread among men until the time of action arrives. Surely this has been so, and truly the time and conditions are ripe for action now.   — 'Abdu'l-Bahá 3

Some things are subject to the free will of man, such as justice, equity, tyranny and injustice, in other words, good and evil actions; it is evident and clear that these actions are, for the most part, left to the will of man. But there are certain things to which man is forced and compelled, such as sleep, death, sickness, decline in power, injuries and misfortunes; these are not subject to the will of man, and he is not responsible for them, for he is compelled to endure them. But in the choice of good and bad actions he is free, and he commits them according to his own will.

For example, if he wishes, he can pass his time in praising God, or he can be occupied with other thoughts. He can be an enkindled light through the fire of the love of God, and a philanthropist loving the world, or he can be a hater of mankind, and engrossed with material things. He can be just or cruel. These actions and these deeds are subject to the control of the will of man himself; consequently, he is responsible for them. . . .

. . . in all the action or inaction of man, he receives power from the help of God; but the choice of good or evil belongs to the man himself.   — 'Abdu'l-Bahá 4

All over the world one hears beautiful sayings extolled and noble precepts admired. All men say they love what is good, and hate everything that is evil! Sincerity is to be admired, whilst lying is despicable. Faith is a virtue, and treachery is a disgrace to humanity. It is a blessed thing to gladden the hearts of men, and wrong to be the cause of pain. To be kind and merciful is right, while to hate is sinful. Justice is a noble quality and injustice an iniquity. That it is one's duty to be pitiful and harm no one, and to avoid jealousy and malice at all costs. Wisdom is the glory of man, not ignorance; light, not darkness! It is a good thing to turn one's face toward God, and foolishness to ignore Him. That it is our duty to guide man upward, and not to mislead him and be the cause of his downfall. There are many more examples like unto these.

But all these sayings are but words and we see very few of them carried into the world of action. On the contrary, we perceive that men are carried away by passion and selfishness, each man thinking only of what will benefit himself even if it means the ruin of his brother. They are all anxious to make their fortune and care little or nothing for the welfare of others. They are concerned about their *own* peace and comfort, while the condition of their fellows troubles them not at all.

Unhappily this is the road most men tread.

—'Abdu'l-Bahá **5**

What profit is there in agreeing that universal friendship is good, and talking of the solidarity of the human race as a grand ideal? Unless these thoughts are translated into the world of action, they are useless.

The wrong in the world continues to exist just because people talk only of their ideals, and do not strive to put them into practice. If actions took the place of words, the world's misery would very soon be changed into comfort.

A man who does great good, and talks not of it, is on the way to perfection.

The man who has accomplished a small good and magnifies it in his speech is worth very little.

If I love you, I need not continually speak of my love—you will know without any words. On the other hand if I love you not, that also will you know—and you would not believe me, were I to tell you in a thousand words, that I loved you.

People make much profession of goodness, multiplying fine words because they wish to be thought greater and better than their fellows, seeking fame in the eyes of the world. Those who do most good use fewest words concerning their actions.

The children of God do the works without boasting, obeying His laws.

My hope for you is that you will ever avoid tyranny and oppression; that you will work without ceasing till justice reigns in every land, that you will keep your hearts pure and your hands free from unrighteousness.

This is what the near approach to God requires from you, and this is what I expect of you.   —*'Abdu'l-Bahá* **6**

Our actions will help on the world, will spread civilization, will help the progress of science, and cause the arts to develop. Without action nothing in the material world can be accomplished, neither can words unaided advance a man in the spiritual Kingdom. It is not through lip service only that the elect of God have attained to holiness, but by patient lives of active service they have brought light into the world.

Therefore strive that your actions day by day may be beautiful prayers. Turn towards God, and seek always to do that which is right and noble. Enrich the poor, raise the fallen, comfort the sorrowful, bring healing to the sick, reassure the fearful, rescue the oppressed, bring hope to the hopeless, shelter the destitute!   —*'Abdu'l-Bahá* **7**

A few, unaware of the power latent in human endeavor, consider this matter* as highly impracticable, nay even beyond the scope of man's utmost efforts. Such is not the case, however. On the contrary, thanks to the unfailing grace of God, the loving kindness of His favored ones, the unrivaled endeavors of wise and capable souls, and the thoughts and ideas of the peerless leaders of this age, nothing whatsoever can be regarded as unattainable. Endeavor, ceaseless endeavor, is required. Nothing short of an indomitable determination can possibly achieve it. Many a cause which past ages have regarded as purely visionary, yet in this day has become most easy and practicable. Why should this most great and lofty Cause—the daystar of the firmament of true civilization and the cause of the glory, the advancement, the well-being and

---

*The Cause of Universal Peace.

the success of all humanity—be regarded as impossible of achievement? Surely the day will come when its beauteous light shall shed illumination upon the assemblage of man.

—*'Abdu'l-Bahá* **8**

Our greatest efforts must be directed towards detachment from the things of the world; we must strive to become more spiritual, more luminous, to follow the counsel of the Divine Teaching, to serve the cause of unity and true equality, to be merciful, to reflect the love of the Highest on all men, so that the light of the Spirit shall be apparent in all our deeds, to the end that all humanity shall be united, the stormy sea thereof calmed, and all rough waves disappear from off the surface of life's ocean henceforth unruffled and peaceful.

—*'Abdu'l-Bahá* **9**

Eliminating Barriers to Peace

Racism

O YE discerning ones! Verily, the words which have descended from the heaven of the Will of God are the source of unity and harmony for the world. Close your eyes to racial differences, and welcome all with the light of oneness.   —*Bahá'u'lláh* **10**

We desire but the good of the world and the happiness of the nations . . . that all nations should become one in faith and all men as brothers; that the bonds of affection and unity between the sons of men should be strengthened; that diversity of religion should cease, and differences of race be annulled.   —*Bahá'u'lláh* **11**

Bahá'u'lláh hath said that the various races of humankind lend a composite harmony and beauty of color to the whole. Let all associate, therefore, in this great human garden even as flowers grow and blend together side by side without discord or disagreement between them.   —*'Abdu'l-Bahá* **12**

Bahá'u'lláh once compared the colored people to the black pupil of the eye surrounded by the white. In this black pupil is seen the reflection of that which is before it, and through it the light of the spirit shineth forth.

—'Abdu'l-Bahá 13

God maketh no distinction between the white and the black. If the hearts are pure both are acceptable unto Him. God is no respecter of persons on account of either color or race. All colors are acceptable unto Him, be they white, black, or yellow. Inasmuch as all were created in the image of God, we must bring ourselves to realize that all embody divine possibilities.   —'Abdu'l-Bahá 14

In the estimation of God all men are equal. There is no distinction or preference for any soul, in the realm of His justice and equity.   —'Abdu'l-Bahá 15

All humanity are the children of God; they belong to the same family, to the same original race. There can be no multiplicity of races, since all are the descendants of Adam. This signifies that racial assumption and distinction are nothing but superstition. In the estimate of God there are no English, French, Germans, Turkish or Persians. All these in the presence of God are equal; they are of one race and creation; God did not make these divisions. These distinctions have had their origin in man himself. Therefore, as they are against the plan and purpose of reality, they are false and imaginary. We are of one physical race, even as we are of one physical plan of material body—each endowed with two eyes, two ears, one head, two feet.   —'Abdu'l-Bahá 16

In the estimation of God there is no distinction of color; all are one in the color and beauty of servitude to Him. Color is not important; the heart is all-important. It mattereth not what the exterior may be if the heart is pure and white within. God doth not behold differences of hue and complexion. He looketh at the hearts. He whose morals and virtues are praiseworthy is preferred in the presence of God; he who is devoted to the Kingdom is most beloved. In the realm of genesis and creation the question of color is of least importance.

— 'Abdu'l-Bahá 17

Excellence does not depend upon color. Character is the true criterion of humanity. Anyone who possesses a good character, who has faith in God and is firm, whose actions are good, whose speech is good—that one is accepted at the threshold of God no matter what color he may be.

— 'Abdu'l-Bahá 18

Indeed, the world of humanity is like one kindred and one family. Because of the climatic differences of the zones, through the passing of ages colors have become different. In the torrid zone, on account of the intensity of the effect of the sun throughout the ages the black race appeared. In the frigid zone, on account of the severity of the cold and the ineffectiveness of the heat of the sun throughout the ages the white race appeared. In the temperate zone, the yellow, brown and red races came into existence. But in reality mankind is one race. Because it is of one race unquestionably there must be unity and harmony and no separation or discord.

Gracious God! The animal, notwithstanding that it is a captive of nature and nature completely dominateth it, attacheth no importance to color. For instance, thou dost behold that the black, white, yellow, blue and other colored pigeons are in utmost harmony with one another. They never give importance to color. Likewise sheep and the beasts, despite differences in color, are in utmost love and unity. It is strange that man hath made color a means of strife.   — 'Abdu'l-Bahá 19

Throughout the animal kingdom we do not find the creatures separated because of color. They recognize unity of species and oneness of kind. If we do not find color distinction drawn in a kingdom of lower intelligence and reason, how can it be justified among human beings, especially when we know that all have come from the same source and belong to the same household? In origin and intention of creation mankind is one. Distinctions of race and color have arisen afterward.

—'Abdu'l-Bahá **20**

Man is endowed with superior reasoning power and the faculty of perception; he is the manifestation of divine bestowals. Shall racial ideas prevail and obscure the creative purpose of unity in his kingdom? *—'Abdu'l-Bahá* **21**

One of the important questions which affect the unity and the solidarity of mankind is the fellowship and equality of the white and colored races. Between these two races certain points of agreement and points of distinction exist which warrant just and mutual consideration. The points of contact are many. . . . In this country, the United States of America, patriotism is common to both races; all have equal rights to citizenship, speak one language, receive the blessings of the same civilization, and follow the precepts of the same religion. In fact numerous points of partnership and agreement exist between the two races, whereas the one point of distinction is that of color. Shall this, the least of all distinctions, be allowed to separate you as races and individuals? *—'Abdu'l-Bahá* **22**

If you go into a garden and find all the flowers alike in form, species and color, the effect is wearisome to the eye. The garden is more beautiful when the flowers are many-colored and different; the variety lends charm and adornment. In a flock of doves some are white, some black, red, blue; yet they make no distinction among themselves. All are doves no matter what the color.

This variety in forms and colorings which is manifest in all the kingdoms is according to creative wisdom and has a divine purpose. Nevertheless, whether the creatures be all alike or all different should not be the cause of strife and quarreling among them. Especially why should man find cause for discord in the color or race of his fellow creature? No

educated or illumined mind will allow that this differentiation and discord should exist or that there is any ground for it.
—'Abdu'l-Bahá   **23**

The diversity in the human family should be the cause of love and harmony, as it is in music where many different notes blend together in the making of a perfect chord. If you meet those of different race and color from yourself, do not mistrust them and withdraw yourself into your shell of conventionality, but rather be glad and show them kindness. Think of them as different colored roses growing in the beautiful garden of humanity, and rejoice to be among them.   —'Abdu'l-Bahá   **24**

In the world of being the meeting is blessed when the white and colored races meet together with infinite spiritual love and heavenly harmony. When such meetings are established, and the participants associate with each other with perfect love, unity and kindness, the angels of the Kingdom praise them, and the Beauty of Bahá'u'lláh addresseth them, "Blessed are ye! Blessed are ye!"   —'Abdu'l-Bahá   **25**

It is God's purpose that in the West union and harmony may day by day increase among the friends of God and the handmaids of the Merciful. Not until this is realized can any advance be achieved. And the greatest means for the union and harmony of all is the gathering of the friends in spiritual meetings. This matter is very important and is a magnet which will attract divine confirmations.   —'Abdu'l-Bahá   **26**

Strive earnestly and put forth your greatest endeavor toward the accomplishment of this fellowship and the cementing of this bond of brotherhood between you. Such an attainment is not possible without will and effort on the part of each; from one, expressions of gratitude and appreciation; from the other, kindliness and recognition of equality. Each one should endeavor to develop and assist the other toward mutual advancement. . . . Love and unity will be fostered between you, thereby bringing about the oneness of mankind. For the ac-

complishment of unity between the colored and white will be
an assurance of the world's peace.   —'Abdu'l-Bahá 27

This question of the union of the white and the black is
very important, for if it is not realized, erelong great difficulties
will arise, and harmful results will follow.   —'Abdu'l-Bahá 28

If this matter remaineth without change, enmity will be
increased day by day, and the final result will be hardship and
may end in bloodshed.   —'Abdu'l-Bahá 29

Let the white make a supreme effort in their resolve to
contribute their share to the solution of this problem, to abandon once for all their usually inherent and at times subcon-
scious sense of superiority, to correct their tendency towards
revealing a patronizing attitude towards the members of the
other race, to persuade them through their intimate, spontaneous and informal association with them of the genuineness
of their friendship and the sincerity of their intentions, and to
master their impatience of any lack of responsiveness on the
part of a people who have received, for so long a period, such
grievous and slow-healing wounds. Let the Negroes, through a
corresponding effort on their part, show by every means in
their power the warmth of their response, their readiness to
forget the past, and their ability to wipe out every trace of
suspicion that may still linger in their hearts and minds. Let
neither think that the solution of so vast a problem is a matter
that exclusively concerns the other. Let neither think that such
a problem can either easily or immediately be resolved. . . .
Let neither think that anything short of genuine love, extreme
patience, true humility, consummate tact, sound initiative, ma-
ture wisdom, and deliberate, persistent, and prayerful effort,
can succeed in blotting out the stain which this patent evil has
left on the fair name of their common country.* Let them rather
believe, and be firmly convinced, that on their mutual under-

---

*The United States.

standing, their amity, and sustained cooperation, must depend
. . . the deflection of that dangerous course so greatly feared
by 'Abdu'l-Bahá. . . .   —*Shoghi Effendi* **30**

Racism, one of the most baneful and persistent evils, is a
major barrier to peace. Its practice perpetrates too outrageous
a violation of the dignity of human beings to be countenanced
under any pretext. Racism retards the unfoldment of the
boundless potentialities of its victims, corrupts its perpetrators, and blights human progress. Recognition of the oneness
of mankind, implemented by appropriate legal measures, must
be universally upheld if this problem is to be overcome.
                     —*The Universal House of Justice* **31**

Intense is the hatred, in America, between black and
white, but my hope is that the power of the Kingdom will bind
these two in friendship, and serve them as a healing balm.
Let them look not upon a man's color but upon his heart.
If the heart be filled with light, that man is nigh unto the
threshold of his Lord; but if not, that man is careless of his
Lord, be he white or be he black.   —*'Abdu'l-Bahá* **32**

In the world of humanity it is wise and seemly that all
the individual members should manifest unity and affinity. In
the clustered jewels of the races may the blacks be as sap-
phires and rubies and the whites as diamonds and pearls. The
composite beauty of humanity will be witnessed in their unity
and blending. How glorious the spectacle of real unity among
mankind! How conducive to peace, confidence and happiness
if races and nations were united in fellowship and accord! The
Prophets of God were sent into the world upon this mission
of unity and agreement: that these long-separated sheep might
flock together. When the sheep separate, they are exposed to
danger, but in a flock and under protection of the shepherd
they are safe from the attack of all ferocious enemies.
When the racial elements of the American nation unite in
actual fellowship and accord, the lights of the oneness of

humanity will shine, the day of eternal glory and bliss will dawn, the spirit of God encompass, and the divine favors descend. Under the leadership and training of God, the real Shepherd, all will be protected and preserved. He will lead them in green pastures of happiness and sustenance, and they will attain to the real goal of existence. This is the blessing and benefit of unity; this is the outcome of love. This is the sign of the Most Great Peace; this is the star of the oneness of the human world. Consider how blessed this condition will be. I pray for you and ask the confirmation and assistance of God in your behalf.   —'Abdu'l-Bahá **33**

Extremes of Wealth and Poverty

Preventing Economic Disparity. O son of man! If thine eyes be turned towards mercy, forsake the things that profit thee and cleave unto that which will profit mankind. And if thine eyes be turned towards justice, choose thou for thy neighbor that which thou choosest for thyself. Humility exalteth man to the heaven of glory and power, whilst pride abaseth him to the depths of wretchedness and degradation.   —Bahá'u'lláh **34**

O Son of Man! Bestow My wealth upon My poor, that in heaven thou mayest draw from stores of unfading splendor and treasures of imperishable glory.   —Bahá'u'lláh **35**

Wealth is praiseworthy in the highest degree, if it is acquired by an individual's own efforts and the grace of God, in commerce, agriculture, art and industry, and if it be expended for philanthropic purposes. Above all, if a judicious and resourceful individual should initiate measures which would universally enrich the masses of the people, there could be no undertaking greater than this, and it would rank in the sight of God as the supreme achievement, for such a benefactor would supply the needs and ensure the comfort and well-being of a great multitude. Wealth is most commendable, provided the entire population is wealthy. If, however, a few have inordinate riches while the rest are impoverished, and no fruit or benefit accrues from that wealth, then it is only a liability to its possessor. If, on the other hand, it is expended for the promotion of knowledge, the founding of elementary and other schools, the encouragement of art and industry, the training of orphans and the poor—in brief, if it is dedicated to the welfare of society—its possessor will stand out before God and man as the most excellent of all who live on earth and will be accounted as one of the people of paradise.

—*Abdu'l-Bahá* **36**

Every human being has the right to live; they have a right to rest, and to a certain amount of well-being. As a rich man is able to live in his palace surrounded by luxury and the greatest comfort, so should a poor man be able to have the necessaries of life. Nobody should die of hunger; everybody should have sufficient clothing; one man should not live in excess while another has no possible means of existence.

—*Abdu'l-Bahá* **37**

We see amongst us men who are overburdened with riches on the one hand, and on the other those unfortunate ones who starve with nothing; those who possess several stately palaces, and those who have not where to lay their head. Some we find with numerous courses of costly and dainty food; whilst others can scarce find sufficient crusts to keep them alive. Whilst some are clothed in velvets, furs and fine linen, others have insufficient, poor and thin garments with which to protect them from the cold.

This condition of affairs is wrong, and must be remedied.

—*Abdu'l-Bahá* **38**

It is important to limit riches, as it is also of importance to limit poverty. Either extreme is not good. To be seated in the mean is most desirable.* If it be right for a capitalist to

---

* "Give me neither poverty nor riches" (Prov. 30:8).

possess a large fortune, it is equally just that his workman should have a sufficient means of existence.

A financier with colossal wealth should not exist whilst near him is a poor man in dire necessity. When we see poverty allowed to reach a condition of starvation it is a sure sign that somewhere we shall find tyranny. Men must bestir themselves in this matter, and no longer delay in altering conditions which bring the misery of grinding poverty to a very large number of the people. The rich must give of their abundance, they must soften their hearts and cultivate a compassionate intelligence, taking thought for those sad ones who are suffering from lack of the very necessities of life.

There must be special laws made, dealing with these extremes of riches and of want. The members of the Government should consider the laws of God when they are framing plans for the ruling of the people. The general rights of mankind must be guarded and preserved.

The government of the countries should conform to the Divine Law which gives equal justice to all. This is the only way in which the deplorable superfluity of great wealth and miserable, demoralizing, degrading poverty can be abolished. Not until this is done will the Law of God be obeyed.

—'Abdu'l-Bahá **39**

Under present systems and conditions of government the poor are subject to the greatest need and distress while others more fortunate live in luxury and plenty far beyond their actual necessities. This inequality of portion and privilege is one of the deep and vital problems of human society. That there is need of an equalization and apportionment by which all may possess the comforts and privileges of life is evident. The remedy must be legislative readjustment of conditions. The rich too must be merciful to the poor, contributing from willing hearts to their needs without being forced or compelled to do so. The composure of the world will be assured by the establishment of this principle in the religious life of mankind.

—'Abdu'l-Bahá **40**

The laws of the present civilization . . . lead to a small number of individuals accumulating incomparable fortunes, beyond their needs, while the greater number remain destitute, stripped and in the greatest misery. This is contrary to justice, to humanity, to equity; it is the height of iniquity, the opposite to what causes divine satisfaction.

This contrast is peculiar to the world of man: with other creatures—that is to say, with nearly all animals—there is a kind of justice and equality. Thus equality exists in a shepherd's flock and in a herd of deer in the country. Likewise, among the birds of the prairie, of the plain, of the hills or of the orchard, and among every kind of animal some kind of equality prevails. With them such a difference in the means of existence is not to be found; so they live in the most complete peace and joy.

It is quite otherwise with the human species, which persists in the greatest error, and in absolute iniquity. Consider an individual who has amassed treasures by colonizing a country for his profit: he has obtained an incomparable fortune and has secure profits and incomes which flow like a river, while a hundred thousand unfortunate people, weak and powerless, are in need of a mouthful of bread. There is neither equality nor benevolence. So you see that general peace and joy are destroyed, and the welfare of humanity is negated to such an extent as to make fruitless the lives of many. For fortune, honors, commerce, industry are in the hands of some industrialists, while other people are submitted to quite a series of difficulties and to limitless troubles: they have neither advantages, nor profits, nor comforts, nor peace.

Then rules and laws should be established to regulate the excessive fortunes of certain private individuals and meet the needs of millions of the poor masses; thus a certain moderation would be obtained. However, absolute equality is just as impossible, for absolute equality in fortunes, honors, commerce, agriculture, industry would end in disorderliness, in chaos, in disorganization of the means of existence, and in universal disappointment: the order of the community would be quite destroyed. Thus difficulties will also arise when unjustified equality is imposed. It is, therefore, preferable for moderation to be established by means of laws and regulations to hinder the constitution of the excessive fortunes of certain individuals, and to protect the essential needs of the masses. For instance, the manufacturers and the industrialists heap up a treasure each day, and the poor artisans do not gain their daily sustenance: that is the height of iniquity, and no just man can accept it. Therefore, laws and regulations should be established which would permit the workmen to receive from the factory owner their wages and a share in the fourth or the fifth part of the profits, according to the capacity of the factory; or in some other way the body of workmen and the manufacturers should share equitably the profits and advantages. Indeed, the capital and management come from the owner of the factory, and the work and labor, from the body of the workmen. Either the workmen should receive wages which assure them an adequate support and, when they cease work, becoming feeble or helpless, they should have sufficient benefits from the income of the industry; or the wages should be high enough to satisfy the workmen with the amount they receive so that they may themselves be able to put a little aside for days of want and helplessness.

When matters will be thus fixed, the owner of the factory will no longer put aside daily a treasure which he has absolutely no need of (for, if the fortune is disproportionate, the capitalist succumbs under a formidable burden and gets into the greatest difficulties and troubles; the administration of an excessive fortune is very difficult and exhausts man's natural strength). And the workmen and artisans will no longer be in the greatest misery and want; they will no longer be submitted to the worst privations at the end of their life.

It is, then, clear and evident that the repartition of excessive fortunes among a small number of individuals, while the masses are in need, is an iniquity and an injustice. In the same way, absolute equality would be an obstacle to life, to welfare, to order and to the peace of humanity. In such a question moderation is preferable. It lies in the capitalists' being moderate in the acquisition of their profits, and in their having a consideration for the welfare of the poor and needy—that is to say, that the workmen and artisans receive a fixed and established daily wage—and have a share in the general profits of the factory.

It would be well, with regard to the common rights of manufacturers, workmen and artisans, that laws be established, giving moderate profits to manufacturers, and to workmen the necessary means of existence and security for the future. Thus when they become feeble and cease working, get old and helpless, or leave behind children under age, they and their children will not be annihilated by excess of poverty.

—'Abdu'l-Bahá   **41**

The inordinate disparity between rich and poor, a source of acute suffering, keeps the world in a state of instability, virtually on the brink of war. Few societies have dealt effectively with this situation. The solution calls for the combined application of spiritual, moral and practical approaches. A fresh look at the problem is required, entailing consultation with experts from a wide spectrum of disciplines, devoid of economic and ideological polemics, and involving the people directly affected in the decisions that must urgently be made. It is an issue that is bound up not only with the necessity for eliminating extremes of wealth and poverty but also with those spiritual verities the understanding of which can produce a new universal attitude. Fostering such an attitude is itself a major part of the solution.

—The Universal House of Justice   **42**

Fostering Altruism and Philanthropy. O Ye Rich Ones on Earth! The poor in your midst are My trust; guard ye My trust, and be not intent only on your own ease.   *—Bahá'u'lláh*   **43**

Charity is pleasing and praiseworthy in the sight of God and is regarded as a prince among goodly deeds. Consider ye and call to mind that which the All-Merciful hath revealed in the Qur'án: "They prefer them before themselves, though poverty be their own lot. And with such as are preserved from their own covetousness shall it be well." . . . Blessed is he who preferreth his brother before himself.   —Bahá'u'lláh 44

If ye meet the abased or the downtrodden, turn not away disdainfully from them, for the King of Glory* ever watcheth over them and surroundeth them with such tenderness as none can fathom except them that have suffered their wishes and desires to be merged in the Will of your Lord, the Gracious, the All-Wise. O ye rich ones of the earth! Flee not from the face of the poor that lieth in the dust, nay rather befriend him and suffer him to recount the tale of the woes with which God's inscrutable Decree hath caused him to be afflicted. By the righteousness of God! Whilst ye consort with him, the Concourse on high will be looking upon you, will be interceding for you, will be extolling your names and glorifying your action.   —Bahá'u'lláh 45

The Teachings of Bahá'u'lláh advocate voluntary sharing, and this is a greater thing than the equalization of wealth. For equalization must be imposed from without, while sharing is a matter of free choice.

Man reacheth perfection through good deeds, voluntarily performed, not through good deeds the doing of which was forced upon him. And sharing is a personally chosen righteous act: that is, the rich should extend assistance to the poor, they should expend their substance for the poor, but of their own free will, and not because the poor have gained this end by force. For the harvest of force is turmoil and the ruin of the social order. On the other hand voluntary sharing, the freely chosen expending of one's substance, leadeth to society's comfort and peace. It lighteth up the world; it bestoweth honor upon humankind.   —'Abdu'l-Bahá 46

_____
*God.

The fundamentals of the whole economic condition are divine in nature and are associated with the world of the heart and spirit. . . . Hearts must be so cemented together, love must become so dominant that the rich shall most willingly extend assistance to the poor and take steps to establish these economic adjustments permanently. If it is accomplished in this way, it will be most praiseworthy because then it will be for the sake of God and in the pathway of His service. For example, it will be as if the rich inhabitants of a city should say, "It is neither just nor lawful that we should possess great wealth while there is abject poverty in this community," and then willingly give their wealth to the poor, retaining only as much as will enable them to live comfortably.

Strive, therefore, to create love in the hearts in order that they may become glowing and radiant. When that love is shining, it will permeate other hearts even as this electric light illumines its surroundings. When the love of God is established, everything else will be realized. This is the true foundation of all economics.   —'Abdu'l-Bahá **47**

Among the results of the manifestation of spiritual forces will be that the human world will adapt itself to a new social form, the justice of God will become manifest throughout human affairs, and human equality will be universally established. The poor will receive a great bestowal, and the rich attain eternal happiness. For although at the present time the rich enjoy the greatest luxury and comfort, they are nevertheless deprived of eternal happiness; for eternal happiness is contingent upon giving, and the poor are everywhere in the state of abject need. Through the manifestation of God's great equity the poor of the world will be rewarded and assisted fully, and there will be a readjustment in the economic conditions of mankind so that in the future there will not be the abnormally rich nor the abject poor. The rich will enjoy the privilege of this new economic condition as well as the poor, for owing to certain provisions and restrictions they will not be able to accumulate so much as to be burdened by its management, while the poor will be relieved from the stress of want and misery. The rich will enjoy his palace, and the poor will have his comfortable cottage.

The essence of the matter is that divine justice will become manifest in human conditions and affairs, and all mankind will find comfort and enjoyment in life. It is not meant that all will be equal, for inequality in degree and capacity is a property of nature. Necessarily there will be rich people and also those who will be in want of their livelihood, but in the aggregate community there will be equalization and readjustment of values and interests. In the future there will be no very rich nor extremely poor. There will be an equilibrium of interests, and a condition will be established which will make both rich and poor comfortable and content. This will be an eternal and blessed outcome of the glorious twentieth century which will be realized universally.   —'Abdu'l-Bahá **48**

Man is he who forgets his own interests for the sake of others. His own comfort he forfeits for the well-being of all. Nay, rather, his own life must he be willing to forfeit for the life of mankind. Such a man is the honor of the world of humanity. Such a man is the glory of the world of mankind. Such a man is the one who wins eternal bliss. Such a man is near to the threshold of God. Such a man is the very manifestation of eternal happiness. Otherwise, men are like animals, exhibiting the same proclivities and propensities as the world of animals. What distinction is there? What prerogatives, what perfections? None whatever! Animals are better even—thinking only of themselves and negligent of the needs of others. . . .

We ask God to endow human souls with justice so that they may be fair, and may strive to provide for the comfort of all, that each member of humanity may pass his life in the utmost comfort and welfare. Then this material world will become the very paradise of the Kingdom, this elemental earth will be a heavenly state and all the servants of God will live in the utmost joy, happiness and gladness. We must all strive and concentrate all our thoughts in order that such happiness may accrue to the world of humanity.

—'Abdu'l-Bahá **49**

Unbridled Nationalism

O YE men of wisdom among nations! Shut your eyes to estrangement, then fix your gaze upon unity. Cleave tenaciously unto that which will lead to the well-being and tranquillity of all mankind. This span of earth is but one homeland and one habitation. It behooveth you to abandon vainglory which causeth alienation and to set your hearts on whatever will ensure harmony. In the estimation of the people of Bahá* man's glory lieth in his knowledge, his upright conduct, his praiseworthy character, his wisdom, and not in his nationality or rank.
—*Bahá'u'lláh* **50**

That one indeed is a man who, today, dedicateth himself to the service of the entire human race. The Great Being saith: Blessed and happy is he that ariseth to promote the best interests of the peoples and kindreds of the earth. In another passage He hath proclaimed: It is not for him to pride himself who loveth his own country, but rather for him who loveth the whole world. The earth is but one country, and mankind its citizens.   —*Bahá'u'lláh* **51**

Consider the prejudice of patriotism. This is one globe, one land, one country. God did not divide it into national boundaries. He created all the continents without national divisions. Why should we make such division ourselves? These are but imaginary lines and boundaries.   —*'Abdu'l-Bahá* **52**

All mankind are of one nation; all have sprung from the tree of Adam, and Adam is the root of the tree. That tree is one and all these nations are like branches, while the individuals of humanity are like leaves, blossoms and fruits thereof. Then the establishment of various nations and the consequent shedding of blood and destruction of the edifice of humanity result from human ignorance and selfish motives.   —*'Abdu'l-Bahá* **53**

---

*Bahá'ís, followers of Bahá'u'lláh.

As to the patriotic prejudice, this is also due to absolute ignorance, for the surface of the earth is one native land. Everyone can live in any spot on the terrestrial globe. Therefore all the world is man's birthplace. These boundaries and outlets have been devised by man. In the creation, such boundaries and outlets were not assigned. Europe is one continent, Asia is one continent, Africa is one continent, Australia is one continent, but some of the souls, from personal motives and selfish interests, have divided each one of these continents and considered a certain part as their own country. God has set up no frontier between France and Germany; they are continuous. Yea, in the first centuries, selfish souls, for the promotion of their own interests, have assigned boundaries and outlets and have, day by day, attached more importance to these, until this led to intense enmity, bloodshed and rapacity in subsequent centuries. In the same way this will continue indefinitely, and if this conception of patriotism remains limited within a certain circle, it will be the primary cause of the world's destruction. No wise and just person will acknowledge these imaginary distinctions. Every limited area which we call our native country we regard as our motherland, whereas the terrestrial globe is the motherland of all, and not any restricted area. In short, for a few days we live on this earth and eventually we are buried in it, it is our eternal tomb. Is it worthwhile that we should engage in bloodshed and tear one another to pieces for this eternal tomb? Nay, far from it, neither is God pleased with such conduct nor would any sane man approve of it.

Consider! The blessed animals engage in no patriotic quarrels. They are in the utmost fellowship with one another and live together in harmony. For example, if a dove from the east and a dove from the west, a dove from the north and a dove from the south chance to arrive, at the same time, in one spot, they immediately associate in harmony. So is it with all the blessed animals and birds. But the ferocious animals, as soon as they meet, attack and fight with each other, tear each other to pieces and it is impossible for them to live peaceably

together in one spot. They are all unsociable and fierce, savage
and combative fighters.   —'Abdu'l-Bahá **54**

If the various races and distinct types of mankind had
each proceeded from a different original paternity—in other
words, if we had two or more Adams for our human fathers—
there might be reasonable ground for difference and divergence in humanity today; but inasmuch as we belong to one
progeny and one family, all names which seek to differentiate
and distinguish mankind as Italian, German, French, Russian
and so on are without significance and sanction. We are all
human, all servants of God and all come from Mr. Adam's
family. Why, then, all these fallacious national and racial distinctions? These boundary lines and artificial barriers have
been created by despots and conquerors who sought to attain
dominion over mankind, thereby engendering patriotic feeling and rousing selfish devotion to merely local standards of
government. As a rule they themselves enjoyed luxuries in
palaces, surrounded by conditions of ease and affluence, while
armies of soldiers, civilians and tillers of the soil fought and
died at their command upon the field of battle, shedding their
innocent blood for a delusion such as "we are Germans," "our
enemies are French," etc., when, in reality, all are humankind,
all belong to the one family and posterity of Adam, the original
father. This prejudice or limited patriotism is prevalent
throughout the world, while man is blind to patriotism in the
larger sense which includes all races and native lands. From
every real standpoint there must and should be peace among
all nations.

God created one earth and one mankind to people it.
Man has no other habitation, but man himself has come forth
and proclaimed imaginary boundary lines and territorial restrictions, naming them Germany, France, Russia, etc. And
torrents of precious blood are spilled in defense of these
imaginary divisions of our one human habitation, under the
delusion of a fancied and limited patriotism.

After all, a claim and title to territory or native land is but
a claim and attachment to the dust of earth. We live upon this

earth for a few days and then rest beneath it forever. So it is our graveyard eternally. Shall man fight for the tomb which devours him, for his eternal sepulcher? What ignorance could be greater than this? To fight over his grave, to kill another for his grave! What heedlessness! What a delusion!

—'Abdu'l-Bahá **55**

Man is endowed with powers to investigate reality, and the reality is that humanity is one in kind and equal in the creative plan. Therefore, false distinctions of race and native land, which are factors and causes of warfare, must be abandoned. *—'Abdu'l-Bahá* **56**

Let there be no misgivings as to the animating purpose of the worldwide Law of Bahá'u'lláh. Far from aiming at the subversion of the existing foundations of society, it seeks to broaden its basis, to remold its institutions in a manner consonant with the needs of an ever-changing world. It can conflict with no legitimate allegiances, nor can it undermine essential loyalties. Its purpose is neither to stifle the flame of a sane and intelligent patriotism in men's hearts, nor to abolish the system of national autonomy so essential if the evils of excessive centralization are to be avoided. It does not ignore, nor does it attempt to suppress, the diversity of ethnical origins, of climate, of history, of language and tradition, of thought and habit, that differentiate the peoples and nations of the world. It calls for a wider loyalty, for a larger aspiration than any that has animated the human race. It insists upon the subordination of national impulses and interests to the imperative claims of a unified world. *—Shoghi Effendi* **57**

Unbridled nationalism, as distinguished from a sane and legitimate patriotism, must give way to a wider loyalty, to the love of humanity as a whole. Bahá'u'lláh's statement is: "The earth is but one country, and mankind its citizens." The concept of world citizenship is a direct result of the contraction of the world into a single neighborhood through scientific advances and of the indisputable interdependence of nations.

Love of all the world's peoples does not exclude love of one's country. The advantage of the part in a world society is best served by promoting the advantage of the whole. Current international activities in various fields which nurture mutual affection and a sense of solidarity among peoples need greatly to be increased.   *—The Universal House of Justice* **58**

O contending peoples and kindreds of the earth! Set your faces towards unity, and let the radiance of its light shine upon you. Gather ye together and for the sake of God resolve to root out whatever is the source of contention amongst you. Then will the effulgence of the world's great Luminary envelop the whole earth, and its inhabitants become the citizens of one city, and the occupants of one and the same throne.
                                           —Bahá'u'lláh **59**

Religious Strife

CONSORT with all religions with amity and concord, that they may inhale from you the sweet fragrance of God.
                                           —Bahá'u'lláh **60**

Through each and every one of the verses which the Pen of the Most High hath revealed, the doors of love and unity have been unlocked and flung open to the face of men. We have erewhile declared—and Our Word is the truth—: "Consort with the followers of all religions in a spirit of friendliness and fellowship." Whatsoever hath led the children of men to shun one another, and hath caused dissensions and divisions amongst them, hath, through the revelation of these words, been nullified and abolished.   *—Bahá'u'lláh* **61**

That the divers communions of the earth, and the manifold systems of religious belief, should never be allowed to foster the feelings of animosity among men, is, in this Day, of the essence of the Faith of God and His Religion. These principles and laws, these firmly established and mighty systems, have proceeded from one Source, and are the rays of one Light. That they differ one from another is to be attributed to the varying requirements of the ages in which they are promulgated. —*Bahá'u'lláh* **62**

If religion proves to be the source of hatred, enmity and contention, if it becomes the cause of warfare and strife and influences men to kill each other, its absence is preferable. For that which is productive of hatred amongst the people is rejected by God, and that which establishes fellowship is beloved and sanctioned by Him. Religion and divine teachings are like unto a remedy. A remedy must produce the condition of health. If it occasions sickness, it is wiser and better to have no remedy whatever. —*'Abdu'l-Bahá* **63**

From the beginning of human history to the present time the various religions of the world have anathematized and accused each other of falsity. Each religion has considered the others bereft of the face of God, deprived of His mercy and in the direct line of divine wrath. Therefore, they have shunned each other most rigidly, exercising mutual animosity and rancor. Consider the record of religious warfare, the battles between nations, the bloodshed and destruction in the name of religion. One of the greatest religious wars, the Crusades, extended over a period of two hundred years. In this succession of great campaigns the western crusaders were constantly invading the Orient, bent upon recovering the Holy City from the hands of the Islamic people. Army after army raised in Europe poured its fanatical legions into the East. The kings of European nations personally led these crusades, killing and shedding the blood of the Orientals. During this period of two hundred years the East and West were in a state of violence and commotion. Sometimes the crusaders were successful, killing, pillaging and taking captive the Muslim people; sometimes the Muslims were victorious, inflicting bloodshed, death and ruin in turn upon the invaders. So they continued for two centuries, alternately fighting with fury and relaxing from weakness, until the European religionists withdrew from the East, leaving ashes of desolation behind them and finding their own nations in a condition of turbulence and upheaval. Hundreds of thousands of human beings were killed and untold wealth wasted in this fruitless religious warfare. How many fathers mourned the loss of their sons! How many mothers and wives lamented the absence of their dear ones! Yet this was only one of the "holy" wars. Consider and reflect.

Religious wars have been many. Nine hundred thousand martyrs to the Protestant cause was the record of conflict and difference between that sect of Christians and the Catholics. Consult history and confirm this. How many languished in prisons! How merciless the treatment of captives! All in the name of religion! Consider and estimate the outcome of other wars between the people and sects of religious belief.

From the beginning of human history down to this time the world of humanity has not enjoyed a day of absolute rest and relaxation from conflict and strife. Most of the wars have been caused by religious prejudice, fanaticism and sectarian hatred. Religionists have anathematized religionists, each considering the other as deprived of the mercy of God, abiding in gross darkness and the children of Satan. For example, the Christians and Muslims considered the Jews satanic and the enemies of God. Therefore, they cursed and persecuted them. Great numbers of Jews were killed, their houses burned and pillaged, their children carried into captivity. The Jews in turn regarded the Christians as infidels and the Muslims as enemies and destroyers of the law of Moses. Therefore, they call down vengeance upon them and curse them even to this day.

Consider what injuries, ordeals and calamities have been inflicted upon mankind since the beginning of history. Every city, country, nation and people has been subjected to the destruction and havoc of war. Each one of the divine religions considers itself as belonging to a goodly and blessed tree, the tree of the Merciful, and all other religious systems as belonging to a tree of evil, the tree of Satan. For this reason they heap execration and abuse upon each other. This is clearly apparent in books of historical record. . . .   *—'Abdu'l-Bahá* **64**

The world of humanity is one, and God is equally kind to all. What, then, is the source of unkindness and hatred in the human world? This real Shepherd loves all His sheep. He leads them in green pastures. He rears and protects them. What, then, is the source of enmity and alienation among humankind? Whence this conflict and strife? The real underlying cause is lack of religious unity and association, for in each of the great religions we find superstition, blind imitation of creeds, and theological formulas adhered to instead of the divine fundamentals, causing difference and divergence among mankind instead of agreement and fellowship. Consequently, strife, hatred and warfare have arisen, based upon this divergence and separation. If we investigate the foundations of the divine religions, we find them to be one, absolutely changeless and never subject to transformation. —*'Abdu'l-Bahá* **65**

The divine Manifestations since the day of Adam have striven to unite humanity so that all may be accounted as one soul. The function and purpose of a shepherd is to gather and not disperse his flock. The Prophets of God have been divine Shepherds of humanity. They have established a bond of love and unity among mankind, made scattered peoples one nation and wandering tribes a mighty kingdom. They have laid the foundation of the oneness of God and summoned all to universal peace. All these holy, divine Manifestations are one. They have served one God, promulgated the same truth, founded the same institutions and reflected the same light. Their appearances have been successive and correlated; each One has announced and extolled the One Who was to follow, and all laid the foundation of reality. They summoned and invited the people to love and made the human world a mirror of the Word of God. Therefore, the divine religions They established have one foundation; Their teachings, proofs and evidences are one; in name and form They differ, but in reality They agree and are the same. —*'Abdu'l-Bahá* **66**

All the holy ones of God have tried with heart and soul to spread the light of love and unity throughout the world, so that the darkness of materiality might disappear and the light of spirituality might shine forth among the children of men. Then would hate, slander and murder disappear, and in their stead love, unity and peace would reign.

All the Manifestations of God came with the same purpose, and they have all sought to lead men into the paths of virtue. Yet we, their servants, still dispute among ourselves! Why is it thus? Why do we not love one another and live in unity?

It is because we have shut our eyes to the underlying principle of all religions, that God is one, that He is the Father of us all, that we are all immersed in the ocean of His mercy and sheltered and protected by His loving care.

The glorious Sun of Truth shines for all alike, the waters of Divine Mercy immerse each one, and His Divine favor is bestowed on all His children.

This loving God desires peace for all His creatures— why, then, do they spend their time in war?

He loves and protects all His children—why do they forget Him?

He bestows His Fatherly care on us all—why do we neglect our brothers?

Surely, when we realize how God loves and cares for us, we should so order our lives that we may become more like Him.

God has created us, one and all—why do we act in opposition to His wishes, when we are all His children, and love the same Father? All these divisions we see on all sides, all these disputes and opposition, are caused because men cling to *ritual* and outward observances, and forget the simple, underlying truth. It is the *outward practices* of religion that are so different, and it is they that cause disputes and enmity—while the *reality* is always the same, and one. The Reality is the Truth, and truth has no division. Truth is God's guidance, it is the light of the world, it is love, it is mercy. These attributes of truth are also human virtues inspired by the Holy Spirit.

So let us one and all hold fast to truth, and we shall be free indeed!

The day is coming when all the religions of the world will unite, for in principle they are one already. There is no need for division, seeing that it is only the outward forms that separate them. Among the sons of men some souls are suffering through ignorance, let us hasten to teach them; others are like children needing care and education until they are grown, and some are sick—to these we must carry Divine healing.

Whether ignorant, childish or sick, they must be loved and helped, and not disliked because of their imperfection.

Doctors of religion were instituted to bring spiritual healing to the peoples and to be the cause of unity among the nations. If they become the cause of division they had better not exist! A remedy is given to cure a disease, but if it only succeeds in aggravating the complaint, it is better to leave it alone. If religion is only to be a cause of disunion it had better not exist.

All the Divine Manifestations sent by God into the world would have gone through their terrible hardships and sufferings for the single hope of spreading Truth, unity and concord among men. Christ endured a life of sorrow, pain and grief, to bring a perfect example of love into the world—and in spite of this we continue to act in a contrary spirit one towards the other! . . .

I beseech you, one and all, to add your prayers to mine to the end that war and bloodshed may cease, and that love, friendship, peace and unity may reign in the world.

All down the ages we see how blood has stained the surface of the earth; but now a ray of greater light has come, man's intelligence is greater, spirituality is beginning to grow, and a time is *surely* coming when the religions of the world will be at peace. Let us leave the discordant arguments concerning outward forms, and let us join together to hasten forward the Divine Cause of unity, until all humanity knows itself to be one family, joined together in love.

—*'Abdu'l-Bahá* 67

Man must cut himself free from all prejudice and from the result of his own imagination, so that he may be able to search for truth unhindered. Truth is one in all religions, and by means of it the unity of the world can be realized.

All the peoples have a fundamental belief in common. Being one, truth cannot be divided, and the differences that appear to exist among the nations only result from their attachment to prejudice. If only men would search out truth, they would find themselves united.   — *'Abdu'l-Bahá* **68**

The strife between religions, nations and races arises from misunderstanding. If we investigate the religions to discover the principles underlying their foundations, we will find they agree; for the fundamental reality of them is one and not multiple. By this means the religionists of the world will reach their point of unity and reconciliation. They will ascertain the truth that the purpose of religion is the acquisition of praiseworthy virtues, the betterment of morals, the spiritual development of mankind, the real life and divine bestowals. All the Prophets have been the promoters of these principles; none of Them has been the promoter of corruption, vice or evil. They have summoned mankind to all good. They have united people in the love of God, invited them to the religions of the unity of mankind and exhorted them to amity and agreement.
— *'Abdu'l-Bahá* **69**

The divine origin of all the Prophets of God—including Jesus Christ and the Apostle of God,* the two greatest Manifestations preceding the Revelation of the Báb—is unreservedly and unshakably upheld by each and every follower of the Bahá'í religion. The fundamental unity of these Messengers of God is clearly recognized, the continuity of their Revelations is affirmed, the God-given authority and correlative character of their Books is admitted, the singleness of their aims and purposes is proclaimed, the uniqueness of their influence

---

*Muhammad.

emphasized, the ultimate reconciliation of their teachings and followers taught and anticipated. "They all," according to Bahá'u'lláh's testimony, "abide in the same tabernacle, soar in the same heaven, are seated upon the same throne, utter the same speech, and proclaim the same Faith."

The Faith standing identified with the name of Bahá'u'lláh disclaims any intention to belittle any of the Prophets gone before Him, to whittle down any of their teachings, to obscure, however slightly, the radiance of their Revelations, to oust them from the hearts of their followers, to abrogate the fundamentals of their doctrines, to discard any of their revealed Books, or to suppress the legitimate aspirations of their adherents. Repudiating the claim of any religion to be the final revelation of God to man, disclaiming finality for His own Revelation, Bahá'u'lláh inculcates the basic principle of the relativity of religious truth, the continuity of Divine Revelation, the progressiveness of religious experience. His aim is to widen the basis of all revealed religions and to unravel the mysteries of their scriptures. He insists on the unqualified recognition of the unity of their purpose, restates the eternal verities they enshrine, coordinates their functions, distinguishes the essential and the authentic from the nonessential and spurious in their teachings, separates the God-given truths from the priest-prompted superstitions, and on this as a basis proclaims the possibility, and even prophesies the inevitability, of their unification, and the consummation of their highest hopes. *—Shoghi Effendi* **70**

Religious strife, throughout history, has been the cause of innumerable wars and conflicts, a major blight to progress, and is increasingly abhorrent to the people of all faiths and no faith. Followers of all religions must be willing to face the basic questions which this strife raises, and to arrive at clear answers. How are the differences between them to be resolved, both in theory and in practice? The challenge facing the religious leaders of mankind is to contemplate, with hearts filled with the spirit of compassion and a desire for truth, the plight of humanity, and to ask themselves whether they cannot, in humility before their Almighty Creator, submerge their theological differences in a great spirit of mutual forbearance that will enable them to work together for the advancement of human understanding and peace.

—The Universal House of Justice **71**

The Lord of mankind has caused His holy, divine Manifestations to come into the world. He has revealed His heavenly Books in order to establish spiritual brotherhood and through the power of the Holy Spirit has made it practicable for perfect fraternity to be realized among mankind. And when through the breaths of the Holy Spirit this perfect fraternity and agreement are established amongst men—this brotherhood and love being spiritual in character, this loving kindness being heavenly, these constraining bonds being divine—a unity appears which is indissoluble, unchanging and never subject to transformation. It is ever the same and will forever remain the same.   *—'Abdu'l-Bahá* **72**

There can be no doubt whatever that the peoples of the world, of whatever race or religion, derive their inspiration from one heavenly Source, and are the subjects of one God. The difference between the ordinances under which they abide should be attributed to the varying requirements and exigencies of the age in which they were revealed. All of them, except a few which are the outcome of human perversity, were ordained of God, and are a reflection of His Will and Purpose. Arise and, armed with the power of faith, shatter to pieces the gods of your vain imaginings, the sowers of dissension amongst you. Cleave unto that which draweth you together and uniteth you.   *—Bahá'u'lláh* **73**

Denial of the Equality of Men and Women

WOMEN and men have been and will always be equal in the sight of God. The Dawning-Place of the Light of God sheddeth its radiance upon all with the same effulgence. Verily God created women for men, and men for women. The most beloved of people before God are the most steadfast and those who have surpassed others in their love for God, exalted be His glory. *—Bahá'u'lláh* **74**

In this Day the Hand of divine grace hath removed all distinction. The servants of God and His handmaidens are regarded on the same plane. Blessed is the servant who hath attained unto that which God hath decreed, and likewise the leaf moving in accordance with the breezes of His will. This favor is great and this station lofty. *—Bahá'u'lláh* **75**

In the sight of Bahá,* women are accounted the same as men, and God hath created all humankind in His own image, and after His own likeness. That is, men and women alike are the revealers of His names and attributes, and from the spiritual viewpoint there is no difference between them. Whosoever draweth nearer to God, that one is the most favored, whether man or woman. How many a handmaid, ardent and devoted, hath, within the sheltering shade of Bahá, proved superior to the men, and surpassed the famous of the earth. *—'Abdu'l-Bahá* **76**

In past ages it was held that woman and man were not equal—that is to say, woman was considered inferior to man, even from the standpoint of her anatomy and creation. She was considered especially inferior in intelligence, and the idea prevailed universally that it was not allowable for her to step into the arena of important affairs. In some countries man went so far as to believe and teach that woman belonged to a sphere lower than human. But in this century, which is the century of light and the revelation of mysteries, God is proving to the satisfaction of humanity that all this is ignorance and error; nay, rather, it is well established that mankind and womankind as parts of composite humanity are coequal and that

---

*Bahá'u'lláh.

no difference in estimate is allowable, for all are human. The conditions in past centuries were due to woman's lack of opportunity. She was denied the right and privilege of education and left in her undeveloped state. Naturally, she could not and did not advance. In reality, God has created all mankind, and in the estimation of God there is no distinction as to male and female. The one whose heart is pure is acceptable in His sight, be that one man or woman. God does not inquire, "Art thou woman or art thou man?" He judges human actions. If these are acceptable in the threshold of the Glorious One, man and woman will be equally recognized and rewarded.

—'Abdu'l-Bahá **77**

In this Revelation of Bahá'u'lláh, the women go neck and neck with the men. In no movement will they be left behind. Their rights with men are equal in degree. They will enter all the administrative branches of politics. They will attain in all such a degree as will be considered the very highest station of the world of humanity and will take part in all affairs. Rest ye assured. Do ye not look upon the present conditions; in the not far distant future the world of women will become all-refulgent and all-glorious. . . . At the time of elections the right to vote is the inalienable right of women, and the entrance of women into all human departments is an irrefutable and incontrovertible question. No soul can retard or prevent it.

—'Abdu'l-Bahá **78**

Divine Justice demands that the rights of both sexes should be equally respected since neither is superior to the other in the eyes of Heaven. Dignity before God depends, not on sex, but on purity and luminosity of heart. Human virtues belong equally to all!   —'Abdu'l-Bahá **79**

If we say man and woman differ in creational endowment, it is contrary to divine justice and intention. Both are human. If God has created one perfect and the other defective, He is unjust. But God is just; all are perfect in His intention and creative endowment. To assume imperfection in the crea-

ture is to presuppose imperfection in the almighty Creator.
The soul that excels in attainment of His attributes and graces
is most acceptable before God.   —'Abdu'l-Bahá **80**

In brief, the assumption of superiority by man will continue to be depressing to the ambition of woman, as if her
attainment to equality was creationally impossible; woman's
aspiration toward advancement will be checked by it, and she
will gradually become hopeless. On the contrary, we must
declare that her capacity is equal, even greater than man's.
This will inspire her with hope and ambition, and her susceptibilities for advancement will continually increase. She must
not be told and taught that she is weaker and inferior in
capacity and qualification. If a pupil is told that his intelligence
is less than his fellow pupils, it is a very great drawback and
handicap to his progress. He must be encouraged to advance
by the statement, "You are most capable, and if you endeavor,
you will attain the highest degree."   —'Abdu'l-Bahá **81**

Until the reality of equality between man and woman is
fully established and attained, the highest social development
of mankind is not possible. Even granted that woman is inferior to man in some degree of capacity or accomplishment,
this or any other distinction would continue to be productive
of discord and trouble. The only remedy is education, opportunity; for equality means equal qualification. . . .
. . . And let it be known once more that until woman and
man recognize and realize equality, social and political progress here* or anywhere will not be possible.
                                        —'Abdu'l-Bahá **82**

The world of humanity consists of two parts: male and
female. Each is the complement of the other. Therefore, if one
is defective, the other will necessarily be incomplete, and
perfection cannot be attained. There is a right hand and a left

---

*This talk was delivered in Chicago on 2 May 1912.

hand in the human body, functionally equal in service and administration. If either proves defective, the defect will naturally extend to the other by involving the completeness of the whole; for accomplishment is not normal unless both are perfect. If we say one hand is deficient, we prove the inability and incapacity of the other; for single-handed there is no full accomplishment. Just as physical accomplishment is complete with two hands, so man and woman, the two parts of the social body, must be perfect. It is not natural that either should remain undeveloped; and until both are perfected, the happiness of the human world will not be realized.

—'Abdu'l-Bahá **83**

The world of humanity is possessed of two wings: the male and the female. So long as these two wings are not equivalent in strength, the bird will not fly. Until womankind reaches the same degree as man, until she enjoys the same arena of activity, extraordinary attainment for humanity will not be realized; humanity cannot wing its way to heights of real attainment. When the two wings or parts become equivalent in strength, enjoying the same prerogatives, the flight of man will be exceedingly lofty and extraordinary. Therefore, woman must receive the same education as man and all inequality be adjusted. Thus, imbued with the same virtues as man, rising through all the degrees of human attainment, women will become the peers of men, and until this equality is established, true progress and attainment for the human race will not be facilitated.

—'Abdu'l-Bahá **84**

The sex distinction which exists in the human world is due to the lack of education for woman, who has been denied equal opportunity for development and advancement. Equality of the sexes will be established in proportion to the increased opportunities afforded woman in this age, for man and woman are equally the recipients of powers and endowments from God, the Creator. God has not ordained distinction between them in His consummate purpose.

—'Abdu'l-Bahá **85**

If woman be fully educated and granted her rights, she will attain the capacity for wonderful accomplishments and prove herself the equal of man. She is the coadjutor of man, his complement and helpmeet. Both are human; both are endowed with potentialities of intelligence and embody the virtues of humanity. In all human powers and functions they are partners and coequals. At present in spheres of human activity woman does not manifest her natal prerogatives, owing to lack of education and opportunity. Without doubt education will establish her equality with men. Consider the animal kingdom, where no distinction is observed between male and female. They are equal in powers and privileges. Among birds of the air no distinction is evidenced. Their powers are equal; they dwell together in complete unity and mutual recognition of rights. Shall we not enjoy the same equality? Its absence is not befitting to mankind.   —'Abdu'l-Bahá **86**

In ancient times and medieval ages woman was completely subordinated to man. The cause of this estimate of her inferiority was her lack of education. A woman's life and intellect were limited to the household. Glimpses of this may be found even in the Epistles of Saint Paul. In later centuries the scope and opportunities of a woman's life broadened and increased. Her mind unfolded and developed; her perceptions awakened and deepened. The question concerning her was: Why should a woman be left mentally undeveloped? Science is praiseworthy—whether investigated by the intellect of man or woman. So, little by little, woman advanced, giving increasing evidence of equal capabilities with man—whether in scientific research, political ability or any other sphere of human activity. The conclusion is evident that woman has been outdistanced through lack of education and intellectual facilities. If given the same educational opportunities or course of study, she would develop the same capacity and abilities.
          —'Abdu'l-Bahá **87**

Furthermore, the education of woman is more necessary and important than that of man, for woman is the trainer of the

child from its infancy. If she be defective and imperfect herself, the child will necessarily be deficient; therefore, imperfection of woman implies a condition of imperfection in all
mankind, for it is the mother who rears, nurtures and guides
the growth of the child. This is not the function of the father.
If the educator be incompetent, the educated will be correspondingly lacking. This is evident and incontrovertible. Could
the student be brilliant and accomplished if the teacher is
illiterate and ignorant? The mothers are the first educators of
mankind; if they be imperfect, alas for the condition and future
of the race.　　　　　　　　　　　　　—'Abdu'l-Bahá　**88**

The woman is indeed of the greater importance to the
race. She has the greater burden and the greater work. Look at
the vegetable and the animal worlds. The palm which carries
the fruit is the tree most prized by the date grower. The Arab
knows that for a long journey the mare has the longest wind.
For her greater strength and fierceness, the lioness is more
feared by the hunter than the lion.
　. . . The woman has greater moral courage than the man;
she has also special gifts which enable her to govern in mo-
ments of danger and crisis.　　　　　　—'Abdu'l-Bahá　**89**

In proclaiming the oneness of mankind He* taught that
men and women are equal in the sight of God and that there
is no distinction to be made between them. The only difference between them now is due to lack of education and
training. If woman is given equal opportunity of education,
distinction and estimate of inferiority will disappear. . . .
　He promulgated the adoption of the same course of education for man and woman. Daughters and sons must follow
the same curriculum of study, thereby promoting unity of the
sexes. When all mankind shall receive the same opportunity
of education and the equality of men and women be realized,

---

*Bahá'u'lláh.

the foundations of war will be utterly destroyed. Without equality this will be impossible because all differences and distinction are conducive to discord and strife. Equality between men and women is conducive to the abolition of warfare for the reason that women will never be willing to sanction it. *—'Abdu'l-Bahá* **90**

In past ages humanity has been defective and inefficient because it has been incomplete. War and its ravages have blighted the world; the education of woman will be a mighty step toward its abolition and ending, for she will use her whole influence against war. Woman rears the child and educates the youth to maturity. She will refuse to give her sons for sacrifice upon the field of battle. In truth, she will be the greatest factor in establishing universal peace and international arbitration. Assuredly, woman will abolish warfare among mankind. *—'Abdu'l-Bahá* **91**

Consider a son reared and trained twenty years by a devoted mother. What sleepless nights and restless, anxious days she has spent! Having brought him through dangers and difficulties to the age of maturity, how agonizing then to sacrifice him upon the battlefield! Therefore, the mothers will not sanction war nor be satisfied with it. So it will come to pass that when women participate fully and equally in the affairs of the world, when they enter confidently and capably the great arena of laws and politics, war will cease; for woman will be the obstacle and hindrance to it. This is true and without doubt. *—'Abdu'l-Bahá* **92**

The world in the past has been ruled by force, and man has dominated over woman by reason of his more forceful and aggressive qualities both of body and mind. But the balance is already shifting; force is losing its dominance, and mental alertness, intuition, and the spiritual qualities of love and service, in which woman is strong, are gaining ascendancy. Hence the new age will be an age less masculine and more permeated with the feminine ideals, or, to speak more exactly, will be an age in which the masculine and feminine elements of civilization will be more evenly balanced.   —'Abdu'l-Bahá **93**

The realities of things have been revealed in this radiant century, and that which is true must come to the surface. Among these realities is the principle of the equality of man and woman—equal rights and prerogatives in all things appertaining to humanity. . . . But while this principle of equality is true, it is likewise true that woman must prove her capacity and aptitude, must show forth the evidences of equality. She must become proficient in the arts and sciences and prove by her accomplishments that her abilities and powers have merely been latent. Demonstrations of force . . . are neither becoming nor effective in the cause of womanhood and equality. Woman must especially devote her energies and abilities toward the industrial and agricultural sciences, seeking to assist mankind in that which is most needful. By this means she will demonstrate capability and ensure recognition of equality in the social and economic equation. Undoubtedly God will confirm her in her efforts and endeavors, for in this century of radiance Bahá'u'lláh has proclaimed the reality of the oneness of the world of humanity and announced that all nations, peoples and races are one.   —'Abdu'l-Bahá **94**

The emancipation of women, the achievement of full equality between the sexes, is one of the most important, though less acknowledged prerequisites of peace. The denial of such equality perpetrates an injustice against one-half of the world's population and promotes in men harmful attitudes and habits that are carried from the family to the workplace, to political life, and ultimately to international relations. There are no grounds, moral, practical, or biological, upon which such denial can be justified. Only as women are welcomed into full partnership in all fields of human endeavor will the moral and psychological climate be created in which international peace can emerge.   —*The Universal House of Justice* **95**

Woman must endeavor then to attain greater perfection, to be man's equal in every respect, to make progress in all in which she has been backward, so that man will be compelled to acknowledge her equality of capacity and attainment. . . .

Women must make the greatest effort to acquire spiritual power and to increase in the virtue of wisdom and holiness until their enlightenment and striving succeeds in bringing about the unity of mankind.   *—'Abdu'l-Bahá* **96**

Therefore, strive to show in the human world that women are most capable and efficient, that their hearts are more tender and susceptible than the hearts of men, that they are more philanthropic and responsive toward the needy and suffering, that they are inflexibly opposed to war and are lovers of peace. Strive that the ideal of international peace may become realized through the efforts of womankind, for man is more inclined to war than woman, and a real evidence of woman's superiority will be her service and efficiency in the establishment of universal peace.   *—'Abdu'l-Bahá* **97**

Exalted, immensely exalted is He Who hath removed differences and established harmony. Glorified, infinitely glorified is He Who hath caused discord to cease, and decreed solidarity and unity. Praised be God, the Pen of the Most High hath lifted distinctions from between His servants and handmaidens and, through His consummate favors and all-encompassing mercy, hath conferred upon all a station and rank on. the same plane. He hath broken the back of vain imaginings with the sword of utterance and hath obliterated the perils of idle fancies through the pervasive power of His might.
—'Abdu'l-Bahá **98**

Ignorance and Lack of Education

MAN is the supreme Talisman. Lack of a proper education hath, however, deprived him of that which he doth inherently possess. Through a word proceeding out of the mouth of God he was called into being; by one word more he was guided to recognize the Source of his education; by yet another word his station and destiny were safeguarded. The Great Being saith: Regard man as a mine rich in gems of inestimable value. Education can, alone, cause it to reveal its treasures, and enable mankind to benefit therefrom.   *—Bahá'u'lláh* **99**

Man is even as steel, the essence of which is hidden: through admonition and explanation, good counsel and education, that essence will be brought to light. If, however, he be allowed to remain in his original condition, the corrosion of lusts and appetites will effectively destroy him.
—Bahá'u'lláh **100**

Strain every nerve to acquire both inner and outer perfections, for the fruit of the human tree hath ever been and will ever be perfections both within and without. It is not desirable that a man be left without knowledge or skills, for he is then but a barren tree. Then, so much as capacity and capability allow, ye needs must deck the tree of being with fruits such as knowledge, wisdom, spiritual perception and eloquent speech.
—Bahá'u'lláh **101**

Knowledge is as wings to man's life, and a ladder for his ascent. Its acquisition is incumbent upon everyone. The knowledge of such sciences, however, should be acquired as can profit the peoples of the earth, and not those which begin with words and end with words.* Great indeed is the claim of scientists and craftsmen on the peoples of the world. . . .

---

*By "begin with words and end with words" is meant "fruitless excursions into metaphysical hair-splitting," not sound branches of learning (Letter written on behalf of Shoghi Effendi to an individual, 15 February 1947, in Shoghi Effendi, *The Unfolding Destiny of the British Bahá'í Community: The Messages from the Guardian of the Bahá'í Faith to the Bahá'ís of the British Isles* [London: Bahá'í Publishing Trust, 1981], p. 445).

In truth, knowledge is a veritable treasure for man, and a source of glory, of bounty, of joy, of exaltation, of cheer and gladness unto him. —*Bahá'u'lláh* **102**

At the outset of every endeavor, it is incumbent to look to the end of it. Of all the arts and sciences, set the children to studying those which will result in advantage to man, will ensure his progress and elevate his rank. Thus the noisome odors of lawlessness will be dispelled, and thus through the high endeavors of the nation's leaders, all will live cradled, secure and in peace.

The Great Being saith: The learned of the day must direct the people to acquire those branches of knowledge which are of use, that both the learned themselves and the generality of mankind may derive benefits therefrom. Such academic pursuits as begin and end in words alone have never been and will never be of any worth. —*Bahá'u'lláh* **103**

[A] . . . requirement of perfection is to arise with complete sincerity and purity of purpose to educate the masses: to exert the utmost effort to instruct them in the various branches of learning and useful sciences, to encourage the development of modern progress, to widen the scope of commerce, industry and the arts, to further such measures as will increase the people's wealth. For the mass of the population is uninformed as to these vital agencies which would constitute an immediate remedy for society's chronic ills. —*'Abdu'l-Bahá* **104**

Close investigation will show that the primary cause of oppression and injustice, of unrighteousness, irregularity and disorder, is the people's lack of religious faith and the fact that they are uneducated. When, for example, the people are genuinely religious and are literate and well schooled, and a difficulty presents itself, they can apply to the local authorities; if they do not meet with justice and secure their rights and if they see that the conduct of the local government is incompatible with the Divine good pleasure and the king's justice, they can then take their case to higher courts and describe the deviation of the local administration from the spiritual law. Those courts can then send for the local records of the case and in this way justice will be done. At present, however, because of their inadequate schooling, most of the population lack even the vocabulary to explain what they want.

—'Abdu'l-Bahá **105**

The primary, the most urgent requirement is the promotion of education. It is inconceivable that any nation should achieve prosperity and success unless this paramount, this fundamental concern is carried forward. The principal reason for the decline and fall of peoples is ignorance. Today the mass of the people are uninformed even as to ordinary affairs, how much less do they grasp the core of the important problems and complex needs of the time.

It is therefore urgent that beneficial articles and books be written, clearly and definitely establishing what the present-day requirements of the people are, and what will conduce to the happiness and advancement of society. These should be published and spread throughout the nation. . . .

It is, furthermore, a vital necessity to establish schools . . . even in the smallest country towns and villages, and to encourage the people in every possible way to have their children learn to read and write. If necessary, education should even be made compulsory. Until the nerves and arteries of the nation stir into life, every measure that is attempted will prove vain; for the people are as the human body, and determination and the will to struggle are as the soul, and a soulless body does not move. This dynamic power is present . . . in the very nature of the . . . people, and the spread of education will release it.   *—'Abdu'l-Bahá* **106**

Through education the ignorant become learned; the cowardly become valiant. Through cultivation the crooked branch becomes straight; the acid, bitter fruit of the mountains and woods becomes sweet and delicious; and the five-petaled flower becomes hundred petaled. Through education savage nations become civilized, and even the animals become domesticated. Education must be considered as most important, for as diseases in the world of bodies are extremely contagious, so, in the same way, qualities of spirit and heart are extremely contagious. Education has a universal influence, and the differences caused by it are very great.

—'Abdu'l-Bahá **107**

It is education that brings the East and the West under the authority of man; it is education that produces wonderful industries; it is education that spreads great sciences and arts; it is education that makes manifest new discoveries and institutions. If there were no educator, there would be no such things as comforts, civilization or humanity. If a man be left alone in a wilderness where he sees none of his own kind, he will undoubtedly become a mere brute; it is then clear that an educator is needed.

But education is of three kinds: material, human and spiritual. Material education is concerned with the progress and development of the body, through gaining its sustenance, its material comfort and ease. This education is common to animals and man.

Human education signifies civilization and progress— that is to say, government, administration, charitable works, trades, arts and handicrafts, sciences, great inventions and discoveries and elaborate institutions, which are the activities essential to man as distinguished from the animal.

Divine education is that of the Kingdom of God: it consists in acquiring divine perfections, and this is true education; for in this state man becomes the focus of divine blessings, the manifestation of the words, "Let Us make man in Our image, and after Our likeness."* This is the goal of the world of humanity.

—'Abdu'l-Bahá **108**

---

*Cf. Gen. 1:26.

Inasmuch as ignorance and lack of education are barriers of separation among mankind, all must receive training and instruction. Through this provision the lack of mutual understanding will be remedied and the unity of mankind furthered and advanced. Universal education is a universal law. It is, therefore, incumbent upon every father to teach and instruct his children according to his possibilities. If he is unable to educate them, the body politic, the representative of the people, must provide the means for their education.

—'Abdu'l-Bahá 109

Everyone, whether man or woman, should hand over to a trusted person a portion of what he or she earneth through trade, agriculture or other occupation, for the training and education of children. . . . —Bahá'u'lláh 110

The education and training of children is among the most meritorious acts of humankind and draweth down the grace and favor of the All-Merciful, for education is the indispensable foundation of all human excellence and alloweth man to work his way to the heights of abiding glory.

—'Abdu'l-Bahá 111

Were there no educator, all souls would remain savage, and were it not for the teacher, the children would be ignorant creatures.

It is for this reason that, in this new cycle, education and training are recorded in the Book of God as obligatory and not voluntary. That is, it is enjoined upon the father and mother, as a duty, to strive with all effort to train the daughter and the son, to nurse them from the breast of knowledge and to rear them in the bosom of sciences and arts. Should they neglect this matter, they shall be held responsible and worthy of reproach in the presence of the stern Lord. —'Abdu'l-Bahá 112

Every child is potentially the light of the world—and at the same time its darkness; wherefore must the question of education be accounted as of primary importance. From his infancy, the child must be nursed at the breast of God's love, and nurtured in the embrace of His knowledge, that he may radiate light, grow in spirituality, be filled with wisdom and learning, and take on the characteristics of the angelic host.

—'Abdu'l-Bahá **113**

While the children are yet in their infancy feed them from the breast of heavenly grace, foster them in the cradle of all excellence, rear them in the embrace of bounty. Give them the advantage of every useful kind of knowledge. Let them share in every new and rare and wondrous craft and art. Bring them up to work and strive, and accustom them to hardship. Teach them to dedicate their lives to matters of great import, and inspire them to undertake studies that will benefit mankind.   —'Abdu'l-Bahá **114**

The root cause of wrongdoing is ignorance, and we must therefore hold fast to the tools of perception and knowledge. Good character must be taught. Light must be spread afar, so that, in the school of humanity, all may acquire the heavenly characteristics of the spirit, and see for themselves beyond any doubt that there is no fiercer hell, no more fiery abyss, than to possess a character that is evil and unsound; nor more darksome pit nor loathsome torment than to show forth qualities which deserve to be condemned.

The individual must be educated to such a high degree that he would rather have his throat cut than tell a lie, and would think it easier to be slashed with a sword or pierced with a spear than to utter calumny or be carried away by wrath.

Thus will be kindled the sense of human dignity and pride, to burn away the reapings of lustful appetites. Then will each one of God's beloved shine out as a bright moon with qualities of the spirit, and the relationship of each to the Sacred Threshold of his Lord will be not illusory but sound and real, will be as the very foundation of the building, not some embellishment on its facade.

It followeth that the children's school must be a place of utmost discipline and order, that instruction must be thorough, and provision must be made for the rectification and refinement of character; so that, in his earliest years, within the very essence of the child, the divine foundation will be laid and the structure of holiness raised up.

Know that this matter of instruction, of character rectification and refinement, of heartening and encouraging the child is of the utmost importance, for such are basic principles of God.   —'Abdu'l-Bahá **115**

Training in morals and good conduct is far more important than book learning. A child that is cleanly, agreeable, of good character, well-behaved—even though he be ignorant— is preferable to a child that is rude, unwashed, ill-natured, and yet becoming deeply versed in all the sciences and arts. The reason for this is that the child who conducts himself well, even though he be ignorant, is of benefit to others, while an ill-natured, ill-behaved child is corrupted and harmful to others, even though he be learned. If, however, the child be trained to be both learned and good, the result is light upon light.

Children are even as a branch that is fresh and green; they will grow up in whatever way ye train them. Take the utmost care to give them high ideals and goals, so that once they come of age, they will cast their beams like brilliant candles on the world, and will not be defiled by lusts and passions in the way of animals, heedless and unaware, but instead will set their hearts on achieving everlasting honor and acquiring all the excellences of humankind.

                          —'Abdu'l-Bahá **116**

Train these children with divine exhortations. From their childhood instill in their hearts the love of God so they may manifest in their lives the fear of God and have confidence in the bestowals of God. Teach them to free themselves from human imperfections and to acquire the divine perfections latent in the heart of man. The life of man is useful if he attains the perfections of man. If he becomes the center of the imperfections of the world of humanity, death is better than life, and nonexistence better than existence. Therefore make ye an effort in order that these children may be rightly trained and educated and that each one of them may attain perfection in the world of humanity. — *'Abdu'l-Bahá* **117**

The cause of universal education, which has already enlisted in its service an army of dedicated people from every faith and nation, deserves the utmost support that the governments of the world can lend it. For ignorance is indisputably the principal reason for the decline and fall of peoples and the perpetuation of prejudice. No nation can achieve success unless education is accorded all its citizens. Lack of resources limits the ability of many nations to fulfill this necessity, imposing a certain ordering of priorities. The decision-making agencies involved would do well to consider giving first priority to the education of women and girls, since it is through educated mothers that the benefits of knowledge can be most effectively and rapidly diffused throughout society. In keeping with the requirements of the times, consideration should also be given to teaching the concept of world citizenship as part of the standard education of every child.
— *The Universal House of Justice* **118**

Every imperfect soul is self-centered and thinketh only of his own good. But as his thoughts expand a little he will begin to think of the welfare and comfort of his family. If his ideas still more widen, his concern will be the felicity of his fellow citizens; and if still they widen, he will be thinking of the glory of his land and of his race. But when ideas and views reach the utmost degree of expansion and attain the stage of perfection, then will he be interested in the exaltation of humankind. He will then be the well-wisher of all men and the seeker of the weal and prosperity of all lands. This is indicative of perfection. — *'Abdu'l-Bahá* **119**

Is there any deed in the world that would be nobler than service to the common good? Is there any greater blessing conceivable for a man, than that he should become the cause of the education, the development, the prosperity and honor of his fellow creatures? No, by the Lord God! The highest righteousness of all is for blessed souls to take hold of the hands of the helpless and deliver them out of their ignorance and abasement and poverty, and with pure motives, and only for the sake of God, to arise and energetically devote themselves to the service of the masses, forgetting their own worldly advantage and working only to serve the general good.

—'Abdu'l-Bahá **120**

Multiplicity of Languages

FROM the beginning of time the light of unity hath shed its divine radiance upon the world, and the greatest means for the promotion of that unity is for the peoples of the world to understand one another's writing and speech.

—Bahá'u'lláh **121**

Consider the differences that have arisen since the days of Adam. The divers and widely known languages now spoken by the peoples of the earth were originally unknown, as were the varied rules and customs now prevailing amongst them. The people of those times spoke a language different from those now known. Diversities of language arose in a later age, in a land known as Babel. It was given the name Babel, because the term signifieth "the place where the confusion of tongues arose." *—Bahá'u'lláh* **122**

Among the things which are conducive to unity and concord and will cause the whole earth to be regarded as one country is that the divers languages be reduced to one language and in like manner the scripts used in the world be confined to a single script. It is incumbent upon all nations to appoint some men of understanding and erudition to convene a gathering and through joint consultation choose one language from among the varied existing languages, or create a new one, to be taught to the children in all schools of the world.

The day is approaching when all the peoples of the world will have adopted one universal language and one common script. When this is achieved, to whatsoever city a man may journey, it shall be as if he were entering his own home.

—Bahá'u'lláh **123**

One of the great steps towards universal peace would be the establishment of a universal language. Bahá'u'lláh commands that the servants of humanity should meet together, and either choose a language which now exists, or form a new one. This was revealed in the Kitáb-i-Aqdas.* . . . It is there pointed out that the question of diversity of tongues is a very difficult one. There are more than eight hundred languages in the world, and no person could acquire them all.

The races of mankind are not isolated as in former days. Now, in order to be in close relationship with all countries it is necessary to be able to speak their tongues.

A universal language would make intercourse possible with every nation. Thus it would be needful to know two languages only, the mother tongue and the universal speech. The latter would enable a man to communicate with any and every man in the world!

A third language would not be needed. To be able to talk with a member of any race and country without requiring an interpreter, how helpful and restful to all! . . .

Until such a language is in use, the world will continue to feel the vast need of this means of intercourse. Difference of speech is one of the most fruitful causes of dislike and distrust that exists between nations, which are kept apart by their inability to understand each other's language more than by any other reason.

If everybody could speak one language, how much more easy would it be to serve humanity! *—'Abdu'l-Bahá* **124**

---

*The Kitáb-i-Aqdas, or "Most Holy Book" of Bahá'u'lláh, was written *circa* 1873 and is the chief repository of His laws. See Bahá'u'lláh, *A Synopsis and Codification of the Kitáb-i-Aqdas: The Most Holy Book of Bahá'u'lláh*, [comp. the Universal House of Justice] (Haifa: Bahá'í World Centre, 1973).

Diversity of languages has been a fruitful cause of discord. The function of language is to convey the thought and purpose of one to another. Therefore, it matters not what language man speaks or employs. . . . Bahá'u'lláh advocated one language as the greatest means of unity and the basis of international conference. He wrote to the kings and rulers of the various nations, recommending that one language should be sanctioned and adopted by all governments. According to this each nation should acquire the universal language in addition to its native tongue. The world would then be in close communication, consultation would become general, and dissensions due to diversity of speech would be removed.

—*'Abdu'l-Bahá* **125**

Today the greatest need of the world of humanity is discontinuance of the existing misunderstandings among nations. This can be accomplished through the unity of language. Unless the unity of languages is realized, the Most Great Peace and the oneness of the human world cannot be effectively organized and established because the function of language is to portray the mysteries and secrets of human hearts. The heart is like a box, and language is the key. Only by using the key can we open the box and observe the gems it contains. Therefore, the question of an auxiliary international tongue has the utmost importance. Through this means international education and training become possible; the evidence and history of the past can be acquired. The spread of the known facts of the human world depends upon language. The explanation of divine teachings can only be through this medium. As long as diversity of tongues and lack of comprehension of other languages continue, these glorious aims cannot be realized. Therefore, the very first service to the world of man is to establish this auxiliary international means of communication. It will become the cause of the tranquillity of the human commonwealth. Through it sciences and arts will be spread among the nations, and it will prove to be the means of the progress and development of all races. We must endeavor with all our powers to establish this international auxiliary language throughout the world.   —*'Abdu'l-Bahá* **126**

A fundamental lack of communication between peoples seriously undermines efforts towards world peace. Adopting an international auxiliary language would go far to resolving this problem and necessitates the most urgent attention.
                    —*The Universal House of Justice* **127**

Bahá'u'lláh has proclaimed the adoption of a universal language. A language shall be agreed upon by which unity will be established in the world. Each person will require training in two languages: his native tongue and the universal auxiliary form of speech. This will facilitate intercommunication and dispel the misunderstandings which the barriers of language have occasioned in the world. All people worship the same God and are alike His servants. When they are able to communicate freely, they will associate in friendship and concord, entertain the greatest love and fellowship for each other, and in reality the Orient and Occident will embrace in unity and agreement.   —*'Abdu'l-Bahá* **128**

Evoking Moral Attitudes Conducive to Enduring Peace

Material Achievements and Spiritual Perfections: Two Wings of Progress

THE betterment of the world can be accomplished through pure and goodly deeds, through commendable and seemly conduct.   —*Bahá'u'lláh* **129**

Whatsoever instilleth assurance into the hearts of men, whatsoever exalteth their station or promoteth their contentment, is acceptable in the sight of God. How lofty is the station which man, if he but choose to fulfill his high destiny, can attain! To what depths of degradation he can sink, depths which the meanest of creatures have never reached! Seize, O friends, the chance which this Day offereth you, and deprive not yourselves of the liberal effusions of His grace.

—Bahá'u'lláh **130**

Wert thou to attain to but a dewdrop of the crystal waters of divine knowledge, thou wouldst readily realize that true life is not the life of the flesh but the life of the spirit. For the life of the flesh is common to both men and animals, whereas the life of the spirit is possessed only by the pure in heart who have quaffed from the ocean of faith and partaken of the fruit of certitude.   *—Bahá'u'lláh* **131**

Man has two powers; and his development, two aspects. One power is connected with the material world, and by it he is capable of material advancement. The other power is spiritual, and through its development his inner, potential nature is awakened. These powers are like two wings. Both must be developed, for flight is impossible with one wing. Praise be to God! Material advancement has been evident in the world, but there is need of spiritual advancement in like proportion. We must strive unceasingly and without rest to accomplish the development of the spiritual nature in man, and endeavor with tireless energy to advance humanity toward the nobility of its true and intended station.   *—'Abdu'l-Bahá* **132**

The primary purpose, the basic objective, in laying down powerful laws and setting up great principles and institutions dealing with every aspect of civilization, is human happiness; and human happiness consists only in drawing closer to the Threshold of Almighty God, and in securing the peace and well-being of every individual member, high and low alike, of the human race; and the supreme agencies for accomplishing these two objectives are the excellent qualities with which humanity has been endowed.

A superficial culture, unsupported by a cultivated morality, is as "a confused medley of dreams,"* and external luster without inner perfection is "like a vapor in the desert which the thirsty dreameth to be water."† For results which would win the good pleasure of God and secure the peace and well-being of man, could never be fully achieved in a merely external civilization. . . .

There is the . . . case of the ruler who is fostering peace and tranquillity and at the same time devoting more energy than the warmongers to the accumulation of weapons and the building up of a larger army, on the grounds that peace and harmony can only be brought about by force. Peace is the pretext, and night and day they are all straining every nerve to pile up more weapons of war, and to pay for this their wretched people must sacrifice most of whatever they are able to earn by their sweat and toil. How many thousands have given up their work in useful industries and are laboring day and night to produce new and deadlier weapons which would spill out the blood of the race more copiously than before.

Each day they invent a new bomb or explosive and then the governments must abandon their obsolete arms and begin producing the new, since the old weapons cannot hold their own against the new. For example at this writing, in the year 1292 A.H.‡ they have invented a new rifle in Germany and a bronze cannon in Austria, which have greater firepower than the Martini-Henry rifle and the Krupp cannon, are more rapid in their effects and more efficient in annihilating humankind. The staggering cost of it all must be borne by the hapless masses.

Be just: can this nominal civilization, unsupported by a genuine civilization of character, bring about the peace and well-being of the people or win the good pleasure of God? Does it not, rather, connote the destruction of man's estate and pull down the pillars of happiness and peace?

— 'Abdu'l-Bahá   **133**

---

*Qur'án 12:44; 21:5.
†Qur'án 24:39.
‡1875.

What result is forthcoming from material rest, tranquillity, luxury and attachment to this corporeal world! It is evident that the man who pursues these things will in the end become afflicted with regret and loss.

Consequently, one must close his eyes wholly to these thoughts, long for eternal life, the sublimity of the world of humanity, the celestial developments, the Holy Spirit, the promotion of the Word of God, the guidance of the inhabitants of the globe, the promulgation of Universal Peace and the proclamation of the oneness of the world of humanity! *This is the work!* Otherwise like unto other animals and birds one must occupy himself with the requirements of this physical life, the satisfaction of which is the highest aspiration of the animal kingdom, and one must stalk across the earth like unto the quadrupeds.   —*'Abdu'l-Bahá* 134

Know ye, verily, that the happiness of mankind lieth in the unity and the harmony of the human race, and that spiritual and material developments are conditioned upon love and amity among all men. Consider ye the living creatures, namely those which move upon the earth and those which fly, those which graze and those which devour. Among the beasts of prey each kind liveth apart from other species of its genus, observing complete antagonism and hostility; and whenever they meet they immediately fight and draw blood, gnashing their teeth and baring their claws. This is the way in which ferocious beasts and bloodthirsty wolves behave, carnivorous animals that live by themselves and fight for their lives. But the docile, good-natured and gentle animals, whether they belong to the flying or grazing species, associate with one another in complete affinity, united in their flocks, and living their lives with enjoyment, happiness and contentment. Such are the birds that are satisfied with and grateful for a few grains; they live in complete gladness, and break into rich and melodious song while soaring over meadows, plains, hills and mountains. Similarly those animals which graze, like the sheep, the antelope and the gazelle, consort in the greatest amity, intimacy and unity while living in their plains and prairies in a condition of complete contentment. But dogs, wolves, tigers, hyenas and those other beasts of prey, are alienated from each other as they hunt and roam about alone. The creatures of the fields and birds of the air do not even shun or molest one another when they come upon their mutual grazing and rest-ing grounds but accept each other with friendliness, unlike the devouring beasts who immediately tear each other apart when one intrudes upon the other's cave or lair; yea, even if one merely passeth by the abode of another the latter at once rusheth out to attack and if possible kill the former.

Therefore, it hath been made clear and manifest that in the animal kingdom also love and affinity are the fruits of a gentle disposition, a pure nature and praiseworthy character, while discord and isolation are characteristic of the fierce beasts of the wild. — *'Abdu'l-Bahá* **135**

Love and good faith must so dominate the human heart that men will regard the stranger as a familiar friend, the malefactor as one of their own, the alien even as a loved one, the enemy as a companion dear and close. Who killeth them, him will they call a bestower of life; who turneth away from them, him will they regard as turning towards them; who denieth their message, him will they consider as one acknowl-edging its truth. The meaning is that they must treat all human-kind even as they treat their sympathizers, their fellow believ-ers, their loved ones and familiar friends.

Should such a torch light up the world community, ye. will find that the whole earth is sending forth a fragrance, that it hath become a delightsome paradise, and the face of it the image of high heaven. Then will the whole world be one native land, its diverse peoples one single kind, the nations of both east and west one household. — *'Abdu'l-Bahá* **136**

Question: Is peace a greater word than love?

Answer: No! Love is greater than peace, for peace is founded upon love. Love is the objective point of peace, and peace is an outcome of love. Until love is attained, peace cannot be; but there is a so-called peace without love. The love which is from God is the fundamental. This love is the object of all human attainment, the radiance of heaven, the light of man.   —'Abdu'l-Bahá **137**

Man is a child of God, most noble, lofty and beloved by God, his Creator. Therefore, he must ever strive that the divine bounties and virtues bestowed upon him may prevail and control him. Just now the soil of human hearts seems like black earth, but in the innermost substance of this dark soil there are thousands of fragrant flowers latent. We must endeavor to cultivate and awaken these potentialities, discover the secret treasure in this very mine and depository of God, bring forth these resplendent powers long hidden in human hearts. Then will the glories of both worlds be blended and increased and the quintessence of human existence be made manifest.
                                    —'Abdu'l-Bahá **138**

All mankind must be awakened to and become conscious of the harm of war, . . . they should be brought to realize the benefits of peace and know that peace is from God while warfare is satanic. Man must emulate the merciful God and turn away from satanic promptings in order that universal inclination shall be toward peace, love and unity and the discord of war vanish.   —'Abdu'l-Bahá **139**

Civilization and material progress should be combined with the Most Great Guidance* so that this nether world may become the scene of the appearance of the bestowals of the Kingdom, and physical achievements may be conjoined with the effulgences of the Merciful. This in order that the beauty and perfection of the world of man may be unveiled and be manifested before all in the utmost grace and splendor. Thus everlasting glory and happiness shall be revealed.
                                    —'Abdu'l-Bahá **140**

---

*The Revelation of Bahá'u'lláh.

The Power of a Moral Character

O PEOPLE of God! Do not busy yourselves in your own concerns; let your thoughts be fixed upon that which will rehabilitate the fortunes of mankind and sanctify the hearts and souls of men. This can best be achieved through pure and holy deeds, through a virtuous life and a goodly behavior.

—Bahá'u'lláh **141**

A good character is, verily, the best mantle for men from God. With it He adorneth the temples of His loved ones. By My life! The light of a good character surpasseth the light of the sun and the radiance thereof. Whoso attaineth unto it is accounted as a jewel among men. The glory and the upliftment of the world must needs depend upon it. A goodly character is a means whereby men are guided to the Straight Path. . . . Well is it with him who is adorned with the saintly attributes and character of the Concourse on High.   *—Bahá'u'lláh* **142**

Honesty, virtue, wisdom and a saintly character redound to the exaltation of man, while dishonesty, imposture, ignorance and hypocrisy lead to his abasement. By My life! Man's distinction lieth not in ornaments or wealth, but rather in virtuous behavior and true understanding. *—Bahá'u'lláh* **143**

Within the very breath of such souls as are pure and sanctified far-reaching potentialities are hidden. So great are these potentialities that they exercise their influence upon all created things.   *—Bahá'u'lláh* **144**

Would that ye had the power to perceive the things your Lord, the All-Merciful, doth see—things that attest the excellence of your rank, that bear witness to the greatness of your worth, that proclaim the sublimity of your station! God grant that your desires and unmortified passions may not hinder you from that which hath been ordained for you.

—Bahá'u'lláh **145**

O my friend! In all circumstances one should seize upon every means which will promote security and tranquillity among the peoples of the world. The Great Being saith: In this glorious Day whatever will purge you from corruption and will lead you towards peace and composure, is indeed the Straight Path. *—Bahá'u'lláh* **146**

O Son of Spirit! There is no peace for thee save by renouncing thyself and turning unto Me; for it behooveth thee to glory in My name, not in thine own; to put thy trust in Me and not in thyself, since I desire to be loved alone and above all that is. *—Bahá'u'lláh* **147**

Today all people are immersed in the world of nature. That is why thou dost see jealousy, greed, the struggle for survival, deception, hypocrisy, tyranny, oppression, disputes, strife, bloodshed, looting and pillaging, which all emanate from the world of nature. Few are those who have been freed from this darkness, who have ascended from the world of nature to the world of man, who have followed the divine Teachings, have served the world of humanity, are resplendent, merciful, illumined and like unto a rose garden. Strive thine utmost to become godlike, characterized with His attributes, illumined and merciful, that thou mayest be freed from every bond and become attached at heart to the Kingdom of the incomparable Lord. *—'Abdu'l-Bahá* **148**

[To "oppose one's passions"] . . . is the very foundation of every laudable human quality; indeed, these few words embody the light of the world, the impregnable basis of all the spiritual attributes of human beings. This is the balance wheel of all behavior, the means of keeping all man's good qualities in equilibrium.

For desire is a flame that has reduced to ashes uncounted lifetime harvests of the learned, a devouring fire that even the vast sea of their accumulated knowledge could never quench. How often has it happened that an individual who was graced with every attribute of humanity and wore the jewel of true understanding, nevertheless followed after his passions until his excellent qualities passed beyond moderation and he was forced into excess. His pure intentions changed to evil ones, his attributes were no longer put to uses worthy of them, and the power of his desires turned him aside from righteousness and its rewards into ways that were dangerous and dark. A good character is in the sight of God and His chosen ones and the possessors of insight, the most excellent and praiseworthy of all things, but always on condition that its center of emanation should be reason and knowledge and its base should be true moderation.   — 'Abdu'l-Bahá **149**

The happiness and greatness, the rank and station, the pleasure and peace, of an individual have never consisted in his personal wealth, but rather in his excellent character, his high resolve, the breadth of his learning, and his ability to solve difficult problems. How well has it been said: "On my back is a garment which, were it sold for a penny, that penny would be worth far more; yet within the garment is a soul which, if you weighed it against all the souls in the world, would prove greater and nobler."   — 'Abdu'l-Bahá **150**

O ye friends, exert ye an effort! Every expenditure is in need of an income. This day, in the world of humanity, men are all the time expending, for war is nothing but the consumption of men and of wealth. At least engage ye in a deed of profit to the world of humanity that ye may partially compensate for that loss. Perchance, through the divine confirmations, ye may be assisted in promulgating amity and concord among men, in substituting love for enmity, in causing universal peace to result from universal war and in converting loss and rancor into profit and love. This wish will be realized through the power of the Kingdom.   — 'Abdu'l-Bahá **151**

O ye the beloved of the one true God! Pass beyond the narrow retreats of your evil and corrupt desires, and advance into the vast immensity of the realm of God, and abide ye in the meads of sanctity and of detachment, that the fragrance of your deeds may lead the whole of mankind to the ocean of God's unfading glory. —*Bahá'u'lláh* **152**

O Son of Spirit! With the joyful tidings of light I hail thee: rejoice! To the court of holiness I summon thee; abide therein that thou mayest live in peace for evermore.

—*Bahá'u'lláh* **153**

Chapter 5

Constructing a Peaceful and Global Civilization

Recognizing the Oneness of Humanity: The Fundamental Prerequisite

HE Who is your Lord, the All-Merciful, cherisheth in His heart the desire of beholding the entire human race as one soul and one body. Haste ye to win your share of God's good grace and mercy in this Day that eclipseth all other created Days. How great the felicity that awaiteth the man that forsaketh all he hath in a desire to obtain the things of God! Such a man, We testify, is among God's blessed ones.

—Bahá'u'lláh 1

Regard ye the world as a man's body, which is afflicted with divers ailments, and the recovery of which dependeth upon the harmonizing of all of its component elements. Gather ye around that which We have prescribed unto you, and walk not in the ways of such as create dissension. Meditate on the world and the state of its people. *—Bahá'u'lláh* 2

O Brethren! Be forbearing one with another and set not your affections on things below. Pride not yourselves in your glory, and be not ashamed of abasement. By My beauty! I have created all things from dust, and to dust will I return them again. *—Bahá'u'lláh* 3

God, the Almighty, has created all mankind from the dust of earth. He has fashioned them all from the same elements; they are descended from the same race and live upon the same globe. He has created them to dwell beneath the one heaven. As members of the human family and His children He has endowed them with equal susceptibilities. He maintains, protects and is kind to all. He has made no distinction in mercies and graces among His children. With impartial love and wisdom He has sent forth His Prophets and divine teachings. His teachings are the means of establishing union and fellowship among mankind and awakening love and kindness in human hearts. He proclaims the oneness of the kingdom of humanity. He rebukes those things which create differences and destroy harmony; He commends and praises every means that will conduce to the solidarity of the human race. He encourages man in every step of advancement which leads to ultimate union. *— 'Abdu'l-Bahá* **4**

[A principle of Bahá'u'lláh] . . . is the oneness of mankind: that all men are the sheep of God, and God is their loving Shepherd, caring most tenderly for all without favoring one or another. "No difference canst thou see in the creation of the God of mercy";* all are His servants, all implore His grace. *— 'Abdu'l-Bahá* **5**

The divine policy is the oneness of humanity. God is just and kind to all. He considers all as His servants. He excludes none, and His judgments are correct and true. No matter how complete human policy and foresight may appear, they are imperfect. If we do not seek the counsel of God or if we refuse to follow His dictates, it is presumptive evidence that we are knowing and wise, whereas God is ignorant; that we are sagacious and God is not. God forbid! We seek shelter in His mercy for this suggestion! No matter how far the human intelligence may advance, it is still but a drop, while divine omniscience is the ocean. Shall we say that a drop is imbued or endowed with qualities of which the ocean is devoid? Shall we believe that the policy and plan of this atom of a human soul are superior to the wisdom of the Omniscient? There is no greater ignorance than this. *— 'Abdu'l-Bahá* **6**

---

*Qur'án 67:3.

There is perfect brotherhood underlying humanity, for all are servants of one God and belong to one family under the protection of divine providence. The bond of fraternity exists in humanity because all are intelligent beings. . . . There is brotherhood potential in humanity because all inhabit this earthly globe under the one canopy of heaven. There is brotherhood natal in mankind because all are elements of one human society subject to the necessity of agreement and co-operation. There is brotherhood intended in humanity because all are waves of one sea, leaves and fruit of one tree. This is physical fellowship which ensures material happiness in the human world. The stronger it becomes, the more will mankind advance and the circle of materiality be enlarged.

—'Abdu'l-Bahá 7

When the light of Bahá'u'lláh dawned from the East, He proclaimed the promise of the oneness of humanity. He addressed all mankind, saying, "Ye are all the fruits of one tree. There are not two trees: one a tree of divine mercy, the other the tree of Satan." Again He said, "Ye are all the fruits of one tree, the leaves of one branch." This was His announcement; this was His promise of the oneness of the world of humanity. Anathema and execration were utterly abrogated. He said, "It is not becoming in man to curse another; it is not befitting that man should attribute darkness to another; it is not meet that one human being should consider another human being as bad; nay, rather, all mankind are the servants of one God; God is the Father of all; there is not a single exception to that law. There are no people of Satan; all belong to the Merciful. There is no darkness; all is light. All are the servants of God, and man must love humanity from his heart. He must, verily, behold humanity as submerged in the divine mercy."

Bahá'u'lláh has made no exception to this rule. He said that among mankind there may be those who are ignorant; they must be trained. Some are sick; they must be treated. Some are immature; they must be helped to attain maturity. In other respects humanity is submerged in the ocean of divine mercy. God is the Father of all. He educates, provides for and loves all; for they are His servants and His creation. Surely the Creator loves His creatures. It would be impossible to find an artist who does not love his own production. Have you ever seen a man who did not love his own actions? Even though they be bad actions, he loves them. How ignorant, therefore, the thought that God, Who created man, educated and nurtured him, surrounded him with all blessings, made the sun and all phenomenal existence for his benefit, bestowed upon him tenderness and kindness and then did not love him. This is palpable ignorance, for no matter to what religion a man belongs, even though he be an atheist or materialist, nevertheless, God nurtures him, bestows His kindness and sheds upon him His light. How then can we believe God is wrathful and unloving? How can we even imagine this, when as a matter of fact we are witnesses of the tenderness and mercy of God upon every hand? All about us we behold manifestations of the love of God. If, therefore, God be loving, what should we do? We have nothing else to do but to emulate Him. Just as God loves all and is kind to all, so must we really love and be kind to everybody. We must consider none bad, none worthy of detestation, no one as an enemy. We must love all; nay, we must consider everyone as related to us, for all are the servants of one God. All are under the instructions of one Educator. We must strive day and night that love and amity may increase, that this bond of unity may be strengthened, that joy and happiness may more and more prevail, that in unity and solidarity all mankind may gather beneath the shadow of God, that people may turn to God for their sustenance, finding in Him the life that is everlasting. Thus may they be confirmed in the Kingdom of God and live forever through His grace and bounty.   —'Abdu'l-Bahá **8**

Today the world of humanity is walking in darkness because it is out of touch with the world of God. That is why we do not see the signs of God in the hearts of men. The power of the Holy Spirit has no influence. When a divine spiritual illumination becomes manifest in the world of humanity, when divine instruction and guidance appear, then enlightenment follows, a new spirit is realized within, a new power descends, and a new life is given. It is like the birth from the animal kingdom into the kingdom of man. When man acquires these virtues, the oneness of the world of humanity will be revealed, the banner of international peace will be upraised, equality between all mankind will be realized, and the Orient and Occident will become one. Then will the justice of God become manifest, all humanity will appear as the members of one family, and every member of that family will be consecrated to cooperation and mutual assistance. The lights of the love of God will shine; eternal happiness will be unveiled; everlasting joy and spiritual delight will be attained.

I will pray, and you must pray, likewise, that such heavenly bounty may be realized; that strife and enmity may be banished, warfare and bloodshed taken away; that hearts may attain ideal communication and that all people may drink from the same fountain. May they receive their knowledge from the same divine source. May all hearts become illumined with the rays of the Sun of Reality; may all of them enter the university of God, acquire spiritual virtues and seek for themselves heavenly bounties. Then this material, phenomenal world will become the mirror of the world of God, and within this pure mirror the divine virtues of the realm of might will be reflected.

—'Abdu'l-Bahá **9**

Quench ye the fires of war, lift high the banners of peace, work for the oneness of humankind and remember that religion is the channel of love unto all peoples. Be ye aware that the children of men are sheep of God and He their loving Shepherd, that He careth tenderly for all His sheep and maketh them to feed in His own green pastures of grace and giveth them to drink from the wellspring of life. Such is the way of the Lord. Such are His bestowals. Such, from among His teachings, is His precept of the oneness of mankind.

The portals of His blessings are opened wide and His signs are published abroad and the glory of truth is blazing forth; inexhaustible are the blessings. Know ye the value of this time. Strive ye with all your hearts, raise up your voices and shout, until this dark world be filled with light, and this narrow place of shadows be widened out, and this dust heap of a fleeting moment be changed into a mirror for the eternal gardens of heaven, and this globe of earth receive its portion of celestial grace.

Then will aggression crumble away, and all that maketh for disunity be destroyed, and the structure of oneness be raised—that the Blessed Tree may cast its shade over east and west, and the Tabernacle of the singleness of man be set up on the high summits, and flags that betoken love and fellowship flutter from their staffs around the world until the sea of truth lift high its waves, and earth bring forth the roses and sweet herbs of blessings without end, and become from pole to pole the Abhá Paradise.*   —'Abdu'l-Bahá **10**

The principle of the Oneness of Mankind—the pivot round which all the teachings of Bahá'u'lláh revolve—is no mere outburst of ignorant emotionalism or an expression of vague and pious hope. Its appeal is not to be merely identified with a reawakening of the spirit of brotherhood and goodwill among men, nor does it aim solely at the fostering of harmonious cooperation among individual peoples and nations. Its implications are deeper, its claims greater than any which the Prophets of old were allowed to advance. Its message is applicable not only to the individual, but concerns itself primarily with the nature of those essential relationships that must bind all the states and nations as members of one human family. It does not constitute merely the enunciation of an ideal, but stands inseparably associated with an institution adequate to embody its truth, demonstrate its validity, and perpetuate its influence. It implies an organic change in the structure of present-day society, a change such as the world has not yet

---

*The "most glorious paradise," the establishment of the Kingdom of God on earth.

experienced. It constitutes a challenge, at once bold and universal, to outworn shibboleths of national creeds—creeds that have had their day and which must, in the ordinary course of events as shaped and controlled by Providence, give way to a new gospel, fundamentally different from, and infinitely superior to, what the world has already conceived. It calls for no less than the reconstruction and the demilitarization of the whole civilized world—a world organically unified in all the essential aspects of its life, its political machinery, its spiritual aspiration, its trade and finance, its script and language, and yet infinite in the diversity of the national characteristics of its federated units.

It represents the consummation of human evolution—an evolution that has had its earliest beginnings in the birth of family life, its subsequent development in the achievement of tribal solidarity, leading in turn to the constitution of the city-state, and expanding later into the institution of independent and sovereign nations.

The principle of the Oneness of Mankind, as proclaimed by Bahá'u'lláh, carries with it no more and no less than a solemn assertion that attainment to this final stage in this stupendous evolution is not only necessary but inevitable, that its realization is fast approaching, and that nothing short of a power that is born of God can succeed in establishing it.

—Shoghi Effendi **11**

O Children of Men! Know ye not why We created you all from the same dust? That no one should exalt himself over the other. Ponder at all times in your hearts how ye were created. Since We have created you all from one same substance it is incumbent on you to be even as one soul, to walk with the same feet, eat with the same mouth and dwell in the same land, that from your inmost being, by your deeds and actions, the signs of oneness and the essence of detachment may be made manifest. Such is My counsel to you, O concourse of light! Heed ye this counsel that ye may obtain the fruit of holiness from the tree of wondrous glory.   *—Bahá'u'lláh* **12**

Your efforts must be lofty. Exert yourselves with heart and soul so that, perchance, through your efforts the light of universal peace may shine and this darkness of estrangement and enmity may be dispelled from amongst men, that all men may become as one family and consort together in love and kindness, that the East may assist the West and the West give help to the East, for all are the inhabitants of one planet, the people of one original native land and the flocks of one Shepherd.

—*'Abdu'l-Bahá* **13**

Abandoning All Forms of Prejudice

O HUMANKIND! Verily, ye are all the leaves and fruits of one tree; ye are all one. Therefore, associate in friendship; love one another; abandon prejudices of race; dispel forever this gloomy darkness of human ignorance, for the century of light, the Sun of Reality hath appeared. Now is the time for affiliation, and now is the period of unity and concord. For thousands of years ye have been contending in warfare and strife. It is enough. Now is the time for unity. Lay aside all self-purposes, and know for a certainty that all men are the servants of one God Who will bind them together in love and agreement.

—*Bahá'u'lláh* **14**

The most important teaching of Bahá'u'lláh is to leave behind racial, religious, national and patriotic prejudices. Until these prejudices are entirely removed mankind will not find rest. Nay, rather, discord and bloodshed will increase day by day, and the foundation of the prosperity of the world of man will be destroyed.   —*'Abdu'l-Bahá* **15**

God has created His servants in order that they may love and associate with each other. He has revealed the glorious splendor of His sun of love in the world of humanity. The cause of the creation of the phenomenal world is love. All the Prophets have promulgated the law of love. Man has opposed the will of God and acted in opposition to the plan of God. Therefore, from the beginning of history to the present time the world of humanity has had no lasting rest; warfare and strife have continuously prevailed, and hearts have manifested hatred toward each other. The cause of bloodshed and battle, strife and hatred throughout the past has been either religious, racial, patriotic or political prejudice. Therefore, the world of humanity has ever been in torment. —'Abdu'l-Bahá 16

For a period of 6,000 years history informs us about the world of humanity. During these 6,000 years the world of humanity has not been free from war, strife, murder and blood-thirstiness. In every period war has been waged in one country or another and that war was due to either religious prejudice, racial prejudice, political prejudice or patriotic prejudice. It has therefore been ascertained and proved that all prejudices are destructive of the human edifice. As long as these prejudices persist, the struggle for existence must remain dominant, and bloodthirstiness and rapacity continue. Therefore, even as was the case in the past, the world of humanity cannot be saved from the darkness of nature and cannot attain illumination except through the abandonment of prejudices and the acquisition of the morals of the Kingdom. —'Abdu'l-Bahá 17

When thou traversest the regions of the world, thou shalt conclude that all progress is the result of association and cooperation, while ruin is the outcome of animosity and hatred. Notwithstanding this, the world of humanity doth not take warning, nor doth it awake from the slumber of heedlessness. Man is still causing differences, quarrels and strife in order to marshal the cohorts of war and, with his legions, rush into the field of bloodshed and slaughter. —'Abdu'l-Bahá 18

Ye observe how the world is divided against itself, how many a land is red with blood and its very dust is caked with human gore. The fires of conflict have blazed so high that never in early times, not in the Middle Ages, not in recent centuries hath there ever been such a hideous war, a war that is even as millstones, taking for grain the skulls of men. Nay, even worse, for flourishing countries have been reduced to rubble, cities have been leveled with the ground, and many a once prosperous village hath been turned into ruin. Fathers have lost their sons, and sons their fathers. Mothers have wept away their hearts over dead children. Children have been orphaned, women left to wander, vagrants without a home. From every aspect, humankind hath sunken low. Loud are the piercing cries of fatherless children; loud the mothers' anguished voices, reaching to the skies.

And the breeding-ground of all these tragedies is prejudice: prejudice of race and nation, of religion, of political opinion; and the root cause of prejudice is blind imitation of the past—imitation in religion, in racial attitudes, in national bias, in politics. So long as this aping of the past persisteth, just so long will the foundations of the social order be blown to the four winds, just so long will humanity be continually exposed to direst peril.   —'Abdu'l-Bahá **19**

For blind imitation of the past will stunt the mind. But once every soul inquireth into truth, society will be freed from the darkness of continually repeating the past.
                                        —'Abdu'l-Bahá **20**

Contemplate first the prejudice of religion: consider the nations of so-called religious people; if they were truly worshipers of God they would obey His law which forbids them to kill one another.

If priests of religion really adored the God of love and served the Divine Light, they would teach their people to keep the chief Commandment, "To be in love and charity with all men." But we find the contrary, for it is often the priests who encourage nations to fight. Religious hatred is ever the most cruel!

All religions teach that we should love one another; that we should seek out our own shortcomings before we presume to condemn the faults of others, that we must not consider ourselves superior to our neighbors! We must be careful not to exalt ourselves lest we be humiliated.

Who are *we* that we should judge? How shall *we* know

who, in the sight of God, is the most upright man? God's thoughts are not like our thoughts! How many men who have seemed saintlike to their friends have fallen into the greatest humiliation. Think of Judas Iscariot; he began well, but remember his end! On the other hand, Paul, the Apostle, was in his early life an enemy of Christ, whilst later he became His most faithful servant. How then can we flatter ourselves and despise others?

Let us therefore be humble, without prejudices, preferring others' good to our own! Let us never say, "I am a believer but he is an infidel," "I am near to God, whilst he is an outcast." We can never know what will be the final judgment! Therefore let us help all who are in need of any kind of assistance.

Let us teach the ignorant, and take care of the young child until he grows to maturity. When we find a person fallen into the depths of misery or sin we must be kind to him, take him by the hand, help him to regain his footing, his strength; we must guide him with love and tenderness, treat him as a friend not as an enemy.

We have no right to look upon any of our fellow mortals as evil.

Concerning the prejudice of race: it is an illusion, a superstition pure and simple! For God created us all of one race. There were no differences in the beginning, for we are all descendants of Adam. In the beginning, also, there were no limits and boundaries between the different lands; no part of the earth belonged more to one people than to another. In the sight of God there is no difference between the various races. Why should man invent such a prejudice? How can we uphold war caused by an illusion?

God has not created men that they should destroy one another. All races, tribes, sects and classes share equally in the Bounty of their Heavenly Father.

The only difference lies in the degree of faithfulness, of obedience to the laws of God. There are some who are as lighted torches, there are others who shine as stars in the sky of humanity. The lovers of mankind, these are the superior men, of whatever nation, creed, or color they may be. For it is they to whom God will say these blessed words, "Well done, My good and faithful servants." In that day He will not ask, "Are you English, French, or perhaps Persian? Do you come from the East, or from the West?"

The only division that is real is this: There are heavenly men and earthly men; self-sacrificing servants of humanity in the love of the Most High, bringing harmony and unity, teaching peace and goodwill to men. On the other hand there are those selfish men, haters of their brethren, in whose hearts prejudice has replaced loving kindness, and whose influence breeds discord and strife.

To which race or to which color belong these two divisions of men, to the White, to the Yellow, to the Black, to the East or to the West, to the North or to the South? If these are God's divisions, why should we invent others? Political prejudice is equally mischievous, it is one of the greatest causes of bitter strife amongst the children of men. There are people who find pleasure in breeding discord, who constantly endeavor to goad their country into making war upon other nations—and why? They think to advantage their own country to the detriment of others. They send armies to harass and destroy the land, in order to become famous in the world, for the joy of conquest. That it may be said: "Such a country has defeated another, and brought it under the yoke of their stronger, more superior rule." This victory, bought at the price of much bloodshed, is not lasting! The conqueror shall one day be conquered; and the vanquished ones victorious! Remember the history of the past: did not France conquer Germany more than once—then did not the German nation overcome France?

We learn also that France conquered England; then was the English nation victorious over France!

These glorious conquests are so ephemeral! Why attach so great importance to them and to their fame, as to be willing to shed the blood of the people for their attainment? Is any victory worth the inevitable train of evils consequent upon human slaughter, the grief and sorrow and ruin which must overwhelm so many homes of both nations? For it is not possible that one country alone should suffer.

Oh! why will man, the disobedient child of God, who should be an example of the power of the spiritual law, turn his face away from the Divine Teaching and put all his effort into destruction and war?

My hope is that in this enlightened century the Divine Light of love will shed its radiance over the whole world, seeking out the responsive heart's intelligence of every human being; that the light of the Sun of Truth will lead politicians to shake off all the claims of prejudice and superstition, and with freed minds to follow the Policy of God: for Divine Politics are mighty, man's politics are feeble! . . .

Are we not the servants of God? Shall we neglect to follow our Master's Example,* and ignore His Commands?

I pray that the Kingdom shall come on Earth, and that all darkness shall be driven away by the effulgence of the Heavenly Sun. —'Abdu'l-Bahá 21

The earth is one native land, one home; and all mankind are the children of one Father. God has created them, and they are the recipients of His compassion. Therefore, if anyone offends another, he offends God. It is the wish of our heavenly Father that every heart should rejoice and be filled with happiness, that we should live together in felicity and joy. The obstacle to human happiness is racial or religious prejudice, the competitive struggle for existence and inhumanity toward each other. —'Abdu'l-Bahá 22

Therefore, it has been decreed by God in this day that these prejudices and differences shall be laid aside. All are commanded to seek the good pleasure of the Lord of unity, to follow His command and obey His will; in this way the world of humanity shall become illumined with the reality of love and reconciliation. —'Abdu'l-Bahá 23

---

*God's.

Ye who are servants of the human race, strive ye with all your heart to deliver mankind out of this darkness and these prejudices that belong to the human condition and the world of nature, so that humanity may find its way into the light of the world of God. . . .

Strive ye, therefore, with the help of God, with illumined minds and hearts and a strength born of heaven, to become a bestowal from God to man, and to call into being for all humankind, comfort and peace.   —'Abdu'l-Bahá   **24**

Reducing the World's Armaments

WE cherish the hope that through the earnest endeavors of such as are the exponents of the power of God—exalted be His glory—the weapons of war throughout the world may be converted into instruments of reconstruction and that strife and conflict may be removed from the midst of men.

—*Bahá'u'lláh*   **25**

O ye rulers of the earth! Wherefore have ye clouded the radiance of the Sun, and caused it to cease from shining? Hearken unto the counsel given you by the Pen of the Most High, that haply both ye and the poor may attain unto tranquillity and peace. We beseech God to assist the kings of the earth to establish peace on earth. He, verily, doth what He willeth.

O kings of the earth! We see you increasing every year your expenditures, and laying the burden thereof on your subjects. This, verily, is wholly and grossly unjust. Fear the sighs and tears of this Wronged One, and lay not excessive burdens on your peoples. Do not rob them to rear palaces for yourselves; nay rather choose for them that which ye choose for yourselves. Thus We unfold to your eyes that which profiteth you, if ye but perceive. Your people are your treasures. Beware lest your rule violate the commandments of God, and ye deliver your wards to the hands of the robber. By them ye rule, by their means ye subsist, by their aid ye conquer. Yet, how disdainfully ye look upon them! How strange, how very strange! . . .

O rulers of the earth! Be reconciled among yourselves, that ye may need no more armaments save in a measure to safeguard your territories and dominions. Beware lest ye disregard the counsel of the All-Knowing, the Faithful.

Be united, O kings of the earth, for thereby will the tempest of discord be stilled amongst you, and your peoples find rest, if ye be of them that comprehend. Should any one among you take up arms against another, rise ye all against him, for this is naught but manifest justice. —*Bahá'u'lláh* **26**

The cause of peace is a very great cause; it is the Cause of God, and all the forces of the world are opposed to it. Governments, for instance, consider militarism as the step to human progress, that division among men and nations is the cause of patriotism and honor, that if one nation attack and conquer another, gaining wealth, territory and glory thereby, this warfare and conquest, this bloodshed and cruelty are the cause of that victorious nation's advancement and prosperity. This is an utter mistake. —*'Abdu'l-Bahá* **27**

A conquest can be a praiseworthy thing, and there are times when war becomes the powerful basis of peace, and ruin the very means of reconstruction. If, for example, a high-minded sovereign marshals his troops to block the onset of the insurgent and the aggressor, or again, if he takes the field and distinguishes himself in a struggle to unify a divided state and people, if, in brief, he is waging war for a righteous purpose, then this seeming wrath is mercy itself, and this apparent tyranny the very substance of justice and this warfare the cornerstone of peace. Today, the task befitting great rulers is to establish universal peace, for in this lies the freedom of all peoples. —*'Abdu'l-Bahá* **28**

How is universal peace to be established? By the education of the public with the sentiments of peace. Today the full

realization of universal peace is the panacea of every disease.
What are the diseases?

One of the diseases is the impoverishment of the farmers
and the middle classes through the unbearable burden of war
taxes.

This wave of military craze has reached its height. It shall
soon recede. The income of the farmers and others is taken by
the force of a military government and expended foolishly
over useless instruments of destruction. The prospect of every
government becomes gloomier every year, because the war
budget of every government is being increased without regard
to the feverish signs of social unrest and industrial upheavals.
The people are seething with ideas of insurrection and agitation. The burden has become too heavy. The patience of mankind is exhausted. They groan under this load, and they grope
in the darkness seeking the light of peace and brotherhood.
Their pitiful cries ascend to the throne of the Almighty. Lo! Lo!
He has listened to them; He has answered their prayers. The
dawn of peace hath appeared. The lights of brotherhood are
breaking through the dark clouds of human prejudices. Lovers
of peace, rejoice! O ye who are heavy laden, be happy, be
happy! Weep no more, for your loads will be taken from you!

This military and naval expenditure is a great disease.
Look at the results of the war between Italy and Turkey*—
how dreadful they are! The fathers hear the news of the death
of their sons. The sons are grieved through the death of their
fathers. How many peaceful villages are laid waste! How the
wealth of two nations is exhausted!

The remedy of this disease is through universal peace.
This will ensure public safety. Today that which is the cause of
dispersion is war. If the nations enter into a faithful agreement
to leave off all warlike preparations at once, they shall secure
for themselves and their posterity eternal welfare. They shall
become freed from every difficulty and international confusion. This end must be obtained through the development of

---

*The Italo-Turkish War of 1911–12.

the intellects and the inculcation of peaceful ideals in all the institutions of modern civilization. —*'Abdu'l-Bahá* **29**

Once . . . the governments of the world . . . [have] entered into a covenant of eternal friendship [they] will have no need of keeping large standing armies and navies. A few battalions to preserve internal order, and an International Police to keep the highways of the seas clear, are all that will be necessary. Then these huge sums will be diverted to other more useful channels, pauperism will disappear, knowledge will increase, the victories of Peace will be sung by poets and bards, knowledge will improve the conditions and mankind will be rocked in the cradle of felicity and bliss. Then, whether a government is constitutional or republican, hereditary monarchy or democratic, the rulers will devote their time to the prosperity of their nations, the legislation of just and sane laws and the fostering of closer and more amicable relations with their neighbors—thus will the world of humanity become a mirror reflecting the virtues and attributes of the Kingdom of God. . . .

. . . By a general agreement all the governments of the world must disarm simultaneously. . . . It will not do if one lays down the arms and the other refuses to do so. The nations of the world must concur with each other concerning this supremely important subject, thus they may abandon together the deadly weapons of human slaughter. As long as one nation increases her military and naval budget, another nation will be forced into this crazed competition through her natural and supposed interests. . . .

Now the question of disarmament must be put into practice by all the nations and not only by one or two. Consequently the advocates of Peace must strive day and night, so that the individuals of every country may become peace loving, public opinion may gain a strong and permanent footing, and day by day the army of International Peace be increased, complete disarmament be realized and the Flag of Universal Conciliation be waving on the summit of the mountains of the earth. . . .

. . . The ideals of Peace must be nurtured and spread among the inhabitants of the world; they must be instructed in the school of Peace and the evils of war. First: The financiers and bankers must desist from lending money to any government contemplating to wage an unjust war upon an innocent nation. Second: The presidents and managers of the railroads and steamship companies must refrain from transporting war ammunition, infernal engines, guns, and cannons and powder from one country into another. Third: The soldiers must petition, through their representatives, the Ministers of War, the politicians, the Congressmen and the generals to put forth in a clear, intelligible language the reasons and the causes which have brought them to the brink of such a national calamity. The soldiers must *demand* this as one of the prerogatives. "Demonstrate to us," they must say, "that this is a just war, and we will then enter into the battlefield[;] otherwise we will not take one step. . . . Come forth from your hiding-places, enter into the battlefield if you like to attack each other and tear each other to pieces if you desire to air your so-called contentions. The discord and feud are between you; why do you make us, innocent people, a party to it? If fighting and bloodshed are good things, then lead us into the fray by your presence!"

In short, every means that produces war must be checked and the causes that prevent the occurrence of war be advanced—so that physical conflict may become an impossibility. On the other hand, every country must be properly delimited, its exact frontiers marked, its national integrity secured, its permanent independence protected, and its vital interests honored by the family of nations. These services ought to be rendered by an impartial, international Commission. In this manner all causes of friction and differences will be removed. And in the case there should arise some disputes between them, they could arbitrate before the Parliament of Man, the representatives of which should be chosen from among the wisest and most judicious men of all the nations of the world.

—'Abdu'l-Bahá **30**

"As to the question of disarmament, all nations must disarm at the same time. It will not do at all, and it is not proposed, that some nations shall lay down their arms while others, their neighbors, remain armed. The peace of the world must be brought about by international agreement. All nations must agree to disarm simultaneously. . . . No nation can follow a peace policy while its neighbor remains warlike. . . . There is no justice in that. Nobody would dream of suggesting that the peace of the world could be brought about by any such line of action. It is to be brought about by a general and comprehensive international agreement, and in no other way. . . .

"Simultaneous action," he* went on, "is necessary in any scheme of disarmament. All the governments of the world must transform their battleships and warcraft into merchant vessels. But no one nation can by itself start in upon such a policy and it would be folly should one power attempt to do so. . . . it would simply invite destruction." . . .

"Are there any signs that the permanent peace of the world will be established in anything like a reasonable period?" 'Abdu'l-Bahá was asked.

"It will be established in this century," he answered. "It will be universal in the twentieth century. All nations will be forced into it."

"Economic pressure will tell?"

"Yes: the nations will be forced to come to peace and to agree to the abolition of war. The awful burdens of taxation for war purposes will get beyond human endurance. . . .

"No," said 'Abdu'l-Bahá in conclusion, "I repeat, no nation can disarm under these circumstances. Disarmament is surely coming, but it must come, and it will come, by the universal consent of the civilized nations of the earth. By international agreement they will lay down their arms and the great era of peace will be ushered in.

"In this and no other way can peace be established upon the earth."   —'Abdu'l-Bahá **31**

---

*'Abdu'l-Bahá.

Convoking an Assembly to Establish a Global Union of Nations

THE Great Being, wishing to reveal the prerequisites of the peace and tranquillity of the world and the advancement of its peoples, hath written: The time must come when the imperative necessity for the holding of a vast, an all-embracing assemblage of men will be universally realized. The rulers and kings of the earth must needs attend it, and, participating in its deliberations, must consider such ways and means as will lay the foundations of the world's Great Peace amongst men. Such a peace demandeth that the Great Powers should resolve, for the sake of the tranquillity of the peoples of the earth, to be fully reconciled among themselves. Should any king take up arms against another, all should unitedly arise and prevent him. If this be done, the nations of the world will no longer require any armaments, except for the purpose of preserving the security of their realms and of maintaining internal order within their territories. This will ensure the peace and composure of every people, government and nation. We fain would hope that the kings and rulers of the earth, the mirrors of the gracious and almighty name of God, may attain unto this station, and shield mankind from the onslaught of tyranny.

—*Bahá'u'lláh* **32**

Any king who will arise and carry out this task, he, verily will, in the sight of God, become the cynosure of all kings. Happy is he, and great is his blessedness!   —*Bahá'u'lláh* **33**

We pray God . . . and cherish the hope that He may graciously assist . . . the kings of the earth . . . to establish the Lesser Peace. This, indeed, is the greatest means for ensuring the tranquillity of the nations. It is incumbent upon the Sovereigns of the world . . . unitedly to hold fast unto this Peace, which is the chief instrument for the protection of all mankind. It is Our hope that they will arise to achieve what will be conducive to the well-being of man. It is their duty to convene an all-inclusive assembly, which either they themselves or their ministers will attend, and to enforce whatever measures are required to establish unity and concord amongst men. They must put away the weapons of war, and turn to the instruments of universal reconstruction. Should one king rise up against another, all the other kings must arise to deter him. Arms and armaments will, then, be no more needed beyond that which is necessary to ensure the internal security of their respective countries. If they attain unto this all-surpassing blessing, the people of each nation will pursue, with tranquillity and contentment, their own occupations, and the groanings and lamentations of most men would be silenced. We beseech God to aid them to do His will and pleasure. He, verily, is the Lord of the throne on high and of earth below, and the Lord of this world and of the world to come.   —*Bahá'u'lláh* **34**

Every century holds the solution of one predominating problem. Although there may be many problems, yet one of the innumerable problems will loom large and become the most important of all. . . . in this luminous century the greatest bestowal of the world of humanity is Universal Peace, which must be founded, so that the realm of creation may obtain composure, the East and the West, which include in their arms the five continents of the globe, may embrace each other, mankind may rest beneath the tent of oneness of the world of humanity, and the flag of universal peace may wave over all the regions. . . .

Today the true duty of a powerful king is to establish a universal peace; for verily it signifies the freedom of all the people of the world. Some persons who are ignorant of the world of true humanity and its high ambitions for the general good, reckon such a glorious condition of life to be very difficult, nay rather impossible to compass. But it is not so, far from it.   —*'Abdu'l-Bahá* **35**

The body politic may be likened to the human organism. As long as the various members and parts of that organism are coordinated and cooperating in harmony, we have as a result the expression of life in its fullest degree. When these members lack coordination and harmony, we have the reverse, which in the human organism is disease, dissolution, death. Similarly, in the body politic of humanity dissension, discord and warfare are always destructive and inevitably fatal. All created beings are dependent upon peace and coordination, for every contingent and phenomenal being is a composition of distinct elements. As long as there is affinity and cohesion among these constituent elements, strength and life are manifest; but when dissension and repulsion arise among them, disintegration follows. This is proof that peace and amity, which God has willed for His children, are the saving factors of human society, whereas war and strife, which violate His ordinances, are the cause of death and destruction.

—'Abdu'l-Bahá **36**

Note ye how easily, where unity existeth in a given family, the affairs of that family are conducted; what progress the members of that family make, how they prosper in the world. Their concerns are in order, they enjoy comfort and tranquillity, they are secure, their position is assured, they come to be envied by all. Such a family but addeth to its stature and its lasting honor, as day succeedeth day. And if we widen out the sphere of unity a little to include the inhabitants of a village who seek to be loving and united, who associate with and are kind to one another, what great advances they will be seen to make, how secure and protected they will be. Then let us widen out the sphere a little more, let us take the inhabitants of a city, all of them together: if they establish the strongest bonds of unity among themselves, how far they will progress, even in a brief period and what power they will exert. And if the sphere of unity be still further widened out, that is, if the inhabitants of a whole country develop peaceable hearts, and if with all their hearts and souls they yearn to cooperate with one another and to live in unity, and if they become kind and loving to one another, that country will achieve undying joy and lasting glory. Peace will it have, and plenty, and vast wealth.

Note then: if every clan, tribe, community, every nation, country, territory on earth should come together under the single-hued pavilion of the oneness of mankind, and by the dazzling rays of the Sun of Truth should proclaim the universality of man; if they should cause all nations and all creeds to open wide their arms to one another, establish a World Council, and proceed to bind the members of society one to another by strong mutual ties, what would happen then? There is no doubt whatsoever that the divine Beloved, in all His endearing beauty, and with Him a massive host of heavenly confirmations and human blessings and bestowals, would appear in His full glory before the assemblage of the world.   —'Abdu'l-Bahá 37

True civilization will unfurl its banner in the midmost heart of the world whenever a certain number of its distinguished and high-minded sovereigns—the shining exemplars of devotion and determination—shall, for the good and happiness of all mankind, arise, with firm resolve and clear vision, to establish the Cause of Universal Peace. They must make the Cause of Peace the object of general consultation, and seek by every means in their power to establish a Union of the nations of the world. They must conclude a binding treaty and establish a covenant, the provisions of which shall be sound, inviolable and definite. They must proclaim it to all the world and obtain for it the sanction of all the human race. This supreme and noble undertaking—the real source of the peace and well-being of all the world—should be regarded as sacred by all that dwell on earth. All the forces of humanity must be mobilized to ensure the stability and permanence of this Most Great Covenant. In this all-embracing Pact the limits and frontiers of each and every nation should be clearly fixed, the principles underlying the relations of governments towards one another definitely laid down, and all international agreements and obligations ascertained. In like manner, the size of the armaments of every government should be strictly limited, for if the preparations for war and the military forces of any nation should be allowed to increase, they will arouse the suspicion of others. The fundamental principle underlying this solemn Pact should be so fixed that if any government later violate any one of its provisions, all the governments on earth should arise to reduce it to utter submission, nay the human race as a whole should resolve, with every power at its disposal, to destroy that government. Should this greatest of all remedies be applied to the sick body of the world, it will assuredly recover from its ills and will remain eternally safe and secure.

Observe that if such a happy situation be forthcoming, no government would need continually to pile up the weapons of war, nor feel itself obliged to produce ever new military weapons with which to conquer the human race. A small force for the purposes of internal security, the correction of criminal and disorderly elements and the prevention of local disturbances, would be required—no more. In this way the entire population would, first of all, be relieved of the crushing burden of expenditure currently imposed for military purposes, and secondly, great numbers of people would cease to devote their time to the continual devising of new weapons of destruction—those testimonials of greed and bloodthirstiness, so inconsistent with the gift of life—and would instead bend their efforts to the production of whatever will foster human existence and peace and well-being, and would become the cause of universal development and prosperity. Then every nation on earth will reign in honor, and every people will be cradled in tranquillity and content.   —*'Abdu'l-Bahá* **38**

"The Tongue of Grandeur," Bahá'u'lláh Himself affirms, "hath . . . in the Day of His Manifestation proclaimed: 'It is not his to boast who loveth his country, but it is his who loveth the world.' " "Through the power," He adds, "released by these exalted words He hath lent a fresh impulse, and set a new direction, to the birds of men's hearts, and hath obliterated every trace of restriction and limitation from God's Holy Book."
. . . The love of one's country, instilled and stressed by

the teaching of Islám, as "an element of the Faith of God," has not, through this declaration, this clarion-call of Bahá'u'lláh, been either condemned or disparaged. It should not, indeed it cannot, be construed as a repudiation, or regarded in the light of a censure, pronounced against a sane and intelligent patriotism, nor does it seek to undermine the allegiance and loyalty of any individual to his country, nor does it conflict with the legitimate aspirations, rights, and duties of any individual state or nation. All it does imply and proclaim is the insufficiency of patriotism, in view of the fundamental changes effected in the economic life of society and the interdependence of the nations, and as the consequence of the contraction of the world, through the revolution in the means of transportation and communication—conditions that did not and could not exist either in the days of Jesus Christ or of Muḥammad. It calls for a wider loyalty, which should not, and indeed does not, conflict with lesser loyalties. It instills a love which, in view of its scope, must include and not exclude the love of one's own country. It lays, through this loyalty which it inspires, and this love which it infuses, the only foundation on which the concept of world citizenship can thrive, and the structure of world unification can rest. It does insist, however, on the subordination of national considerations and particularistic interests to the imperative and paramount claims of humanity as a whole, inasmuch as in a world of interdependent nations and peoples the advantage of the part is best to be reached by the advantage of the whole.   —*Shoghi Effendi* **39**

The issue of paramount importance in the world today is international peace. . . . Even now war is raging furiously in some places, the blood of innocent people is being shed, children are made captive, women are left without support, and homes are being destroyed. Therefore, the greatest need in the world today is international peace. The time is ripe. It is time for the abolition of warfare, the unification of nations and governments. It is the time for love. It is time for cementing together the East and the West.   —*'Abdu'l-Bahá* **40**

Governing the Affairs of Humanity
The Standard of Justice

GOVERNMENTS should fully acquaint themselves with the conditions of those they govern, and confer upon them positions according to desert and merit. It is enjoined upon every ruler and sovereign to consider this matter with the utmost care that the traitor may not usurp the position of the faithful, nor the despoiler rule in the place of the trustworthy. —*Bahá'u'lláh* 41

We cherish the hope that the light of justice may shine upon the world and sanctify it from tyranny. If the rulers and kings of the earth, the symbols of the power of God, exalted be His glory, arise and resolve to dedicate themselves to whatever will promote the highest interests of the whole of humanity, the reign of justice will assuredly be established amongst the children of men, and the effulgence of its light will envelop the whole earth. The Great Being saith: The structure of world stability and order hath been reared upon, and will continue to be sustained by, the twin pillars of reward and punishment. And in another connection He hath uttered the following . . . : Justice hath a mighty force at its command. It is none other than reward and punishment for the deeds of men. By the power of this force the tabernacle of order is established throughout the world, causing the wicked to restrain their natures for fear of punishment. —*Bahá'u'lláh* 42

Justice and equity are two guardians for the protection of man. They have appeared arrayed in their mighty and sacred names to maintain the world in uprightness and protect the nations. —*Bahá'u'lláh* 43

The Great Being saith: The heaven of statesmanship is made luminous and resplendent by the brightness of the light of these blessed words which hath dawned from the dayspring of the Will of God: It behooveth every ruler to weigh his own being every day in the balance of equity and justice and then to judge between men and counsel them to do that which would direct their steps unto the path of wisdom and understanding. This is the cornerstone of statesmanship and the essence thereof. From these words every enlightened man of wisdom will readily perceive that which will foster such aims as the welfare, security and protection of mankind and the safety of human lives. Were men of insight to quaff their fill from the ocean of inner meanings which lie enshrined in these words and become acquainted therewith, they would bear witness to the sublimity and the excellence of this utterance. . . . The secrets of statesmanship and that of which the people are in need lie enfolded within these words. This lowly servant earnestly entreateth the One true God—exalted be His glory—to illumine the eyes of the people of the world with the splendor of the light of wisdom that they, one and all, may recognize that which is indispensable in this day.

—Bahá'u'lláh **44**

It beseemeth you to fix your gaze under all conditions upon justice and fairness. In the Hidden Words* this exalted utterance hath been revealed from Our Most August Pen: "O Son of Spirit! The best beloved of all things in My sight is Justice; turn not away therefrom if thou desirest Me, and neglect it not that I may confide in thee. By its aid thou shalt see with thine own eyes and not through the eyes of others, and shalt know of thine own knowledge and not through the knowledge of thy neighbor. Ponder this in thy heart; how it behooveth thee to be. Verily justice is My gift to thee and the sign of My loving kindness. Set it then before thine eyes."

They that are just and fair-minded in their judgment occupy a sublime station and hold an exalted rank. The light of piety and uprightness shineth resplendent from these souls.

---

* *The Hidden Words of Bahá'u'lláh* (Wilmette, Ill.: Bahá'í Publishing Trust, 1939) is a collection of brief, penetrating meditations that Bahá'ís believe express the essence of all revealed truth.

We earnestly hope that the peoples and countries of the world may not be deprived of the splendors of these two luminaries.
—*Bahá'u'lláh* **45**

No radiance can compare with that of justice. The organization of the world and the tranquillity of mankind depend upon it. —*Bahá'u'lláh* **46**

It is incumbent upon everyone to observe God's holy commandments, inasmuch as they are the wellspring of life unto the world. The heaven of divine wisdom is illumined with the two luminaries of consultation and compassion and the canopy of world order is upraised upon the two pillars of reward and punishment. —*Bahá'u'lláh* **47**

The tent of the order of the world is raised and established on the two pillars of "Reward and Retribution."
In despotic Governments carried on by men without Divine faith, where no fear of spiritual retribution exists, the execution of the laws is tyrannical and unjust.
There is no greater prevention of oppression than these two sentiments, hope and fear. They have both political and spiritual consequences.
If administrators of the law would take into consideration the spiritual consequences of their decisions, and follow the guidance of religion, "They would be Divine agents in the world of action, the representatives of God for those who are on earth, and they would defend, for the love of God, the interests of His servants as they would defend their own." If a governor realizes his responsibility, and fears to defy the Divine Law, his judgments will be just. Above all, if he believes that the consequences of his actions will follow him beyond his earthly life, and that "as he sows so must he reap," such a man will surely avoid injustice and tyranny.
Should an official, on the contrary, think that all responsibility for his actions must end with his earthly life, knowing and believing nothing of Divine favors and a spiritual kingdom

of joy, he will lack the incentive to just dealing, and the inspiration to destroy oppression and unrighteousness.

When a ruler knows that his judgments will be weighed in a balance by the Divine Judge, and that if he be not found wanting he will come into the Celestial Kingdom and that the light of the Heavenly Bounty will shine upon him, then will he surely act with justice and equity. Behold how important it is that Ministers of State should be enlightened by religion!

—'Abdu'l-Bahá **48**

[An] . . . attribute of perfection is justice and impartiality. This means to have no regard for one's own personal benefits and selfish advantages, and to carry out the laws of God without the slightest concern for anything else. It means to see one's self as only one of the servants of God, the All-Possessing, and except for aspiring to spiritual distinction, never attempting to be singled out from the others. It means to consider the welfare of the community as one's own. It means, in brief, to regard humanity as a single individual, and one's own self as a member of that corporeal form, and to know of a certainty that if pain or injury afflicts any member of that body, it must inevitably result in suffering for all the rest.

—'Abdu'l-Bahá **49**

Justice is not limited, it is a universal quality. Its operation must be carried out in all classes, from the highest to the lowest. Justice must be sacred, and the rights of all the people must be considered. Desire for others only that which you desire for yourselves. Then shall we rejoice in the Sun of Justice, which shines from the Horizon of God.

Each man has been placed in a post of honor, which he must not desert. A humble workman who commits an injustice is as much to blame as a renowned tyrant. Thus we all have our choice between justice and injustice. *—'Abdu'l-Bahá* **50**

Kings must rule with wisdom and justice; prince, peer and peasant alike have equal rights to just treatment, there must be no favor shown to individuals. A judge must be no "respecter of persons," but administer the law with strict impartiality in every case brought before him.

— *'Abdu'l-Bahá* **51**

When perfect justice reigns in every country of the Eastern and Western World, then will the earth become a place of beauty. The dignity and equality of every servant of God will be acknowledged; the ideal of the solidarity of the human race, the true brotherhood of man, will be realized; and the glorious light of the Sun of Truth will illumine the souls of all men.   — *'Abdu'l-Bahá* **52**

There are two mighty banners which, when they cast their shadow across the crown of any king, will cause the influence of his government quickly and easily to penetrate the whole earth, even as if it were the light of the sun: the first of these two banners is wisdom; the second is justice. Against these two most potent forces, the iron hills cannot prevail, and Alexander's wall will break before them. It is clear that life in this fast-fading world is as fleeting and inconstant as the morning wind, and this being so, how fortunate are the great who leave a good name behind them, and the memory of a lifetime spent in the pathway of the good pleasure of God.

— *'Abdu'l-Bahá* **53**

Take heed, O concourse of the rulers of the world! There is no force on earth that can equal in its conquering power the force of justice and wisdom. I, verily, affirm that there is not, and hath never been, a host more mighty than that of justice and wisdom. Blessed is the king who marcheth with the ensign of wisdom unfurled before him, and the battalions of justice massed in his rear. He verily is the ornament that adorneth the brow of peace and the countenance of security. There can be no doubt whatever that if the daystar of justice, which the clouds of tyranny have obscured, were to shed its light upon men, the face of the earth would be completely transformed.   — *Bahá'u'lláh* **54**

The light of men is justice. Quench it not with the contrary winds of oppression and tyranny. The purpose of justice is the appearance of unity among men. —*Bahá'u'lláh* **55**

The Qualities of Statesmanship

SAY: The beginning of Wisdom and the origin thereof is to acknowledge whatsoever God hath clearly set forth, for through its potency the foundation of statesmanship, which is a shield for the preservation of the body of mankind, hath been firmly established. . . . every matter related to state affairs which ye raise for discussion falls under the shadow of one of the words sent down from the heaven of His glorious and exalted utterance. —*Bahá'u'lláh* **56**

O concourse of kings! . . . your glory consisteth not in your sovereignty, but rather in your nearness unto God and your observance of His command as sent down in His holy and preserved Tablets. Should any one of you rule over the whole earth, and over all that lieth within it and upon it, its seas, its lands, its mountains, and its plains, and yet be not remembered by God, all these would profit him not, could ye but know it. . . . Arise, then, and make steadfast your feet, and make ye amends for that which hath escaped you, and set then yourselves towards His holy Court, on the shore of His mighty Ocean, so that the pearls of knowledge and wisdom, which God hath stored up within the shell of His radiant heart, may be revealed unto you. . . . Beware lest ye hinder the breeze of God from blowing over your hearts, the breeze through which the hearts of such as have turned unto Him can be quickened. . . .

Beware not to deal unjustly with any one that appealeth to you, and entereth beneath your shadow. Walk ye in the fear of God, and be ye of them that lead a godly life. Rest not on your power, your armies, and treasures. Put your whole trust and confidence in God, Who hath created you, and seek ye His help in all your affairs. Succor cometh from Him alone. He succoreth whom He willeth with the hosts of the heavens and of the earth.   —*Bahá'u'lláh* **57**

We have also heard that thou* hast entrusted the reins of counsel into the hands of the representatives of the people. Thou, indeed, hast done well, for thereby the foundations of the edifice of thine affairs will be strengthened, and the hearts of all that are beneath thy shadow, whether high or low, will be tranquillized. It behooveth them, however, to be trustworthy among His servants, and to regard themselves as the representatives of all that dwell on earth. This is what counselleth them, in this Tablet, He Who is the Ruler, the All-Wise. . . . Blessed is he that entereth the assembly for the sake of God, and judgeth between men with pure justice. He, indeed, is of the blissful. . . .   —*Bahá'u'lláh* **58**

While the setting up of parliaments, the organizing of assemblies of consultation, constitutes the very foundation and bedrock of government, there are several essential requirements which these institutions must fulfill. First, the elected members must be righteous, God-fearing, high-minded, incorruptible. Second, they must be fully cognizant, in every particular, of the laws of God, informed as to the highest principles of law, versed in the rules which govern the management of internal affairs and the conduct of foreign relations, skilled in the useful arts of civilization, and content with their lawful emoluments.

Let it not be imagined that members of this type would be impossible to find. Through the grace of God and His chosen ones, and the high endeavors of the devoted and the consecrated, every difficulty can be easily resolved, every problem however complex will prove simpler than blinking an eye.

If, however, the members of these consultative assemblies are inferior, ignorant, uninformed of the laws of government and administration, unwise, of low aim, indifferent, idle,

---

*Queen Victoria.

self-seeking, no benefit will accrue from the organizing of
such bodies.   — 'Abdu'l-Bahá **59**

If any one of you be employed in government offices let
him discharge his responsibilities with absolute truthfulness,
with moral rectitude, integrity, uprightness, sanctity and detachment. Let him uphold undeviating justice and fairmind-
edness. Should anyone, God forbid, manifest one iota of dishonesty, or show laxity and negligence in carrying out his
duties, or unlawfully exact money from the people, be it even
a single penny, or secure private gains for himself, or seek
personal benefits, such a person will surely be deprived of the
blessings of the Almighty. Beware, beware, lest ye fall short of
what hath been set forth in this letter.   — 'Abdu'l-Bahá **60**

It is unquestionable that the object in establishing parliaments is to bring about justice and righteousness, but everything hinges on the efforts of the elected representatives. If
their intention is sincere, desirable results and unforeseen
improvements will be forthcoming; if not, it is certain that the
whole thing will be meaningless, the country will come to a
standstill and public affairs will continuously deteriorate. "I
see a thousand builders unequal to one subverter; what then
of the one builder who is followed by a thousand subverters?"
                                                 — 'Abdu'l-Bahá **61**

The world of politics is like the world of man; he is seed
at first, and then passes by degrees to the condition of embryo
and foetus, acquiring a bone structure, being clothed with
flesh, taking on his own special form, until at last he reaches
the plane where he can befittingly fulfill the words: "the most
excellent of Makers."* Just as this is a requirement of creation
and is based on the universal Wisdom, the political world in
the same way cannot instantaneously evolve from the nadir of
defectiveness to the zenith of rightness and perfection. Rather,

---

*Qur'án 23:14: "Blessed therefore be God, the most excellent of
Makers."

qualified individuals must strive by day and by night, using all those means which will conduce to progress, until the government and the people develop along every line from day to day and even from moment to moment. . . .

. . . when the pure intentions and the justice of the ruler, the wisdom and consummate skill and statecraft of the governing authorities, and the determination and unstinted efforts of the people, are all combined . . . then day by day the effects of the advancement, of the far-reaching reforms, of the pride and prosperity of government and people alike, will become clearly manifest.   —'Abdu'l-Bahá **62**

The Process of Consultation

O ye the elected representatives of the people in every land! Take ye counsel together, and let your concern be only for that which profiteth mankind, and bettereth the condition thereof, if ye be of them that scan heedfully.   —Bahá'u'lláh **63**

O people of God! Give ear unto that which, if heeded, will ensure the freedom, well-being, tranquillity, exaltation and advancement of all men. Certain laws and principles are necessary and indispensable for Persia. However, it is fitting that these measures should be adopted in conformity with the considered views of His Majesty*—may God aid him through His grace—and of the learned divines and of the high-ranking rulers. Subject to their approval a place should be fixed where they would meet. There they should hold fast to the cord of consultation and adopt and enforce that which is conducive to the security, prosperity, wealth and tranquillity of the people. For were any measure other than this to be adopted, it could not but result in chaos and commotion.   —Bahá'u'lláh **64**

No man can attain his true station except through his justice. No power can exist except through unity. No welfare

---

*Náṣiri'd-Dín Sháh, the sovereign of Persia from 1848 to 1896.

and no well-being can be attained except through consultation. —*Bahá'u'lláh* **65**

Consultation bestoweth greater awareness and transmut-
eth conjecture into certitude. It is a shining light which, in a
dark world, leadeth the way and guideth. For everything there
is and will continue to be a station of perfection and maturity.
The maturity of the gift of understanding is made manifest
through consultation. —*Bahá'u'lláh* **66**

Man must consult on all matters, whether major or minor,
so that he may become cognizant of what is good. Consultation giveth him insight into things and enableth him to delve
into questions which are unknown. The light of truth shineth
from the faces of those who engage in consultation. Such
consultation causeth the living waters to flow in the meadows
of man's reality, the rays of ancient glory to shine upon him,
and the tree of his being to be adorned with wondrous fruit.
The members who are consulting, however, should behave in
the utmost love, harmony and sincerity towards each other.
The principle of consultation is one of the most fundamental
elements of the divine edifice. Even in their ordinary affairs
the individual members of society should consult.
—*'Abdu'l-Bahá* **67**

The purpose of consultation is to show that the views of
several individuals are assuredly preferable to one man, even
as the power of a number of men is of course greater than the
power of one man. Thus consultation is acceptable in the
presence of the Almighty, and hath been enjoined upon the
believers, so that they may confer upon ordinary and personal
matters, as well as on affairs which are general in nature and
universal.

For instance, when a man hath a project to accomplish,
should he consult with some of his brethren, that which is
agreeable will of course be investigated and unveiled to his
eyes, and the truth will be disclosed. Likewise on a higher
level, should the people of a village consult one another about

their affairs, the right solution will certainly be revealed. In like manner, the members of each profession, such as in industry, should consult, and those in commerce should similarly consult on business affairs. In short, consultation is desirable and acceptable in all things and on all issues.

— 'Abdu'l-Bahá **68**

Consultation is of vital importance, but spiritual conference and not the mere voicing of personal views is intended. In France I was present at a session of the senate, but the experience was not impressive.* Parliamentary procedure should have for its object the attainment of the light of truth upon questions presented and not furnish a battleground for opposition and self-opinion. Antagonism and contradiction are unfortunate and always destructive to truth. In the parliamentary meeting mentioned, altercation and useless quibbling were frequent; the result, mostly confusion and turmoil; even in one instance a physical encounter took place between two members. It was not consultation but comedy.

The purpose is to emphasize the statement that consultation must have for its object the investigation of truth. He who expresses an opinion should not voice it as correct and right but set it forth as a contribution to the consensus of opinion, for the light of reality becomes apparent when two opinions coincide. A spark is produced when flint and steel come together. Man should weigh his opinions with the utmost serenity, calmness and composure. Before expressing his own views he should carefully consider the views already advanced by others. If he finds that a previously expressed opinion is more true and worthy, he should accept it immediately and not willfully hold to an opinion of his own. By this excellent method he endeavors to arrive at unity and truth. Opposition and division are deplorable. It is better then to have the opinion of a wise, sagacious man; otherwise, contradiction and altercation, in which varied and divergent views

---

* 'Abdu'l-Bahá visited Paris for nine weeks in 1911.

are presented, will make it necessary for a judicial body to render decision upon the question. Even a majority opinion or consensus may be incorrect. A thousand people may hold to one view and be mistaken, whereas one sagacious person may be right. Therefore, true consultation is spiritual conference in the attitude and atmosphere of love. Members must love each other in the spirit of fellowship in order that good results may be forthcoming. Love and fellowship are the foundation.

—'Abdu'l-Bahá **69**

The prime requisites for them that take counsel together are purity of motive, radiance of spirit, detachment from all else save God, attraction to His Divine Fragrances, humility and lowliness amongst His loved ones, patience and long-suffering in difficulties and servitude to His exalted Threshold. Should they be graciously aided to acquire these attributes, victory from the unseen Kingdom of Bahá* shall be vouch-safed to them. —'Abdu'l-Bahá **70**

They must . . . proceed with the utmost devotion, courtesy, dignity, care and moderation to express their views. They must in every matter search out the truth and not insist upon their own opinion, for stubbornness and persistence in one's views will lead ultimately to discord and wrangling and the truth will remain hidden. The honored members must with all freedom express their own thoughts, and it is in no wise permissible for one to belittle the thought of another, nay, he must with moderation set forth the truth, and should differences of opinion arise a majority of voices must prevail, and all must obey and submit to the majority. It is again not permitted that any one of the honored members object to or censure, whether in or out of the meeting, any decision arrived at previously, though that decision be not right, for such criticism would prevent any decision from being enforced. In short, whatsoever thing is arranged in harmony and with love

---

*The spiritual world beyond the grave.

and purity of motive, its result is light, and should the least trace of estrangement prevail the result shall be darkness upon darkness. . . .   —*'Abdu'l-Bahá* **71**

[They] . . . must take counsel together in such wise that no occasion for ill-feeling or discord may arise. This can be attained when every member expresseth with absolute freedom his own opinion and setteth forth his argument. Should anyone oppose, he must on no account feel hurt for not until matters are fully discussed can the right way be revealed. The shining spark of truth cometh forth only after the clash of differing opinions. If after discussion, a decision be carried unanimously well and good; but if, the Lord forbid, differences of opinion should arise, a majority of voices must prevail.
                                        —*'Abdu'l-Bahá* **72**

Every one of the friends should highly praise the other and each should regard himself as evanescent and as naught in the presence of others. All matters should be consulted upon in the meeting and whatever is the majority vote should be carried out. I swear by the One true God, it is better that all should agree on a wrong decision, than for one right vote to be singled out, inasmuch as single votes can be sources of dissension, which lead to ruin. Whereas, if in one case they take a wrong decision, in a hundred other cases they will adopt right decisions, and concord and unity are preserved. This will offset any deficiency, and will eventually lead to the righting of the wrong.   —*'Abdu'l-Bahá* **73**

It is important to realize that the spirit of Bahá'í consultation is very different from that current in the decision-making processes of non-Bahá'í bodies.
        The ideal of Bahá'í consultation is to arrive at a unanimous decision. When this is not possible a vote must be taken. In the words of the beloved Guardian [Shoghi Effendi]: ". . . when they are called upon to arrive at a certain decision, they should, after dispassionate, anxious and cordial consultation, turn to God in prayer, and with earnestness and conviction

and courage record their vote and abide by the voice of the majority, which we are told by the Master ['Abdu'l-Bahá] to be the voice of truth, never to be challenged, and always to be whole-heartedly enforced."

As soon as a decision is reached it becomes the decision of the whole Assembly,* not merely of those members who happened to be among the majority.

—The Universal House of Justice **74**

Our hope is that the world's religious leaders and the rulers thereof will unitedly arise for the reformation of this age and the rehabilitation of its fortunes. Let them, after meditating on its needs, take counsel together and, through anxious and full deliberation, administer to a diseased and sorely afflicted world the remedy it requireth.

The Great Being saith: The heaven of divine wisdom is illumined with the two luminaries of consultation and compassion. Take ye counsel together in all matters, inasmuch as consultation is the lamp of guidance which leadeth the way, and is the bestower of understanding.   *—Bahá'u'lláh* **75**

Such matters should be determined through consultation, and whatever emergeth from the consultation of those chosen, that indeed is the command of God, the Help in Peril, the Self-Subsisting.   *—Bahá'u'lláh* **76**

A System of World Government

WHAT mankind needeth in this day is obedience unto them that are in authority, and a faithful adherence to the cord of

---

*The Assembly, or "Spiritual Assembly," is a decision-making institution composed of nine adult Bahá'ís. Spiritual Assemblies are elected by Bahá'í communities at both the national and local levels. The National Assemblies in turn elect the Universal House of Justice, the international governing body of the Bahá'í Faith. All Bahá'í elections are by secret ballot; any form of electioneering, including the nomination of candidates, is forbidden.

wisdom. The instruments which are essential to the immediate protection, the security and assurance of the human race have been entrusted to the hands, and lie in the grasp, of the governors of human society. This is the wish of God and His decree. . . .   *—Bahá'u'lláh* **77**

All the governments of the world must be united and organize an assembly the members of which should be elected from the parliaments and the nobles of the nations. These must plan with utmost wisdom and power. . . .
                                        —'Abdu'l-Bahá **78**

In His Epistles He* asked the parliaments of the world to send their wisest and best men to an international world conference which should decide all questions between the peoples and establish universal peace. This would be the highest court of appeal, and the parliament of man so long dreamed of by poets and idealists would be realized. . . .
                                        —'Abdu'l-Bahá **79**

The world is in greatest need of international peace. Until it is established, mankind will not attain composure and tranquillity. It is necessary that the nations and governments organize an international tribunal to which all their disputes and differences shall be referred. The decision of that tribunal shall be final. Individual controversy will be adjudged by a local tribunal. International questions will come before the universal tribunal, and so the cause of warfare will be taken away.   *—'Abdu'l-Bahá* **80**

To remedy this condition [of "continuous and fearsome wars"] there must be universal peace. To bring this about, a Supreme Tribunal must be established, representative of all governments and peoples; questions both national and inter-

---

*Bahá'u'lláh. Examples of such letters can be seen on pages 180–81, extracts 32–34.

national must be referred thereto, and all must carry out the decrees of this Tribunal. Should any government or people disobey, let the whole world arise against that government or people.   — *'Abdu'l-Bahá* **81**

Bahá'u'lláh says that the Supreme Tribunal must be established: although the League of Nations has been brought into existence, yet it is incapable of establishing universal peace.* But the Supreme Tribunal which Bahá'u'lláh has described will fulfill this sacred task with the utmost might and power. And His plan is this: that the national assemblies of each country and nation—that is to say parliaments—should elect two or three persons who are the choicest of that nation, and are well informed concerning international laws and the relations between governments and aware of the essential needs of the world of humanity in this day. The number of these representatives should be in proportion to the number of inhabitants of that country. The election of these souls who are chosen by the national assembly, that is, the parliament, must be confirmed by the upper house, the congress and the cabinet and also by the president or monarch so these persons may be the elected ones of all the nation and the government. The Supreme Tribunal will be composed of these people, and all mankind will thus have a share therein, for every one of these delegates is fully representative of his nation. When the Supreme Tribunal gives a ruling on any international question, either unanimously or by majority rule, there will no longer be any pretext for the plaintiff or ground of objection for the defendant. In case any of the governments or nations, in the execution of the irrefutable decision of the Supreme Tribunal, be negligent or dilatory, the rest of the nations will rise up against it, because all the governments and nations of the world are the supporters of this Supreme Tribunal. Consider

---

*This is an excerpt from 'Abdu'l-Bahá's reply, dated 17 December 1919, to a letter addressed to Him by the Executive Committee of the Central Organization for a Durable Peace, The Hague.

what a firm foundation this is! But by a limited and restricted League the purpose will not be realized as it ought and should. This is the truth about the situation, which has been stated. . . .

— *'Abdu'l-Bahá* **82**

A Supreme Tribunal shall be established by the peoples and Governments of every nation, composed of members elected from each country and Government. The members of this Great Council shall assemble in unity. All disputes of an international character shall be submitted to this Court, its work being to arrange by arbitration everything which otherwise would be a cause of war. The mission of this Tribunal would be to prevent war.   — *'Abdu'l-Bahá* **83**

Some form of a world superstate must needs be evolved, in whose favor all the nations of the world will have willingly ceded every claim to make war, certain rights to impose taxation and all rights to maintain armaments, except for purposes of maintaining internal order within their respective dominions. Such a state will have to include within its orbit an international executive adequate to enforce supreme and unchallengeable authority on every recalcitrant member of the commonwealth; a world parliament whose members shall be elected by the people in their respective countries and whose election shall be confirmed by their respective governments; and a supreme tribunal whose judgment will have a binding effect even in such cases where the parties concerned did not voluntarily agree to submit their case to its consideration. A world community in which all economic barriers will have been permanently demolished and the interdependence of Capital and Labor definitely recognized; in which the clamor of religious fanaticism and strife will have been forever stilled; in which the flame of racial animosity will have been finally extinguished; in which a single code of international law—the product of the considered judgment of the world's federated representatives—shall have as its sanction the instant and coercive intervention of the combined forces of the federated units; and finally a world community in which the fury of a capricious and militant nationalism will have been transmuted into an abiding consciousness of world citizenship—such indeed, appears, in its broadest outline, the Order anticipated by Bahá'u'lláh, an Order that shall come to be regarded as the fairest fruit of a slowly maturing age.   —*Shoghi Effendi* **84**

The long ages of infancy and childhood, through which the human race had to pass, have receded into the background. Humanity is now experiencing the commotions invariably associated with the most turbulent stage of its evolution, the stage of adolescence, when the impetuosity of youth and its vehemence reach their climax, and must gradually be superseded by the calmness, the wisdom, and the maturity that characterize the stage of manhood. Then will the human race reach that stature of ripeness which will enable it to acquire all the powers and capacities upon which its ultimate development must depend.

Unification of the whole of mankind is the hallmark of the stage which human society is now approaching. Unity of family, of tribe, of city-state, and nation have been successively attempted and fully established. World unity is the goal towards which a harassed humanity is striving. Nation-building has come to an end. The anarchy inherent in state sovereignty is moving towards a climax. A world, growing to maturity, must abandon this fetish, recognize the oneness and wholeness of human relationships, and establish once for all the machinery that can best incarnate this fundamental principle of its life. . . .

The unity of the human race, as envisaged by Bahá'u'lláh, implies the establishment of a world commonwealth in which all nations, races, creeds and classes are closely and permanently united, and in which the autonomy of its state members and the personal freedom and initiative of the individuals that compose them are definitely and completely safeguarded. This commonwealth must, as far as we can visualize it, consist of a world legislature, whose members will, as the trustees of the whole of mankind, ultimately control the entire resources of all the component nations, and will enact such laws as shall be required to regulate the life, satisfy the needs and adjust the relationships of all races and peoples. A world executive, backed by an international Force, will carry out the decisions arrived at, and apply the laws enacted by, this world legislature, and will safeguard the organic unity of the whole commonwealth. A world tribunal will adjudicate and deliver its compulsory and final verdict in all and any disputes that may arise between the various elements constituting this universal system. A mechanism of world intercommunication will be devised, embracing the whole planet, freed from national hindrances and restrictions, and functioning with marvelous swiftness and perfect regularity. A world metropolis will act as the nerve center of a world civilization, the focus towards which the unifying forces of life will converge and from which its energizing influences will radiate. A world language will either be invented or chosen from among the existing languages and will be taught in the schools of all the federated nations as an auxiliary to their mother tongue. A world script, a world literature, a uniform and universal system of currency, of weights and measures, will simplify and facilitate intercourse and understanding among the nations and races of mankind. In such a world society, science and religion, the two most potent forces in human life, will be reconciled, will cooperate, and will harmoniously develop. The press will, under such a system, while giving full scope to the expression of the diversified views and convictions of mankind, cease to be mischievously manipulated by vested interests, whether private or public, and will be liberated from the influence of contending governments and peoples. The economic resources of the world will be organized, its sources of raw materials will be tapped and fully utilized, its markets will be coordinated and developed, and the distribution of its products will be equitably regulated.

National rivalries, hatreds, and intrigues will cease, and racial animosity and prejudice will be replaced by racial amity, understanding and cooperation. The causes of religious strife will be permanently removed, economic barriers and restrictions will be completely abolished, and the inordinate distinction between classes will be obliterated. Destitution on the one hand, and gross accumulation of ownership on the other, will disappear. The enormous energy dissipated and wasted on war, whether economic or political, will be consecrated to such ends as will extend the range of human inventions and technical development, to the increase of the productivity of mankind, to the extermination of disease, to the extension of scientific research, to the raising of the standard of physical health, to the sharpening and refinement of the human brain, to the exploitation of the unused and unsuspected resources of the planet, to the prolongation of human life, and to the furtherance of any other agency that can stimulate the intellectual, the moral, and spiritual life of the entire human race.

A world federal system, ruling the whole earth and exercising unchallengeable authority over its unimaginably vast resources, blending and embodying the ideals of both the East and the West, liberated from the curse of war and its miseries, and bent on the exploitation of all the available sources of energy on the surface of the planet, a system in which Force is made the servant of Justice, whose life is sustained by its universal recognition of one God and by its allegiance to one common Revelation—such is the goal towards which humanity, impelled by the unifying forces of life, is moving.

—Shoghi Effendi **85**

The bulk of humanity now realizeth what a great calamity war is and how war turneth man into a ferocious animal, causing prosperous cities and villages to be reduced to ruins and the foundations of the human edifice to crumble. Now since all men have been awakened and their ears are attentive, it is time for the promulgation of universal peace—a peace based on righteousness and justice, that mankind may not be exposed to further dangers in the future. Now is the dawn of universal peace; and the first streaks of its light are beginning to appear. We earnestly hope that its effulgent orb may shine forth and flood the east and the west with its radiance.

—'Abdu'l-Bahá   **86**

The Tabernacle of Unity has been raised; regard ye not one another as strangers. . . . Of one tree are all ye the fruit and of one bough the leaves. . . . The world is but one country and mankind its citizens.   *—Bahá'u'lláh*   **87**

Chapter 6

Securing the Basis of Human Happiness

Achieving the Ultimate Goal: Humanity's Intrinsic Oneness

Acknowledging the Spiritual Foundation of Unity

O YE children of men! The fundamental purpose animating the Faith of God and His Religion is to safeguard the interests and promote the unity of the human race, and to foster the spirit of love and fellowship amongst men. . . . This is the straight Path, the fixed and immovable foundation. Whatsoever is raised on this foundation, the changes and chances of the world can never impair its strength, nor will the revolution of countless centuries undermine its structure.

—Bahá'u'lláh **1**

The well-being of mankind, its peace and security, are unattainable unless and until its unity is firmly established. This unity can never be achieved so long as the counsels which the Pen of the Most High hath revealed are suffered to pass unheeded. *—Bahá'u'lláh* **2**

If any man were to meditate on that which the Scriptures, sent down from the heaven of God's holy Will, have revealed, he would readily recognize that their purpose is that all men shall be regarded as one soul, so that the seal bearing the words "The Kingdom shall be God's" may be stamped on every heart, and the light of Divine bounty, of grace, and mercy may envelop all mankind. The One true God, exalted be His glory, hath wished nothing for Himself. The allegiance of mankind profiteth Him not, neither doth its perversity harm Him. . . . If the learned and worldly wise men of this age were to allow mankind to inhale the fragrance of fellowship and love, every understanding heart would apprehend the meaning of true liberty, and discover the secret of undisturbed peace and absolute composure.   —*Bahá'u'lláh* **3**

It is self-evident that humanity is at variance. Human tastes differ; thoughts, native lands, races and tongues are many. The need of a collective center by which these differences may be counterbalanced and the people of the world be unified is obvious. Consider how nothing but a spiritual power can bring about this unification, for material conditions and mental aspects are so widely different that agreement and unity are not possible through outer means. It is possible, however, for all to become unified through one spirit, just as all may receive light from one sun. Therefore, assisted by the collective and divine center which is the law of God and the reality of His Manifestation, we can overcome these conditions until they pass away entirely and the races advance.

—*'Abdu'l-Bahá* **4**

In the world of existence there are various bonds which unite human hearts, but not one of these bonds is completely effective. The first and foremost is the bond of family relationship, which is not an efficient unity, for how often it happens that disagreement and divergence rend asunder this close tie of association. The bond of patriotism may be a means of fellowship and agreement, but oneness of native land will not completely cement human hearts; for if we review history, we shall find that people of the same race and native land have frequently waged war against each other. Often in civil strife they have shed the same racial blood and destroyed the possessions of their own native kind. Therefore, this bond is not sufficient. Another means of seeming unity is the bond of political association, where governments and rulers have been allied for reasons of intercourse and mutual protection, but which agreement and union afterward became subject to change and violent hatred even to the extreme of war and bloodshed. It is evident that political oneness is not perma-nently effective.

The source of perfect unity and love in the world of existence is the bond and oneness of reality. When the divine and fundamental reality enters human hearts and lives, it con-serves and protects all states and conditions of mankind, estab-lishing that intrinsic oneness of the world of humanity which can only come into being through the efficacy of the Holy Spirit. For the Holy Spirit is like unto the life in the human body, which blends all differences of parts and members in unity and agreement. Consider how numerous are these parts and members, but the oneness of the animating spirit of life unites them all in perfect combination. It establishes such a unity in the bodily organism that if any part is subjected to injury or becomes diseased, all the other parts and functions sympathetically respond and suffer, owing to the perfect one-ness existing. Just as the human spirit of life is the cause of coordination among the various parts of the human organism, the Holy Spirit is the controlling cause of the unity and coor-dination of mankind. That is to say, the bond or oneness of humanity cannot be effectively established save through the power of the Holy Spirit, for the world of humanity is a com-posite body, and the Holy Spirit is the animating principle of its life.   *—'Abdu'l-Bahá* **5**

Reflect ye as to other than human forms of life and be ye admonished thereby: those clouds that drift apart cannot pro-duce the bounty of the rain, and are soon lost; a flock of sheep, once scattered, falleth prey to the wolf, and birds that fly alone will be caught fast in the claws of the hawk. What greater demonstration could there be that unity leadeth to flourishing life, while dissension and withdrawing from the others, will lead only to misery; for these are the sure ways to bitter disappointment and ruin.   *—'Abdu'l-Bahá* **6**

A critic may object, saying that peoples, races, tribes and communities of the world are of different and varied customs, habits, tastes, character, inclinations and ideas, that opinions and thoughts are contrary to one another, and how, therefore, is it possible for real unity to be revealed and perfect accord among human souls to exist?

In answer we say that differences are of two kinds. One is the cause of annihilation and is like the antipathy existing among warring nations and conflicting tribes who seek each other's destruction, uprooting one another's families, depriving one another of rest and comfort and unleashing carnage. The other kind which is a token of diversity is the essence of perfection and the cause of the appearance of the bestowals of the Most Glorious Lord.

Consider the flowers of a garden: though differing in kind, color, form and shape, yet, inasmuch as they are refreshed by the waters of one spring, revived by the breath of one wind, invigorated by the rays of one sun, this diversity increaseth their charm, and addeth unto their beauty. Thus when that unifying force, the penetrating influence of the Word of God, taketh effect, the difference of customs, manners, habits, ideas, opinions and dispositions embellish the world of humanity. This diversity, this difference is like the naturally created dissimilarity and variety of the limbs and organs of the human body, for each one contributeth to the beauty, efficiency and perfection of the whole. When these different limbs and organs come under the influence of man's sovereign soul, and the soul's power pervadeth the limbs and members, veins and arteries of the body, then difference reinforceth harmony, diversity strengtheneth love, and multiplicity is the greatest factor for coordination.

How unpleasing to the eye if all the flowers and plants, the leaves and blossoms, the fruits, the branches and the trees of that garden were all of the same shape and color! Diversity of hues, form and shape, enricheth and adorneth the garden, and heighteneth the effect thereof. In like manner, when divers shades of thought, temperament and character, are brought together under the power and influence of one central agency, the beauty and glory of human perfection will be revealed and made manifest. Naught but the celestial potency of the Word of God, which ruleth and transcendeth the realities of all things, is capable of harmonizing the divergent thoughts, sentiments, ideas, and convictions of the children of men. Verily, it is the penetrating power in all things, the mover of souls and the binder and regulator in the world of humanity.

—*'Abdu'l-Bahá* 7

All mankind must attain to spiritual fraternity—that is to say, fraternity in the Holy Spirit—for patriotic, racial and political fraternity are of no avail. Their results are meager; but divine fraternity, spiritual fraternity, is the cause of unity and amity among mankind. As heretofore material civilization has been extended, the divine civilization must now be promulgated. Until the two agree, real happiness among mankind will be unknown. By mere intellectual development and power of reason, man cannot attain to his fullest degree—that is to say, by means of intellect alone he cannot accomplish the progress effected by religion. For the philosophers of the past strove in vain to revivify the world of mankind through the intellectual faculty. The most of which they were capable was educating themselves and a limited number of disciples; they themselves have confessed failure. Therefore, the world of humanity must be confirmed by the breath of the Holy Spirit in order to receive universal education. Through the infusion of divine power all nations and peoples become quickened, and universal happiness is possible.   —*'Abdu'l-Bahá* 8

Every great Cause in this world of existence findeth a visible expression through three means; first, intention; second, confirmation; third, action. Today on this earth there are many souls who are the spreaders of peace and reconciliation and are longing for the realization of the oneness and unity of the world of man; but this intention needs a dynamic power, so that it may become manifest in the world of being. Today the divine instructions and lordly exhortations of Bahá'u'lláh promulgate this most great aim and the confirmations of the

Kingdom are the supports and defenders of this eminent intention. For the power of the Word of God is penetrative and the existence of the divine Kingdom is uninterrupted. Therefore, erelong it will become evident and clear that the ensign of the Most Great Peace is the teachings of Baha'u'llah. For the intention, the power and the action, all the three essential elements are brought together and the realization of everything in the contingent world dependeth upon these three principles.   —*'Abdu'l-Bahá* **9**

The unity which is productive of unlimited results is first a unity of mankind which recognizes that all are sheltered beneath the overshadowing glory of the All-Glorious, that all are servants of one God; for all breathe the same atmosphere, live upon the same earth, move beneath the same heavens, receive effulgence from the same sun and are under the protection of one God. . . . it is certain that the radiance and favors of God are encompassing, minds have developed, perceptions have become acute, sciences and arts are widespread, and capacity exists for the proclamation and promulgation of the real and ultimate unity of mankind, which will bring forth marvelous results. It will reconcile all religions, make warring nations loving, cause hostile kings to become friendly and bring peace and happiness to the human world. It will cement together the Orient and Occident, remove forever the foundations of war and upraise the ensign of the Most Great Peace.
                    —*'Abdu'l-Bahá* **10**

Forging Enduring Bonds of Unity

THE Great Being saith: O well-beloved ones! The tabernacle of unity hath been raised; regard ye not one another as strangers. Ye are the fruits of one tree, and the leaves of one branch.   —*Bahá'u'lláh* **11**

O ye beloved of the Lord! Commit not that which defileth the limpid stream of love or destroyeth the sweet fragrance of friendship. By the righteousness of the Lord! Ye were created to show love one to another and not perversity and rancor. Take pride not in love for yourselves but in love for your fellow creatures. Glory not in love for your country, but in love for all mankind.   —*Bahá'u'lláh* 12

Beware lest the desires of the flesh and of a corrupt inclination provoke divisions among you. Be ye as the fingers of one hand, the members of one body. Thus counseleth you the Pen of Revelation, if ye be of them that believe.

—*Bahá'u'lláh* 13

They that are endued with sincerity and faithfulness should associate with all the peoples and kindreds of the earth with joy and radiance, inasmuch as consorting with people hath promoted and will continue to promote unity and con-cord, which in turn are conducive to the maintenance of order in the world and to the regeneration of nations. Blessed are such as hold fast to the cord of kindliness and tender mercy and are free from animosity and hatred.

This Wronged One* exhorteth the peoples of the world to observe tolerance and righteousness, which are two lights amidst the darkness of the world and two educators for the edification of mankind. Happy are they who have attained thereto and woe betide the heedless.   —*Bahá'u'lláh* 14

Today the most remarkable favor of God centereth around union and harmony among the friends; so that this unity and concord may be the cause of the promulgation of the oneness of the world of humanity, may emancipate the world from this intense darkness of enmity and rancor, and that the Sun of Truth may shine in full and perfect effulgence.

Today, all the peoples of the world are indulging in self-interest and exert the utmost effort and endeavor to promote

---

*Bahá'u'lláh.

their own material interests. They are worshiping themselves and not the divine reality, nor the world of mankind. They seek diligently their own benefit and not the commonweal. This is because they are captives of the world of nature and unaware of the divine teachings, of the bounty of the Kingdom and of the Sun of Truth.   *—'Abdu'l-Bahá* **15**

The Blessed Beauty* saith: "Ye are all the fruits of one tree, the leaves of one branch." Thus hath He likened this world of being to a single tree, and all its peoples to the leaves thereof, and the blossoms and fruits. It is needful for the bough to blossom, and leaf and fruit to flourish, and upon the interconnection of all parts of the world-tree, dependeth the flourishing of leaf and blossom, and the sweetness of the fruit.

For this reason must all human beings powerfully sustain one another and seek for everlasting life; and for this reason must the lovers of God in this contingent world become the mercies and the blessings sent forth by that clement King of the seen and unseen realms. Let them purify their sight and behold all humankind as leaves and blossoms and fruits of the tree of being. Let them at all times concern themselves with doing a kindly thing for one of their fellows, offering to someone love, consideration, thoughtful help. Let them see no one as their enemy, or as wishing them ill, but think of all humankind as their friends; regarding the alien as an intimate, the stranger as a companion, staying free of prejudice, drawing no lines.

In this day, the one favored at the Threshold of the Lord is he who handeth round the cup of faithfulness; who bestoweth, even upon his enemies, the jewel of bounty, and lendeth, even to his fallen oppressor, a helping hand; it is he who will, even to the fiercest of his foes, be a loving friend. These are the Teachings of the Blessed Beauty, these the counsels of the Most Great Name.†   *—'Abdu'l-Bahá* **16**

---

*Bahá'u'lláh.
† Bahá'u'lláh.

Be in perfect unity. Never become angry with one another. Let your eyes be directed toward the kingdom of truth and not toward the world of creation. Love the creatures for the sake of God and not for themselves. You will never become angry or impatient if you love them for the sake of God. Humanity is not perfect. There are imperfections in every human being, and you will always become unhappy if you look toward the people themselves. But if you look toward God, you will love them and be kind to them, for the world of God is the world of perfection and complete mercy. Therefore, do not look at the shortcomings of anybody; see with the sight of forgiveness. The imperfect eye beholds imperfections. The eye that covers faults looks toward the Creator of souls. He created them, trains and provides for them, endows them with capacity and life, sight and hearing; therefore, they are the signs of His grandeur. You must love and be kind to everybody, care for the poor, protect the weak, heal the sick, teach and educate the ignorant.   —'Abdu'l-Bahá **17**

I charge you all that each one of you concentrate all the thoughts of your heart on love and unity. When a thought of war comes, oppose it by a stronger thought of peace. A thought of hatred must be destroyed by a more powerful thought of love. Thoughts of war bring destruction to all harmony, well-being, restfulness and content.

Thoughts of love are constructive of brotherhood, peace, friendship, and happiness.

When soldiers of the world draw their swords to kill, soldiers of God clasp each other's hands! So may all the savagery of man disappear by the Mercy of God, working through the pure in heart and the sincere of soul. Do not think the peace of the world an ideal impossible to attain!

Nothing is impossible to the Divine Benevolence of God.

If you desire with all your heart, friendship with every race on earth, your thought, spiritual and positive, will spread; it will become the desire of others, growing stronger and stronger, until it reaches the minds of all men.

—'Abdu'l-Bahá **18**

The utterance of God is a lamp, whose light is these words: Ye are the fruits of one tree, and the leaves of one branch. Deal ye one with another with the utmost love and harmony, with friendliness and fellowship. He Who is the Daystar of Truth beareth Me witness! So powerful is the light of unity that it can illuminate the whole earth. The one true God, He Who knoweth all things, Himself testifieth to the truth of these words.

Exert yourselves that ye may attain this transcendent and most sublime station, the station that can ensure the protection and security of all mankind. This goal excelleth every other goal, and this aspiration is the monarch of all aspirations.

—Bahá'u'lláh **19**

Studying a Working Model of Unity and Diversity

Aspects of Bahá'í Character

O YE that dwell on earth! The distinguishing feature that marketh the preeminent character of this Supreme Revelation* consisteth in that We have, on the one hand, blotted out from the pages of God's holy Book whatsoever hath been the cause of strife, of malice and mischief amongst the children of men, and have, on the other, laid down the essential prerequisites of concord, of understanding, of complete and enduring unity. Well is it with them that keep My statutes.

—Bahá'u'lláh **20**

O people of God! Adorn your temples with the adornment of trustworthiness and piety. Help, then, your Lord with the hosts of goodly deeds and a praiseworthy character We have forbidden you dissension and conflict in My Books, and

---

*The Revelation of Bahá'u'lláh.

My Scriptures, and My Scrolls, and My Tablets, and have wished thereby naught else save your exaltation and advancement.
—Bahá'u'lláh **21**

The people of God should make the utmost endeavor that perchance the fire of hatred and malice which smoldereth in the breasts of kindreds and peoples may, through the living waters of utterance and the exhortations of Him Who is the Desire of the world, be quenched and the trees of human existence may be adorned with wondrous and excellent fruit. He is, in truth, the Admonisher, the Compassionate, the All-Bountiful.
—Bahá'u'lláh **22**

It is Our wish and desire that every one of you may become a source of all goodness unto men, and an example of uprightness to mankind. Beware lest ye prefer yourselves above your neighbors. Fix your gaze upon Him Who is the Temple of God amongst men. He, in truth, hath offered up His life as a ransom for the redemption of the world. He, verily, is the All-Bountiful, the Gracious, the Most High. If any differences arise amongst you, behold Me standing before your face, and overlook the faults of one another for My name's sake and as a token of your love for My manifest and resplendent Cause. We love to see you at all times consorting in amity and concord within the paradise of My good pleasure, and to inhale from your acts the fragrance of friendliness and unity, of loving kindness and fellowship.
—Bahá'u'lláh **23**

It behooveth, likewise, the loved ones of God to be forbearing towards their fellowmen, and to be so sanctified and detached from all things, and to evince such sincerity and fairness, that all the peoples of the earth may recognize them as the trustees of God amongst men.
—Bahá'u'lláh **24**

They who are the people of God have no ambition except to revive the world, to ennoble its life, and regenerate its peoples. Truthfulness and goodwill have, at all times, marked their relations with all men. Their outward conduct is but a reflection of their inward life, and their inward life a mirror of their outward conduct. No veil hideth or obscureth the verities on which their Faith is established. Before the eyes of all men these verities have been laid bare, and can be unmistakably recognized. Their very acts attest the truth of these words.

—Bahá'u'lláh **25**

Beware, O people of Bahá,* lest ye walk in the ways of them whose words differ from their deeds. Strive that ye may be enabled to manifest to the peoples of the earth the signs of God, and to mirror forth His commandments. Let your acts be a guide unto all mankind, for the professions of most men, be they high or low, differ from their conduct. It is through your deeds that ye can distinguish yourselves from others. Through them the brightness of your light can be shed upon the whole earth. Happy is the man that heedeth My counsel, and keepeth the precepts prescribed by Him Who is the All-Knowing, the All-Wise.   *—Bahá'u'lláh* **26**

Actions must be more to them† than words. By their actions they must be merciful and not merely by their words. They must on all occasions confirm by their actions what they proclaim in words. Their deeds must prove their fidelity, and their actions must show forth Divine light.

Let your actions cry aloud to the world that you are indeed Bahá'ís, for it is *actions* that speak to the world and are the cause of the progress of humanity.   *—'Abdu'l-Bahá* **27**

The Cause of the Ancient Beauty‡ is the very essence of love, the very channel of oneness, existing only that all may become the waves of one sea, and bright stars of the same endless sky, and pearls within the shell of singleness, and

---

*Bahá'ís, followers of Bahá'u'lláh.
† Bahá'ís.
‡ Bahá'u'lláh.

gleaming jewels quarried from the mines of unity; that they may become servants one to another, adore one another, bless one another, praise one another; that each one may loose his tongue and extol the rest without exception, each one voice his gratitude to all the rest; that all should lift up their eyes to the horizon of glory, and remember that they are linked to the Holy Threshold; that they should see nothing but good in one another, hear nothing but praise of one another, and speak no word of one another save only to praise. — *'Abdu'l-Bahá* **28**

O ye beloved of the Lord! In this sacred Dispensation, conflict and contention are in no wise permitted. Every aggressor deprives himself of God's grace. It is incumbent upon everyone to show the utmost love, rectitude of conduct, straightforwardness and sincere kindliness unto all the peoples and kindreds of the world, be they friends or strangers. So intense must be the spirit of love and loving kindness, that the stranger may find himself a friend, the enemy a true brother, no difference whatsoever existing between them. For universality is of God and all limitations earthly. Thus man must strive that his reality may manifest virtues and perfections, the light whereof may shine upon everyone. The light of the sun shineth upon all the world and the merciful showers of Divine Providence fall upon all peoples. The vivifying breeze reviveth every living creature and all beings endued with life obtain their share and portion at His heavenly board. In like manner, the affections and loving kindness of the servants of the One True God must be bountifully and universally extended to all mankind. — *'Abdu'l-Bahá* **29**

O ye lovers of this wronged one! Cleanse ye your eyes, so that ye behold no man as different from yourselves. See ye no strangers; rather see all men as friends, for love and unity come hard when ye fix your gaze on otherness. And in this new and wondrous age, the Holy Writings say that we must be at one with every people; that we must see neither harshness nor injustice, neither malevolence, nor hostility, nor hate, but rather turn our eyes toward the heaven of ancient glory. For each of the creatures is a sign of God, and it was by the grace of the Lord and His power that each did step into the world; therefore they are not strangers, but in the family; not aliens, but friends, and to be treated as such.   *—'Abdu'l-Bahá* **30**

You must manifest complete love and affection toward all mankind. Do not exalt yourselves above others, but consider all as your equals, recognizing them as the servants of one God. Know that God is compassionate toward all; therefore, love all from the depths of your hearts, prefer all religionists before yourselves, be filled with love for every race, and be kind toward the people of all nationalities. Never speak disparagingly of others, but praise without distinction. Pollute not your tongues by speaking evil of another. Recognize your enemies as friends, and consider those who wish you evil as the wishers of good. You must not see evil as evil and then compromise with your opinion, for to treat in a smooth, kindly way one whom you consider evil or an enemy is hypocrisy, and this is not worthy or allowable. You must consider your enemies as your friends, look upon your evil-wishers as your well-wishers and treat them accordingly. Act in such a way that your heart may be free from hatred. Let not your heart be offended with anyone. If some one commits an error and wrong toward you, you must instantly forgive him. Do not complain of others. Refrain from reprimanding them, and if you wish to give admonition or advice, let it be offered in such a way that it will not burden the bearer. Turn all your thoughts toward bringing joy to hearts. Beware! Beware! lest ye offend any heart. Assist the world of humanity as much as possible. Be the source of consolation to every sad one, assist every weak one, be helpful to every indigent one, care for every sick one, be the cause of glorification to every lowly one, and shelter those who are overshadowed by fear.

In brief, let each one of you be as a lamp shining forth with the light of the virtues of the world of humanity. Be trustworthy, sincere, affectionate and replete with chastity. Be illumined, be spiritual, be divine, be glorious, be quickened of God, be a Bahá'í.   *—'Abdu'l-Bahá* **31**

Wherefore, O ye beloved of the Lord, bestir yourselves, do all in your power to be as one, to live in peace, each with the others: for ye are all the drops from but one ocean, the foliage of one tree, the pearls from a single shell, the flowers and sweet herbs from the same one garden. And achieving that, strive ye to unite the hearts of those who follow other faiths.

For one another must ye give up even life itself. To every human being must ye be infinitely kind. Call none a stranger; think none to be your foe. Be ye as if all men were your close kin and honored friends. Walk ye in such wise that this fleeting world will change into a splendor and this dismal heap of dust become a palace of delights. Such is the counsel of 'Abdu'l-Bahá. . . .   —'Abdu'l-Bahá **32**

Address yourselves to the promotion of the well-being and tranquillity of the children of men. Bend your minds and wills to the education of the peoples and kindreds of the earth, that haply the dissensions that divide it may, through the power of the Most Great Name, be blotted out from its face, and all mankind become the upholders of one Order, and the inhabitants of one City. Illumine and hallow your hearts; let them not be profaned by the thorns of hate or the thistles of malice. Ye dwell in one world, and have been created through the operation of one Will. Blessed is he who mingleth with all men in a spirit of utmost kindliness and love.

          —Bahá'u'lláh **33**

Ideal Characteristics of the Bahá'í Community

THIS people have never been, nor are they now, inclined to mischief. Their hearts are illumined with the light of the fear of God, and adorned with the adornment of His love. Their concern hath ever been and now is for the betterment of the world. Their purpose is to obliterate differences, and quench the flame of hatred and enmity, so that the whole earth may come to be viewed as one country.   —Bahá'u'lláh **34**

The great and fundamental teachings of Bahá'u'lláh are the oneness of God and unity of mankind. This is the bond of union among Bahá'ís all over the world. They become united among themselves, then unite others. It is impossible to unite unless united. Christ said, "Ye are the salt of the earth; but if the salt has lost his savor, wherewith shall it be salted?" This proves there were dissensions and lack of unity among His followers. Hence His admonition to unity of action.

Now must we, likewise, bind ourselves together in the utmost unity, be kind and loving to each other, sacrificing all our possessions, our honor, yea, even our lives for each other. Then will it be proved that we have acted according to the teachings of God, that we have been real believers in the oneness of God and unity of mankind.   —'Abdu'l-Bahá **35**

Bahá'u'lláh appeared from the horizon of the Orient and reestablished the essential foundation of the religious teachings of the world. The worn-out traditional beliefs current among men were removed. He caused fellowship and agreement to exist between the representatives of varying denominations so that love became manifest among the contending religions. He created a condition of harmony among hostile sects and upheld the banner of the oneness of the world of humanity. He established the foundation for international peace, caused the hearts of nations to be cemented together and conferred new life upon the various peoples of the East. Among those who have followed the teachings of Bahá'u'lláh no one says, "I am a Persian," "I am a Turk," "I am a Frenchman," or "I am an Englishman." No one says, "I am a Muslim, upholding the only true religion," "I am a Christian, loyal to my traditional and inherited beliefs," "I am a Jew, following talmudic interpretations," or "I am a Zoroastrian and opposed to all other religions." On the contrary, all have been rescued from religious, racial, political and patriotic prejudices and are now associating in fellowship and love to the extent that if you should attend one of their meetings you would be unable to observe any distinction between Christian and Muslim, Jew and Zoroastrian, Persian and Turk, Arab and European; for their meetings are based upon the essential foundations of religion, and real unity has been established among them. Former antagonisms have passed away; the centuries of sectarian hatred are ended; the period of aversion has gone by; the medieval conditions of ignorance have ceased to exist.

—'Abdu'l-Bahá **36**

The Bahá'í friends in Persia attained such a brotherhood and love that it really became a hindrance in the conduct of material affairs. Each one into whatever house of the friends he went considered himself the owner of the house, so to speak. There was no duality but complete mutuality of interests and love. The visiting friend would have no hesitation in opening the provision box and taking out enough food for his needs. They wore each other's clothes as their own when necessary. If in need of a hat or cloak, they would take and use it. The owner of the clothing would be thankful and grateful that the garment had gone. When he returned home, he would perhaps be told, "So and so was here and took away your coat." He would reply, "Praise be to God! I am so grateful to him. Praise be to God! I am so thankful I have been given this opportunity of showing my love for him." To such an extreme degree this love and fellowship expressed itself that Bahá'u'lláh commanded that no one should take possession of another's belongings unless presented with them. The intention is to show to what extent unity and love prevailed among the Bahá'í friends in the East. *—'Abdu'l-Bahá* **37**

Praise be to God, today the splendor of the Word of God hath illumined every horizon, and from all sects, races, tribes, nations, and communities souls have come together in the light of the Word, assembled, united and agreed in perfect harmony. Oh! What a great number of meetings are held adorned with souls from various races and diverse sects! Anyone attending these will be struck with amazement, and might suppose that these souls are all of one land, one nationality, one community, one thought, one belief and one opinion; whereas, in fact, one is an American, the other an African, one cometh from Asia and another from Europe, one is a native of India, another is from Turkestan, one is an Arab, another a Tajik, another a Persian and yet another a Greek. Notwithstanding such diversity they associate in perfect harmony and unity, love and freedom; they have one voice, one thought and one purpose. Verily, this is from the penetrative power of the Word of God! If all the forces of the universe were to combine they would not be able thus to gather a single assemblage so imbued with the sentiments of love, affection, attraction and enkindlement as to unite the members of different races and to raise up from the heart of the world a voice that shall dispel war and strife, uproot dissension and disputation, usher in the era of universal peace and establish unity and concord amongst men.

Can any power withstand the penetrative influence of the Word of God? Nay, by God! The proof is clear and the evidence is complete! If anyone looketh with the eyes of justice he shall be struck with wonder and amazement and will testify that all the peoples, sects and races of the world should be glad, content and grateful for the teachings and admonitions of Bahá'u'lláh. For these divine injunctions tame every ferocious beast, transform the creeping insect into a soaring bird, cause human souls to become angels of the Kingdom, and make the human world a focus for the qualities of mercy.

—'Abdu'l-Bahá   **38**

The Faith of Bahá'u'lláh has assimilated, by virtue of its creative, its regulative and ennobling energies, the varied races, nationalities, creeds and classes that have sought its shadow, and have pledged unswerving fealty to its cause. It has changed the hearts of its adherents, burned away their prejudices, stilled their passions, exalted their conceptions, ennobled their motives, coordinated their efforts, and transformed their outlook. While preserving their patriotism and safeguarding their lesser loyalties, it has made them lovers of mankind, and the determined upholders of its best and truest interests. While maintaining intact their belief in the Divine origin of their respective religions, it has enabled them to visualize the underlying purpose of these religions, to discover their merits, to recognize their sequence, their interdependence, their wholeness and unity, and to acknowledge the bond that vitally links them to itself. This universal, this transcending love which the followers of the Bahá'í Faith feel for their fellowmen, of whatever race, creed, class or nation, is neither mysterious nor can it be said to have been artificially stimulated. It is both spontaneous and genuine. They whose hearts are warmed by the energizing influence of God's creative love cherish His creatures for His sake, and recognize in every human face a sign of His reflected glory.

Of such men and women it may be truly said that to them "every foreign land is a fatherland, and every fatherland a foreign land." For their citizenship, it must be remembered, is in the Kingdom of Bahá'u'lláh. Though willing to share to the utmost the temporal benefits and the fleeting joys which this earthly life can confer, though eager to participate in whatever activity that conduces to the richness, the happiness and peace of that life, they can, at no time, forget that it constitutes no more than a transient, a very brief stage of their existence, that they who live it are but pilgrims and wayfarers whose goal is the Celestial City, and whose home the Country of never-failing joy and brightness.   —*Shoghi Effendi* **39**

The vitality which the organic institutions of this great, this ever-expanding Order* so strongly exhibit; the obstacles which the high courage, the undaunted resolution of its administrators have already surmounted; the fire of an unquenchable enthusiasm that glows with undiminished fervor in the hearts of its itinerant teachers; the heights of self-sacrifice which its champion-builders are now attaining; the breadth of vision, the confident hope, the creative joy, the inward peace, the uncompromising integrity, the exemplary discipline, the unyielding unity and solidarity which its stalwart defenders manifest; the degree to which its moving Spirit has

---

*The World Order of Bahá'u'lláh.

shown itself capable of assimilating the diversified elements within its pale, of cleansing them of all forms of prejudice and of fusing them with its own structure—these are evidences of a power which a disillusioned and sadly shaken society can ill afford to ignore.   —*Shoghi Effendi* **40**

Strangers and outsiders are astonished at this love and radiant affection existing among the Bahá'ís. They inquire about it. They observe the unity and agreement manifest among them. They say, "What a beautiful spirit shines in their faces!" All envy it and wish that such a bond of love might be witnessed everywhere. Therefore, to you my first admonition is this: Associate most kindly with all; be as one family; pursue the same pathway. Let your intentions be one that your love may permeate and affect the hearts of others so that they may grow to love each other and all attain to this condition of oneness.   —*'Abdu'l-Bahá* **41**

I hope that this same degree and intensity of love may become manifest and apparent here;* that the spirit of God shall so penetrate your hearts that each one of the beloved of God shall be considered as all; that each one may become a cause of unity and center of accord and all mankind be bound together in real fellowship and love.   —*'Abdu'l-Bahá* **42**

Acknowledging the God-Given Capacity for Human Progress
Humanity's Potential for Spiritual Excellence

O SON of Man! Veiled in My immemorial being and in the ancient eternity of My essence, I knew My love for thee; therefore I created thee, have engraved on thee Mine image and revealed to thee My beauty.   —*Bahá'u'lláh* **43**

---

*This talk was delivered in New York City on 20 June 1912.

Upon the inmost reality of each and every created thing He hath shed the light of one of His names, and made it a recipient of the glory of one of His attributes. Upon the reality of man, however, He hath focused the radiance of all of His names and attributes, and made it a mirror of His own Self. Alone of all created things man hath been singled out for so great a favor, so enduring a bounty.   *—Bahá'u'lláh* **44**

How resplendent the luminaries of knowledge that shine in an atom, and how vast the oceans of wisdom that surge within a drop! To a supreme degree is this true of man, who, among all created things, hath been invested with the robe of such gifts, and hath been singled out for the glory of such distinction. For in him are potentially revealed all the attributes and names of God to a degree that no other created being hath excelled or surpassed. All these names and attributes are applicable to him. Even as He hath said: "Man is My mystery, and I am his mystery."   *—Bahá'u'lláh* **45**

A human being is distinguished from an animal in a number of ways. . . . he is made in the image of God, in the likeness of the Supernal Light, even as the Torah saith, "Let us make man in our image, after our likeness."* This divine image betokeneth all the qualities of perfection whose lights, emanating from the Sun of Truth, illumine the realities of men, and are among the perfect attributes that lie within wisdom and knowledge. Ye must therefore put forth a mighty effort, striving by night and day and resting not for a moment, to acquire an abundant share of all the sciences and arts, that the Divine Image, which shineth out from the Sun of Truth, may illumine the mirror of the hearts of men.   *—'Abdu'l-Bahá* **46**

Without doubt each being is the center of the shining forth of the glory of God—that is to say, the perfections of God

---

*Gen. 1:26.

appear from it and are resplendent in it. It is like the sun, which is resplendent in the desert, upon the sea, in the trees, in the fruits and blossoms, and in all earthly things. The world, indeed each existing being, proclaims to us one of the names of God, but the reality of man is the collective reality, the general reality, and is the center where the glory of all the perfections of God shine forth—that is to say, for each name, each attribute, each perfection which we affirm of God there exists a sign in man. If it were otherwise, man could not imagine these perfections and could not understand them. So we say that God is the seer, and the eye is the sign of His vision; if this sight were not in man, how could we imagine the vision of God? for the blind (that is, one born blind) cannot imagine sight; and the deaf (that is, one deaf from birth) cannot imagine hearing; and the dead cannot realize life. Consequently, the Divinity of God, which is the sum of all perfections, reflects itself in the reality of man—that is to say, the Essence of Oneness is the gathering of all perfections, and from this unity He casts a reflection upon the human reality. Man, then, is the perfect mirror facing the Sun of Truth and is the center of radiation: the Sun of Truth shines in this mirror. The reflection of the divine perfections appears in the reality of man, so he is the representative of God, the messenger of God. If man did not exist, the universe would be without result, for the object of existence is the appearance of the perfections of God.   —*'Abdu'l-Bahá* **47**

Praise and thanksgiving be unto Providence that out of all the realities in existence He has chosen the reality of man and has honored it with intellect and wisdom, the two most luminous lights in either world. Through the agency of this great endowment, He has in every epoch cast on the mirror of creation new and wonderful configurations. If we look objectively upon the world of being, it will become apparent that from age to age, the temple of existence has continually been embellished with a fresh grace, and distinguished with an ever-varying splendor, deriving from wisdom and the power of thought.

This supreme emblem of God stands first in the order of creation and first in rank, taking precedence over all created things. Witness to it is the Holy Tradition, "Before all else, God created the mind." From the dawn of creation, it was made to be revealed in the temple of man. —'Abdu'l-Bahá **48**

O My Servant! Thou art even as a finely tempered sword concealed in the darkness of its sheath and its value hidden from the artificer's knowledge. Wherefore come forth from the sheath of self and desire that thy worth may be made resplendent and manifest unto all the world. —Bahá'u'lláh **49**

Knowing and Loving God: The Foundation of Human Well-Being and Development

THE purpose of God in creating man hath been, and will ever be, to enable him to know his Creator and to attain His Presence. To this most excellent aim, this supreme objective, all the heavenly Books and the divinely revealed and weighty Scriptures unequivocally bear witness. —Bahá'u'lláh **50**

O Son of Man! I loved thy creation, hence I created thee. Wherefore, do thou love Me, that I may name thy name and fill thy soul with the spirit of life. —Bahá'u'lláh **51**

Having created the world and all that liveth and moveth therein, He, through the direct operation of His unconstrained and sovereign Will, chose to confer upon man the unique distinction and capacity to know Him and to love Him—a capacity that must needs be regarded as the generating impulse and the primary purpose underlying the whole of creation. . . . —Bahá'u'lláh **52**

God . . . hath singled out for His special favor the pure, the gemlike reality of man, and invested it with a unique capacity of knowing Him and of reflecting the greatness of His glory. This twofold distinction conferred upon him hath cleansed away from his heart the rust of every vain desire, and made him worthy of the vesture with which his Creator hath deigned to clothe him. It hath served to rescue his soul from the wretchedness of ignorance.

This robe with which the body and soul of man hath been adorned is the very foundation of his well-being and development.   —*Bahá'u'lláh* **53**

It is known that the knowledge of God is beyond all knowledge, and it is the greatest glory of the human world. For in the existing knowledge of the reality of things there is material advantage, and through it outward civilization progresses; but the knowledge of God is the cause of spiritual progress and attraction, and through it the perception of truth, the exaltation of humanity, divine civilization, rightness of morals and illumination are obtained.

Second, comes the love of God, the light of which shines in the lamp of the hearts of those who know God; its brilliant rays illuminate the horizon and give to man the life of the Kingdom. In truth, the fruit of human existence is the love of God, for this love is the spirit of life, and the eternal bounty. If the love of God did not exist, the contingent world would be in darkness; if the love of God did not exist, the hearts of men would be dead, and deprived of the sensations of existence; if the love of God did not exist, spiritual union would be lost; if the love of God did not exist, the light of unity would not illuminate humanity; if the love of God did not exist, the East and West, like two lovers, would not embrace each other; if the love of God did not exist, division and disunion would not be changed into fraternity; if the love of God did not exist, indifference would not end in affection; if the love of God did not exist, the stranger would not become the friend. The love of the human world has shone forth from the love of God and has appeared by the bounty and grace of God.

It is clear that the reality of mankind is diverse, that opinions are various and sentiments different; and this difference of opinions, of thoughts, of intelligence, of sentiments among the human species arises from essential necessity; for the differences in the degrees of existence of creatures is one of the necessities of existence, which unfolds itself in infinite forms. Therefore, we have need of a general power which may dominate the sentiments, the opinions and the thoughts of all, thanks to which these divisions may no longer have effect, and all individuals may be brought under the influence of the unity of the world of humanity. It is clear and evident that this greatest power in the human world is the love of God. It brings the different peoples under the shadow of the tent of affection; it gives to the antagonistic and hostile nations and families the greatest love and union.   —'Abdu'l-Bahá **54**

The honor and exaltation of man must be something more than material riches. Material comforts are only a branch, but the root of the exaltation of man is the good attributes and virtues which are the adornments of his reality. These are the divine appearances, the heavenly bounties, the sublime emotions, the love and knowledge of God; universal wisdom, intellectual perception, scientific discoveries, justice, equity, truthfulness, benevolence, natural courage and innate fortitude; the respect for rights and the keeping of agreements and covenants; rectitude in all circumstances; serving the truth under all conditions; the sacrifice of one's life for the good of all people; kindness and esteem for all nations; obedience to the teachings of God; service in the Divine Kingdom; the guidance of the people, and the education of the nations and races. This is the prosperity of the human world! This is the exaltation of man in the world! This is eternal life and heavenly honor!

These virtues do not appear from the reality of man except through the power of God and the divine teachings, for they need supernatural power for their manifestation. It may be that in the world of nature a trace of these perfections may appear, but they are unstable and ephemeral; they are like the rays of the sun upon the wall.

As the compassionate God has placed such a wonderful crown upon the head of man, man should strive that its brilliant jewels may become visible in the world.

—'Abdu'l-Bahá **55**

Although it is necessary for man to strive for material needs and comforts, his real need is the acquisition of the bounties of God. If he is bereft of divine bounties, spiritual susceptibilities and heavenly glad tidings, the life of man in this world has not yielded any worthy fruit. While possessing physical life, he should lay hold of the life spiritual, and together with bodily comforts and happiness, he should enjoy divine pleasures and content. Then is man worthy of the title man; then will he be after the image and likeness of God, for the image of the Merciful consists of the attributes of the heavenly Kingdom. If no fruits of the Kingdom appear in the garden of his soul, man is not in the image and likeness of God. . . .   —'Abdu'l-Bahá **56**

Material civilization alone is not sufficient and will not prove productive. The physical happiness of material conditions was allotted to the animal. Consider how the animal has attained the fullest degree of physical felicity. A bird perches upon the loftiest branch and builds there its nest with consummate beauty and skill. All the grains and seeds of the meadows are its wealth and food; all the fresh water of mountain springs and rivers of the plain are for its enjoyment. Truly, this is the acme of material happiness, to which even a human creature cannot attain. This is the honor of the animal kingdom. But the honor of the human kingdom is the attainment of spiritual happiness in the human world, the acquisition of the knowledge and love of God. The honor allotted to man is the acquisition of the supreme virtues of the human world. This is his real happiness and felicity. But if material happiness and spiritual felicity be conjoined, it will be "delight upon delight," as the Arabs say.   —'Abdu'l-Bahá **57**

O My servants! Could ye apprehend with what wonders of My munificence and bounty I have willed to entrust your souls, ye would, of a truth, rid yourselves of attachment to all created things, and would gain a true knowledge of your own selves—a knowledge which is the same as the comprehension of Mine own Being. Ye would find yourselves independent of all else but Me, and would perceive, with your inner and outer eye, and as manifest as the revelation of My effulgent Name, the seas of My loving kindness and bounty moving within you. Suffer not your idle fancies, your evil passions, your insincerity and blindness of heart to dim the luster, or stain the sanctity of so lofty a station. *—Bahá'u'lláh* **58**

Qualities That Will Advance Civilization

ALL men have been created to carry forward an ever-advancing civilization. The Almighty beareth Me witness: To act like the beasts of the field is unworthy of man. Those virtues that befit his dignity are forbearance, mercy, compassion and loving kindness towards all the peoples and kindreds of the earth. *—Bahá'u'lláh* **59**

The virtues and attributes pertaining unto God are all evident and manifest, and have been mentioned and described in all the heavenly Books. Among them are trustworthiness, truthfulness, purity of heart while communing with God, forbearance, resignation to whatever the Almighty hath decreed, contentment with the things His Will hath provided, patience, nay, thankfulness in the midst of tribulation, and complete reliance, in all circumstances, upon Him. These rank, according to the estimate of God, among the highest and most laudable of all acts. All other acts are, and will ever remain, secondary and subordinate unto them. . . . *—Bahá'u'lláh* **60**

Trustworthiness . . . is the door of security for all that dwell on earth and a token of glory on the part of the All-Merciful. He who partaketh thereof hath indeed partaken of the treasures of wealth and prosperity. Trustworthiness is the greatest portal leading unto the tranquillity and security of the people. In truth the stability of every affair hath depended and doth depend upon it. All the domains of power, of grandeur and of wealth are illumined by its light. *—Bahá'u'lláh* **61**

O friends! Be not careless of the virtues with which ye have been endowed, neither be neglectful of your high destiny. Suffer not your labors to be wasted through the vain imaginations which certain hearts have devised. Ye are the stars of the heaven of understanding, the breeze that stirreth at the break of day, the soft-flowing waters upon which must depend the very life of all men, the letters inscribed upon His sacred scroll. With the utmost unity, and in a spirit of perfect fellowship, exert yourselves, that ye may be enabled to achieve that which beseemeth this Day of God. Verily I say, strife and dissension, and whatsoever the mind of man abhorreth are entirely unworthy of his station.   —*Bahá'u'lláh* **62**

Just as God loves all and is kind to all, so must we really love and be kind to everybody. We must consider none bad, none worthy of detestation, no one as an enemy. We must love all; nay, we must consider everyone as related to us, for all are the servants of one God. All are under the instructions of one Educator. We must strive day and night that love and amity may increase, that this bond of unity may be strengthened, that joy and happiness may more and more prevail, that in unity and solidarity all mankind may gather beneath the shadow of God, that people may turn to God for their sustenance, finding in Him the life that is everlasting. Thus may they be confirmed in the Kingdom of God and live forever through His grace and bounty.   —*'Abdu'l-Bahá* **63**

Verily, it is better a thousand times for a man to die than to continue living without virtue.

We have eyes wherewith to see, but if we do not use them how do they profit us? We have ears wherewith to hear, but if we are deaf of what use are they?

We have a tongue wherewith to praise God and proclaim the good tidings, but if we are dumb how useless it is!

The All-Loving God created man to radiate the Divine light and to illumine the world by his words, action and life. If he is without virtue he becomes no better than a mere animal, and an animal devoid of intelligence is a vile thing.

The Heavenly Father gave the priceless gift of intelligence to man so that he might become a spiritual light, piercing the darkness of materiality, and bringing goodness and truth into the world.   —'Abdu'l-Bahá 64

If we review history, we will observe that human advancement has been greatest in the development of material virtues. Civilization is the sign and evidence of this progression. Throughout the world, material civilization has attained truly wonderful heights and degrees of efficiency—that is to say, the outward powers and virtues of man have greatly developed, but the inner and ideal virtues have been correspondingly delayed and neglected. It is now the time in the history of the world for us to strive and give an impetus to the advancement and development of inner forces—that is to say, we must arise to service in the world of morality, for human morals are in need of readjustment. We must also render sevice to the world of intellectuality in order that the minds of men may increase in power and become keener in perception, assisting the intellect of man to attain its supremacy so that the ideal virtues may appear.   —'Abdu'l-Bahá 65

The world of existence is progressive. It is subject to development and growth. Consider how great has been the progress in this radiant century. Civilization has unfolded. Nations have developed. Industrialism and jurisprudence have expanded. Sciences, inventions and discoveries have increased. All of these show that the world of existence is continuously progressing and developing; and therefore, assuredly, the virtues characterizing the maturity of man must, likewise, expand and grow.   —'Abdu'l-Bahá 66

If the moral precepts and foundations of divine civilization become united with the material advancement of man, there is no doubt that the happiness of the human world will be attained and that from every direction the glad tidings of peace upon earth will be announced. Then humankind will achieve extraordinary progress, the sphere of human intelligence will be immeasurably enlarged, wonderful inventions will appear, and the spirit of God will reveal itself; all men will consort in joy and fragrance, and eternal life will be conferred upon the children of the Kingdom. Then will the power of the divine make itself effective and the breath of the Holy Spirit penetrate the essence of all things. Therefore, the material and the divine, or merciful, civilizations must progress together until the highest aspirations and desires of humanity shall become realized.   —'Abdu'l-Bahá   **67**

No matter how much the physical body of man is trained and developed, there will be no real progression in the human station unless the mind correspondingly advances. No matter how much man may acquire material virtues, he will not be able to realize and express the highest possibilities of life without spiritual graces.   —'Abdu'l-Bahá   **68**

I exhort you to be devoted to your spiritual development. Just as you have striven along material lines and have attained to high degrees of worldly advancement, may you likewise become strengthened and proficient in the knowledge of God. May divine susceptibilities be increased and awakened; may your devotion to the heavenly Kingdom become intense. May you be the recipients of the impulses of the Holy Spirit, be assisted in the world of morality and attain ideal power so that the sublimity of the world of mankind may become apparent in you. Thus may you attain the highest happiness, the eternal life, the everlasting glory, the second birth, and become manifestations of the bestowals of God.   —'Abdu'l-Bahá   **69**

As this is the radiant century, it is my hope that the Sun of Truth may illumine all humanity. May the eyes be opened and the ears become attentive; may souls become resuscitated and consort together in the utmost harmony as recipients of the same light. Perchance, God will remove this strife and warfare of thousands of years. May this bloodshed pass away, this tyranny and oppression cease, this warfare be ended. May the light of love shine forth and illumine hearts, and may human lives be cemented and connected until all of us may find agreement and tranquillity beneath the same tabernacle and with the standard of the Most Great Peace above us move steadily onward. — *'Abdu'l-Bahá* **70**

Transforming Civilization through the Power of Divine Sovereignty

The Revelation of Bahá'u'lláh

I WAS but a man like others, asleep upon My couch, when lo, the breezes of the All-Glorious were wafted over Me, and taught Me the knowledge of all that hath been.* This thing is not from Me, but from One Who is Almighty and All-Knowing. And He bade Me lift up My voice between earth and heaven, and for this there befell Me what hath caused the tears of every man of understanding to flow. The learning current amongst men I studied not; their schools I entered not. Ask of the city wherein I dwelt, that thou mayest be well assured that I am not of them who speak falsely. This is but a leaf which the winds of the will of thy Lord, the Almighty, the All-Praised, have stirred. Can it be still when the tempestuous winds are blowing? Nay, by Him Who is the Lord of all Names and Attributes! They move it as they list. The evanescent is as nothing before Him Who is the Ever-Abiding. His all-compelling summons hath reached Me, and caused Me to speak His

---

*In this passage Bahá'u'lláh describes God's summons to Him while imprisoned in 1852 in the Síyáh-Chál, a subterranean dungeon in Tehran. Of that event Shoghi Effendi, in *God Passes By* (new ed. [Wilmette, Ill.: Bahá'í Publishing Trust, 1974], p. 101), writes: "Wrapped in its stygian gloom, breathing its fetid air, numbed by its humid and icy atmosphere, His feet in stocks, His neck weighed down by a mighty chain, surrounded by criminals and miscreants of the worst order . . . under such appalling circumstances the 'Most Great Spirit,' as designated by Himself, and symbolized in the Zoroastrian, the Mosaic, the Christian, and the Muḥammadan Dispensations by the Sacred Fire, the Burning Bush, the Dove and the Angel Gabriel respectively, descended upon, and revealed itself, personated by a 'Maiden,' to the agonized soul of Bahá'u'lláh."

praise amidst all people. I was indeed as one dead when His behest was uttered. The hand of the will of thy Lord, the Compassionate, the Merciful, transformed Me.

—Bahá'u'lláh 71

God is My witness, O people! I was asleep on My couch, when lo, the Breeze of God wafting over Me roused Me from My slumber. His quickening Spirit revived Me, and My tongue was unloosed to voice His Call. Accuse Me not of having transgressed against God. Behold Me, not with your eyes but with Mine. Thus admonisheth you He Who is the Gracious, the All-Knowing. Think ye, O people, that I hold within My grasp the control of God's ultimate Will and Purpose? Far be it from Me to advance such claim. To this I testify before God, the Almighty, the Exalted, the All-Knowing, the All-Wise. Had the ultimate destiny of God's Faith been in Mine hands, I would have never consented, even though for one moment, to manifest Myself unto you, nor would I have allowed one word to fall from My lips. Of this God Himself is, verily, a witness.

—Bahá'u'lláh 72

I swear by Thy might! Neither the hosts of the earth nor those of heaven can keep me back from revealing the things I am commanded to manifest. I have no will before Thy will, and can cherish no desire in the face of Thy desire. By Thy grace I am, at all times, ready to serve Thee and am rid of all attachment to anyone except Thee.   *—Bahá'u'lláh* 73

The Revelation which, from time immemorial, hath been acclaimed as the Purpose and Promise of all the Prophets of God, and the most cherished Desire of His Messengers, hath now, by virtue of the pervasive Will of the Almighty and at His irresistible bidding, been revealed unto men. The advent of such a Revelation hath been heralded in all the sacred Scriptures.   *—Bahá'u'lláh* 74

In this most mighty Revelation all the Dispensations of the past have attained their highest, their final consummation.

That which hath been made manifest in this preeminent, this most exalted Revelation, standeth unparalleled in the annals of the past, nor will future ages witness its like.

—Bahá'u'lláh **75**

This is the Day whereon the All-Merciful hath come down in the clouds of knowledge, clothed with manifest sovereignty. He well knoweth the actions of men. He it is Whose glory none can mistake, could ye but comprehend it. The heaven of every religion hath been rent, and the earth of human understanding been cleft asunder. . . .   *—Bahá'u'lláh* **76**

Verily I say, this is the Day in which mankind can behold the Face, and hear the Voice, of the Promised One. The Call of God hath been raised, and the light of His countenance hath been lifted up upon men. It behooveth every man to blot out the trace of every idle word from the tablet of his heart, and to gaze, with an open and unbiased mind, on the signs of His Revelation, the proofs of His Mission, and the tokens of His glory.   *—Bahá'u'lláh* **77**

The time foreordained unto the peoples and kindreds of the earth is now come. The promises of God, as recorded in the holy Scriptures, have all been fulfilled. Out of Zion hath gone forth the Law of God, and Jerusalem, and the hills and land thereof, are filled with the glory of His Revelation. Happy is the man that pondereth in his heart that which hath been revealed in the Books of God, the Help in Peril, the Self-Subsisting. Meditate upon this, O ye beloved of God, and let your ears be attentive unto His Word, so that ye may, by His grace and mercy, drink your fill from the crystal waters of constancy, and become as steadfast and immovable as the mountain in His Cause.   *—'Abdu'l-Bahá* **78**

Lend an ear unto the song of David. He saith: "Who will bring me into the Strong City?" The Strong City is 'Akká, which hath been named the Most Great Prison, and which possesseth a fortress and mighty ramparts.*

... Peruse that which Isaiah hath spoken in His Book. He saith: "Get thee up into the high mountain, O Zion, that bringest good tidings; lift up Thy Voice with strength, O Jerusalem, that bringest good tidings. Lift it up, be not afraid; say unto the cities of Judah: 'Behold your God! Behold the Lord God will come with strong hand, and His arm shall rule for Him.'" This Day all the signs have appeared. A Great City† hath descended from heaven, and Zion trembleth and exulteth with joy at the Revelation of God, for it hath heard the Voice of God on every side.   *—Bahá'u'lláh* **79**

The Word which the Son‡ concealed is made manifest. It hath been sent down in the form of the human temple in this day. Blessed be the Lord Who is the Father! He, verily, is come unto the nations in His most great majesty. Turn your faces towards Him, O concourse of the righteous! ... This is the day whereon the Rock [Peter] crieth out and shouteth, and celebrateth the praise of its Lord, the All-Possessing, the Most High, saying: "Lo! The Father is come, and that which ye were promised in the Kingdom is fulfilled!"   *—Bahá'u'lláh* **80**

Rend the veils asunder. He Who is the Lord of Lords is come overshadowed with clouds, and the decree hath been fulfilled by God, the Almighty, the Unrestrained.... He, verily, hath again come down from Heaven even as He came down from it the first time. Beware that thou§ dispute not with Him

---

*Bahá'u'lláh was imprisoned in the barracks of Akka, Palestine, from August 1868 until November 1870. He remained under house confinement at several sites in and around Akka until His death in 1892. See the appendix for an account of His exiles and imprisonments.

†The Law of God brought by Bahá'u'lláh. See 'Abdu'l-Bahá, *Some Answered Questions,* comp. and trans. Laura Clifford Barney, 5th ed. (Wilmette, Ill.: Bahá'í Publishing Trust, 1981), pp. 48, 67–68.

‡Christ.

§Pope Pius IX. Bahá'u'lláh sent him an epistle in 1867.

even as the Pharisees disputed with Him [Jesus] without a clear token or proof.   —*Bahá'u'lláh* **81**

In the divine Holy Books there are unmistakable prophecies giving the glad tidings of a certain Day in which the Promised One of all the Books would appear, a radiant dispensation be established, the banner of the Most Great Peace and conciliation be hoisted and the oneness of the world of humanity proclaimed. Among the various nations and peoples of the world no enmity or hatred should remain. All hearts were to be connected one with another. These things are recorded in the Torah, or Old Testament, in the Gospel, the Qur'án, the Zend-Avesta, the books of Buddha and the book of Confucius. In brief, all the Holy Books contain these glad tidings. They announce that after the world is surrounded by darkness, radiance shall appear. For just as the night, when it becomes excessively dark, precedes the dawn of a new day, so likewise when the darkness of religious apathy and heedlessness overtakes the world, when human souls become negligent of God, when materialistic ideas overshadow spirituality, when nations become submerged in the world of matter and forget God—at such a time as this shall the divine Sun shine forth and the radiant morn appear.   —*'Abdu'l-Bahá* **82**

Praise be to God! The springtime of God is at hand. This century is, verily, the spring season. The world of mind and kingdom of soul have become fresh and verdant by its bestowals. It has resuscitated the whole realm of existence. On one hand, the lights of reality are shining; on the other, the clouds of divine mercy are pouring down the fullness of heavenly bounty. Wonderful material progress is evident, and great spiritual discoveries are being made. Truly, this can be called the miracle of centuries, for it is replete with manifestations of the miraculous. The time has come when all mankind shall be united, when all races shall be loyal to one fatherland, all religions become one religion, and racial and religious bias pass away. It is a day in which the oneness of humankind shall uplift its standard and international peace, like the true morning, flood the world with its light.   — *'Abdu'l-Bahá* **83**

O peoples of the earth! God, the Eternal Truth, is My witness that streams of fresh and soft-flowing waters have gushed from the rocks, through the sweetness of the words uttered by your Lord, the Unconstrained; and still ye slumber. Cast away that which ye possess, and, on the wings of detachment, soar beyond all created things. Thus biddeth you the Lord of creation, the movement of Whose Pen hath revolutionized the soul of mankind.   — *Bahá'u'lláh* **84**

The Sacrifice of Bahá'u'lláh for Establishing Peace

IN these days enemies have compassed Us about, and the fire of hatred is kindled.* O peoples of the earth! By My life and by your own! This Wronged One hath never had, nor hath He now any desire for leadership. Mine aim hath ever been, and still is, to suppress whatever is the cause of contention amidst the peoples of the earth, and of separation amongst the nations, so that all men may be sanctified from every earthly attachment, and be set free to occupy themselves with their own interests. . . .

Gracious God! This is the day whereon the wise should seek the advice of this Wronged One, and ask Him Who is the Truth what things are conducive to the glory and tranquillity of men. And yet, all are earnestly striving to put out this glorious and shining light, and are diligently seeking either to establish Our guilt, or to voice their protest against Us. Matters have come to such a pass, that the conduct of this Wronged One hath, in every way, been grossly misrepresented, and in a manner which it would be unseemly to mention. . . .

---

*Bahá'u'lláh, also referred to as the "Wronged One," the "Ancient Beauty," and the "Abhá Beauty," wrote this epistle in 1891 to Shaykh Muḥammad Taqíy-i-Najafí, a Muslim cleric in Isfahan, Iran. See the appendix for an account of Bahá'u'lláh's exiles and imprisonments.

Briefly, this Wronged One hath, in the face of all that hath befallen Him at their hands, and all that hath been said of Him, endured patiently, and held His peace, inasmuch as it is Our purpose, through the loving providence of God—exalted be His glory—and His surpassing mercy, to abolish, through the force of Our utterance, all disputes, war, and bloodshed, from the face of the earth. Under all conditions We have, in spite of what they have said, endured with seemly patience, and have left them to God.   —*Bahá'u'lláh* 85

That which hath touched this Wronged One is beyond compare or equal. We have borne it all with the utmost willingness and resignation, so that the souls of men may be edified, and the Word of God be exalted. While confined in the prison of the Land of Mím (Mázindarán) We were one day delivered into the hands of the divines.* Thou canst well imagine what befell Us. Shouldst thou at sometime happen to visit the dungeon of His Majesty the Sháh, ask the director and chief jailer to show thee those two chains, one of which is known as Qará-Guhar, and the other as Salásil. I swear by the Daystar of Justice that for four months this Wronged One was tormented and chained by one or the other of them. "My grief exceedeth all the woes to which Jacob gave vent, and all the afflictions of Job are but a part of My sorrows!"
                    —*Bahá'u'lláh* 86

The Ancient Beauty hath consented to be bound with chains that mankind may be released from its bondage, and hath accepted to be made a prisoner within this most mighty Stronghold that the whole world may attain unto true liberty. He hath drained to its dregs the cup of sorrow, that all the peoples of the earth may attain unto abiding joy, and be filled with gladness. This is of the mercy of your Lord, the Compas-

_____

*Mazindaran is a province that borders the Caspian Sea in northern Iran. Bahá'u'lláh was arrested there in 1852 and sent to the Síyáh-Chál, a dungeon in Tehran.

sionate, the Most Merciful. We have accepted to be abased, O believers in the Unity of God, that ye may be exalted, and have suffered manifold afflictions, that ye might prosper and flourish.   *—Bahá'u'lláh* **87**

The aim of this Wronged One in sustaining woes and tribulations, in revealing the Holy Verses and in demonstrating proofs hath been naught but to quench the flame of hate and enmity, that the horizon of the hearts of men may be illumined with the light of concord and attain real peace and tranquillity. From the dawning-place of the divine Tablet the daystar of this utterance shineth resplendent, and it behooveth everyone to fix his gaze upon it: We exhort you, O peoples of the world, to observe that which will elevate your station. Hold fast to the fear of God and firmly adhere to what is right.
                                    —Bahá'u'lláh **88**

The Abhá Beauty Himself . . . bore all manner of ordeals, and willingly accepted for Himself intense afflictions. No torment was there left that His sacred form was not subjected to, no suffering that did not descend upon Him. How many a night, when He was chained, did He go sleepless because of the weight of His iron collar; how many a day the burning pain of the stocks and fetters gave Him no moment's peace. From Níyávarán* to Ṭihrán they made Him run—He, that embodied spirit, He Who had been accustomed to repose against cushions of ornamented silk—chained, shoeless, His head bared; and down under the earth, in the thick darkness of that narrow dungeon, they shut Him up with murderers, rebels and thieves. Ever and again they assailed Him with a new torment, and all were certain that from one moment to the next He would suffer a martyr's death. After some time they banished Him from His native land, and sent Him to countries alien and far away. During many a year in 'Iráq, no moment passed but the

---

*A village in the province of Mazindaran in northern Iran.

arrow of a new anguish struck His holy heart; with every breath a sword came down upon that sacred body, and He could hope for no moment of security and rest. From every side His enemies mounted their attack with unrelenting hate; and singly and alone He withstood them all. After all these tribulations, these body blows, they flung Him out of 'Iráq in the continent of Asia, to the continent of Europe,* and in that place of bitter exile, of wretched hardships, to the wrongs that were heaped upon Him by the people of the Qur'án were now added the virulent persecutions, the powerful attacks, the plottings, the slanders, the continual hostilities, the hate and malice, of the people of the Bayán.† My pen is powerless to tell it all; but ye have surely been informed of it. Then, after twenty-four years in this, the Most Great Prison,‡ in agony and sore affliction, His days drew to a close.

To sum it up, the Ancient Beauty was ever, during His sojourn in this transitory world, either a captive bound with chains, or living under a sword, or subjected to extreme suffering and torment, or held in the Most Great Prison. Because of His physical weakness, brought on by His afflictions, His blessed body was worn away to a breath; it was light as a cobweb from long grieving. And His reason for shouldering this heavy load and enduring all this anguish, which was even as an ocean that hurleth its waves to high heaven—His reason for putting on the heavy iron chains and for becoming the very embodiment of utter resignation and meekness, was to lead every soul on earth to concord, to fellow-feeling, to oneness; to make known amongst all peoples the sign of the singleness of God, so that at last the primal oneness deposited at the heart of all created things would bear its destined fruit, and

---

*Bahá'u'lláh was banished from Iran first to Baghdad (1853–63) and then to Constantinople (1863), to Adrianople, now Edirne, in the European part of Turkey (1863–68), and, finally, to Akka, Palestine (1868–92).
†The followers of the Báb who did not accept Bahá'u'lláh as a new Manifestation of God.
‡The prison-city of Akka, Palestine.

the splendor of "No difference canst thou see in the creation of the God of Mercy,"* would cast abroad its rays.

—'Abdu'l-Bahá **89**

He bore all this that He might purify the world, and deck it out with the tender mercies of the Lord God; that He might set it at rest; that conflict and aggression might be put to flight, the lance and the keen blade be exchanged for loving fellowship, malevolence and war turn into safety and gentleness and love, that battlefields of hate and wrath should become gardens of delight, and places where once the blood-drenched armies clashed, be fragrant pleasure grounds; that warfare should be seen as shame, and the resort to arms, even as a loathsome sickness, be shunned by every people; that universal peace raise its pavilions on the loftiest mounts, and war be made to perish forever from the earth.   —'Abdu'l-Bahá **90**

Because He promulgated the message of universal peace and international agreement, the kings of the Orient arose against Him, for they did not find their personal and national benefits advanced by His admonition and teaching. They persecuted Him bitterly, inflicted upon Him every torment, imprisoned, bastinadoed, banished Him and eventually confined Him in a fortress. Then they arose against His followers. For the establishment of international peace the blood of twenty thousand Bahá'ís was spilled. Their homes were destroyed, their children made captives and their possessions pillaged, yet none of these people waxed cold or wavered in devotion. Even to this day the Bahá'ís are persecuted, and quite recently a number were killed, for wherever they are found they put forth the greatest efforts to establish the peace of the world.†

—'Abdu'l-Bahá **91**

---

*Qur'án 67:3.
†Speaking in 1912, 'Abdu'l-Bahá was probably referring to a fresh storm of persecutions that broke out in response to the constitutional movement in early twentieth-century Iran. The persecution of Iranian Bahá'ís has

All this came about that humankind might be illumined, that ignorance might yield to knowledge, that men of earth become men of heaven, that discord and dissension might be torn out by the roots, and the Kingdom of Peace become established over all the world. Strive ye now that this bounty become manifest, and this best-beloved of all hopes be realized in splendor throughout the community of man.

—'Abdu'l-Bahá 92

Woes and sorrows are powerless to restrain thy Lord, the All-Merciful. Indeed He hath risen to champion the Cause of God in such wise that neither the overpowering might of the world nor the tyranny of the nations can ever alarm Him. He calleth aloud betwixt earth and heaven, saying: The Promised Day is come. —Bahá'u'lláh 93

The Promise of Peace

THIS is the Day whereon the Ocean of God's mercy hath been manifested unto men, the Day in which the Daystar of His loving kindness hath shed its radiance upon them, the Day in which the clouds of His bountiful favor have overshadowed the whole of mankind. Now is the time to cheer and refresh the downcast through the invigorating breeze of love and fellowship, and the living waters of friendliness and charity.

—Bahá'u'lláh 94

Through each and every one of the verses which the Pen of the Most High hath revealed, the doors of love and unity have been unlocked and flung open to the face of men. We have erewhile declared—and Our Word is the truth—: "Consort with the followers of all religions in a spirit of friendliness and fellowship." Whatsoever hath led the children of men to

---

continued into the 1980s. Since 1979, 198 Bahá'ís have been put to death, 767 have been imprisoned, some 10,000 have been made homeless, and more than 25,000 have been forced to flee Iran.

shun one another, and hath caused dissensions and divisions amongst them, hath, through the revelation of these words, been nullified and abolished. From the heaven of God's Will, and for the purpose of ennobling the world of being and of elevating the minds and souls of men, hath been sent down that which is the most effective instrument for the education of the whole human race. The highest essence and most perfect expression of whatsoever the peoples of old have either said or written hath, through this most potent Revelation, been sent down from the heaven of the Will of the All-Possessing, the Ever-Abiding God.   —*Bahá'u'lláh* **95**

The world's equilibrium hath been upset through the vibrating influence of this most great, this new World Order. Mankind's ordered life hath been revolutionized through the agency of this unique, this wondrous System—the like of which mortal eyes have never witnessed.   —*Bahá'u'lláh* **96**

Through the movement of Our Pen of glory We have, at the bidding of the omnipotent Ordainer, breathed a new life into every human frame, and instilled into every word a fresh potency. All created things proclaim the evidences of this worldwide regeneration.   —*Bahá'u'lláh* **97**

O peoples of the world! The Sun of Truth hath risen to illumine the whole earth, and to spiritualize the community of man. Laudable are the results and the fruits thereof, abundant the holy evidences deriving from this grace. This is mercy unalloyed and purest bounty; it is light for the world and all its peoples; it is harmony and fellowship, and love and solidarity; indeed it is compassion and unity, and the end of foreignness; it is the being at one, in complete dignity and freedom, with all on earth.   —*'Abdu'l-Bahá* **98**

From the continual imitation of ancient and worn-out ways, the world had grown dark as darksome night. The fundamentals of the divine Teachings had passed from memory; their pith and heart had been totally forgotten, and the people were holding on to husks. The nations had, like tattered garments long outworn, fallen into a pitiful condition.

Out of this pitch blackness there dawned the morning splendor of the Teachings of Bahá'u'lláh. He hath dressed the world with a garment new and fair, and that new garment is the principles which have come down from God.

Now the new age is here and creation is reborn. Humanity hath taken on new life. The autumn hath gone by, and the reviving spring is here. All things are now made new. Arts and industries have been reborn, there are new discoveries in science, and there are new inventions; even the details of human affairs, such as dress and personal effects—even weapons—all these have likewise been renewed. The laws and procedures of every government have been revised. Renewal is the order of the day.

And all this newness hath its source in the fresh outpourings of wondrous grace and favor from the Lord of the Kingdom, which have renewed the world. The people, therefore, must be set completely free from their old patterns of thought, that all their attention may be focused upon these new principles, for these are the light of this time and the very spirit of this age.

Unless these Teachings are effectively spread among the people, until the old ways, the old concepts, are gone and forgotten, this world of being will find no peace, nor will it reflect the perfections of the Heavenly Kingdom. Strive ye with all your hearts to make the heedless conscious, to waken those who sleep, to bring knowledge to the ignorant, to make the blind to see, the deaf to hear, and restore the dead to life.

—'Abdu'l-Bahá **99**

The call of God, when raised, breathed a new life into the body of mankind, and infused a new spirit into the whole creation. It is for this reason that the world hath been moved to its depths, and the hearts and consciences of men been quickened. Erelong the evidences of this regeneration will be revealed, and the fast asleep will be awakened.

—'Abdu'l-Bahá **100**

Now, in the world of being, the Hand of Divine power hath firmly laid the foundations of this all-highest bounty, and this wondrous gift. Whatsoever is latent in the innermost of this holy Cycle shall gradually appear and be made manifest, for now is but the beginning of its growth, and the dayspring of the revelation of its signs. Ere the close of this century and of this age, it shall be made clear and evident how wondrous was that springtide, and how heavenly was that gift.

—'Abdu'l-Bahá   **101**

Bahá'u'lláh, we should . . . recognize, has not only imbued mankind with a new and regenerating Spirit. He has not merely enunciated certain universal principles, or propounded a particular philosophy, however potent, sound and universal these may be. In addition to these He, as well as 'Abdu'l-Bahá after Him, has, unlike the Dispensations of the past, clearly and specifically laid down a set of Laws, established definite institutions, and provided for the essentials of a Divine Economy. These are destined to be a pattern for future society, a supreme instrument for the establishment of the Most Great Peace, and the one agency for the unification of the world, and the proclamation of the reign of righteousness and justice upon the earth.   —Shoghi Effendi   **102**

Who can doubt that such a consummation—the coming of age of the human race—must signalize, in its turn, the inauguration of a world civilization such as no mortal eye hath ever beheld or human mind conceived? Who is it that can imagine the lofty standard which such a civilization, as it unfolds itself, is destined to attain? Who can measure the heights to which human intelligence, liberated from its shackles, will soar? Who can visualize the realms which the human spirit, vitalized by the outpouring light of Bahá'u'lláh, shining in the plenitude of its glory, will discover?

—Shoghi Effendi   **103**

The age has dawned when human fellowship will become a reality.

The century has come when all religions shall be unified.

The dispensation is at hand when all nations shall enjoy the blessings of international peace.

The cycle has arrived when racial prejudice will be abandoned by tribes and peoples of the world.

The epoch has begun wherein all native lands will be conjoined in one great human family.

For all mankind shall dwell in peace and security beneath the shelter of the great tabernacle of the one living God.

—'Abdu'l-Bahá   104

The Sun of Truth hath risen above the horizon of this world and cast down its beams of guidance. Eternal grace is never interrupted, and a fruit of that everlasting grace is universal peace. Rest thou assured that in this era of the spirit, the Kingdom of Peace will raise up its tabernacle on the summits of the world, and the commandments of the Prince of Peace will so dominate the arteries and nerves of every people as to draw into His sheltering shade all the nations on earth. From springs of love and truth and unity will the true Shepherd give His sheep to drink.   —'Abdu'l-Bahá   105

Then will all humankind . . . be gathered in a single homeland. Then will conflict and dissension vanish from the face of the earth, then will mankind be cradled in love for the beauty of the All-Glorious. Discord will change to accord, dissension to unison. The roots of malevolence will be torn out, the basis of aggression destroyed. The bright rays of union will obliterate the darkness of limitations, and the splendors of heaven will make the human heart to be even as a mine veined richly with the love of God.   —'Abdu'l-Bahá   106

That all nations should become one in faith and all men as brothers; that the bonds of affection and unity between the sons of men should be strengthened; that diversity of religion should cease, and differences of race be annulled—what harm is there in this? . . . Yet so it shall be; these fruitless strifes, these ruinous wars shall pass away, and the "Most Great Peace" shall come. . . .   —Bahá'u'lláh   107

Part Three

PRAYERS
FOR
ACHIEVING
PEACE

Chapter 7

Prayers for Peace

O THOU Who art the Lord of Lords! I testify that Thou art the Lord of all creation, and the Educator of all beings, visible and invisible. I bear witness that Thy power hath encompassed the entire universe, and that the hosts of the earth can never dismay Thee, nor can the dominion of all peoples and nations deter Thee from executing Thy purpose. I confess that Thou hast no desire except the regeneration of the whole world, and the establishment of the unity of its peoples, and the salvation of all them that dwell therein.

—*Bahá'u'lláh* **1**

GLORY to Thee, O God, for Thy manifestation of love to mankind! O Thou Who art our Life and Light, guide Thy servants in Thy way, and make us rich in Thee and free from all save Thee.

O God, teach us Thy Oneness and give us a realization of Thy Unity, that we may see no one save Thee. Thou art the Merciful and the Giver of bounty!

O God, create in the hearts of Thy beloved the fire of Thy love, that it may consume the thought of everything save Thee.

Reveal to us, O God, Thine exalted eternity—that Thou hast ever been and wilt ever be, and that there is no God save Thee. Verily, in Thee will we find comfort and strength.

—*Bahá'u'lláh* **2**

O MY God! O my God! Unite the hearts of Thy servants, and reveal to them Thy great purpose. May they follow Thy commandments and abide in Thy law. Help them, O God, in their endeavor, and grant them strength to serve Thee. O God! Leave them not to themselves, but guide their steps by the light of Thy knowledge, and cheer their hearts by Thy love. Verily, Thou art their Helper and their Lord.

—Bahá'u'lláh **3**

MAGNIFIED be Thy Name, O God. Thine in truth are the Kingdoms of Creation and Revelation, and verily in our Lord have we placed our whole trust. All praise be unto Thee, O God; Thou art the Maker of the heavens and the earth and that which is between them, and Thou in truth art the supreme Ruler, the Fashioner, the All-Wise. Glorified art Thou, O Lord! Thou wilt surely gather mankind for the Day of whose coming there is no doubt—the Day whereon everyone shall appear before Thee and find life in Thee. This is the Day of the One true God—the Day Thou shalt bring about as Thou pleasest through the power of Thy behest.

Thou art the Sovereign, the wondrous Creator, the Mighty, the Best Beloved. *—The Báb* **4**

O THOU compassionate Lord, Thou Who art generous and able! We are servants of Thine sheltered beneath Thy providence. Cast Thy glance of favor upon us. Give light to our eyes, hearing to our ears, and understanding and love to our hearts. Render our souls joyous and happy through Thy glad tidings. O Lord! Point out to us the pathway of Thy kingdom and resuscitate all of us through the breaths of the Holy Spirit. Bestow upon us life everlasting and confer upon us never-ending honor. Unify mankind and illumine the world of humanity. May we all follow Thy pathway, long for Thy good pleasure and seek the mysteries of Thy kingdom. O God! Unite us and connect our hearts with Thy indissoluble bond. Verily, Thou art the Giver, Thou art the Kind One and Thou art the Almighty. *— 'Abdu'l-Bahá* **5**

O Thou kind Lord! O Thou Who art generous and merciful!
We are the servants of Thy threshold and are gathered
beneath the sheltering shadow of Thy divine unity. The sun
of Thy mercy is shining upon all, and the clouds of Thy
bounty shower upon all. Thy gifts encompass all, Thy loving
providence sustains all, Thy protection overshadows all,
and the glances of Thy favor are cast upon all. O Lord! Grant
Thine infinite bestowals, and let the light of Thy guidance
shine. Illumine the eyes, gladden the hearts with abiding joy.
Confer a new spirit upon all people and bestow upon them
eternal life. Unlock the gates of true understanding and
let the light of faith shine resplendent. Gather all people
beneath the shadow of Thy bounty and cause them to unite in
harmony, so that they may become as the rays of one sun, as
the waves of one ocean, and as the fruit of one tree. May they
drink from the same fountain. May they be refreshed by the
same breeze. May they receive illumination from the same
source of light. Thou art the Giver, the Merciful, the
Omnipotent.   —'Abdu'l-Bahá **6**

O my God! O my God! Verily, I invoke Thee and supplicate
before Thy threshold, asking Thee that all Thy mercies
may descend upon these souls. Specialize them for Thy favor
and Thy truth.

    O Lord! Unite and bind together the hearts, join in
accord all the souls, and exhilarate the spirits through the
signs of Thy sanctity and oneness. O Lord! Make these faces
radiant through the light of Thy oneness. Strengthen the loins
of Thy servants in the service of Thy kingdom.

    O Lord, Thou possessor of infinite mercy! O Lord of
forgiveness and pardon! Forgive our sins, pardon our
shortcomings, and cause us to turn to the kingdom of Thy
clemency, invoking the kingdom of might and power, humble
at Thy shrine and submissive before the glory of Thine
evidences.

    O Lord God! Make us as waves of the sea, as flowers of

the garden, united, agreed through the bounties of Thy love.
O Lord! Dilate the breasts through the signs of Thy oneness,
and make all mankind as stars shining from the same
height of glory, as perfect fruits growing upon Thy tree of life.
  Verily, Thou art the Almighty, the Self-Subsistent, the
Giver, the Forgiving, the Pardoner, the Omniscient, the One
Creator.   —'Abdu'l-Bahá 7

O DIVINE Providence! This assemblage is composed of Thy
friends who are attracted to Thy beauty and are set ablaze by
the fire of Thy love. Turn these souls into heavenly angels,
resuscitate them through the breath of Thy Holy Spirit, grant
them eloquent tongues and resolute hearts, bestow upon
them heavenly power and merciful susceptibilities, cause
them to become the promulgators of the oneness of mankind
and the cause of love and concord in the world of humanity,
so that the perilous darkness of ignorant prejudice may
vanish through the light of the Sun of Truth, this dreary world
may become illumined, this material realm may absorb the
rays of the world of spirit, these different colors may
merge into one color and the melody of praise may rise to the
kingdom of Thy sanctity.
  Verily, Thou art the Omnipotent and the Almighty!
                                                         —'Abdu'l-Bahá 8

O THOU kind God! In the utmost state of humility and
submission do we entreat and supplicate at Thy threshold,
seeking Thine endless confirmations and illimitable
assistance. O Thou Lord! Regenerate these souls, and confer
upon them a new life. Animate the spirits, inform the
hearts, open the eyes, and make the ears attentive. From
Thine ancient treasury confer a new being and animus, and
from Thy preexistent abode assist them to attain to new
confirmations.
  O God! Verily, the world is in need of reformation.

Bestow upon it a new existence. Give it newness of thoughts, and reveal unto it heavenly sciences. Breathe into it a fresh spirit, and grant unto it a holier and higher purpose.

O God! Verily, Thou hast made this century radiant, and in it Thou hast manifested Thy merciful effulgence. Thou hast effaced the darkness of superstitions and permitted the light of assurance to shine. O God! Grant that these servants may be acceptable at Thy threshold. Reveal a new heaven, and spread out a new earth for habitation. Let a new Jerusalem descend from on high. Bestow new thoughts, new life upon mankind. Endow souls with new perceptions, and confer upon them new virtues. Verily, Thou art the Almighty, the Powerful. Thou art the Giver, the Generous.

—'Abdu'l-Bahá **9**

O GOD! Thou Who art kind. Verily, certain souls have gathered in this meeting turning to Thee with their hearts and spirits. They are seeking the everlasting bounty. They are in need of Thine infinite mercy.

O Lord! Remove the veils from their eyes, and dispel the darkness of ignorance. Confer upon them the light of knowledge and wisdom. Illumine these contrite hearts with the radiance of the Sun of Reality. Make these eyes perceptive through witnessing the lights of Thy sovereignty. Suffer these spirits to rejoice through the great glad tidings, and receive these souls into Thy supreme Kingdom.

O Lord! Verily, we are weak; make us mighty. We are poor; assist us from the treasury of Thy munificence. We are dead; resuscitate us through the breath of the Holy Spirit. We lack patience in tests and in long-suffering; permit us to attain the lights of oneness.

O Lord! Make this assemblage the cause of upraising the standard of the oneness of the world of humanity, and confirm these souls so that they may become the promoters of international peace.

O Lord! Verily, the people are veiled and in a state of

contention with each other, shedding the blood and
destroying the possessions of each other. Throughout the
world there is war and conflict. In every direction there
is strife, bloodshed and ferocity.

O Lord! Guide human souls in order that they may turn
away from warfare and battle, that they may become loving
and kind to each other, that they may enter into affiliation and
serve the oneness and solidarity of humanity.

O Lord! The horizons of the world are darkened by this
dissension. O God! Illumine them, and through the lights
of Thy love let the hearts become radiant. Through the
blessing of Thy bestowal resuscitate the spirits until every
soul shall perceive and act in accordance with Thy teachings.
Thou art the Almighty. Thou art the Omniscient. Thou art
the Seer. O Lord, be compassionate to all.   —'Abdu'l-Bahá   **10**

O THOU kind Lord! Thou hast created all humanity from
the same stock. Thou hast decreed that all shall belong to the
same household. In Thy Holy Presence they are all Thy
servants, and all mankind are sheltered beneath Thy
Tabernacle; all have gathered together at Thy Table of
Bounty; all are illumined through the light of Thy Providence.

O God! Thou art kind to all, Thou hast provided for all,
dost shelter all, conferrest life upon all. Thou hast endowed
each and all with talents and faculties, and all are submerged
in the Ocean of Thy Mercy.

O Thou kind Lord! Unite all. Let the religions agree and
make the nations one, so that they may see each other as
one family and the whole earth as one home. May they live
together in perfect harmony.

O God! Raise aloft the banner of the oneness of
mankind.

O God! Establish the Most Great Peace.

Cement Thou, O God, the hearts together.

O Thou kind Father, God! Gladden our hearts through
the fragrance of Thy love. Brighten our eyes through the Light

of Thy Guidance. Delight our ears with the melody of Thy Word, and shelter us all in the Stronghold of Thy Providence.

Thou art the Mighty and Powerful, Thou art the Forgiving and Thou art the One Who overlooketh the shortcomings of all mankind. *—'Abdu'l-Bahá* **11**

Appendix

Appendix

The Bahá'í Faith

Firuz Kazemzadeh

BAHÁ'Í FAITH is a religion founded by Mírzá Ḥu-
sayn-'Alí (1817–92; known as . . . Bahá'u'lláh, Glory of God). The
word Bahá'í derives from *bahá* ("glory, splendor") and signifies a
follower of Bahá'u'lláh. The religion stemmed from the Bábí faith—
founded in 1844 by Mírzá (Siyyid) 'Alí Muhammad of Shiraz, known
as the Báb—which emphasized the forthcoming appearance of "Him
Whom God Shall Make Manifest," a new prophet or messenger of
God. The Bábí faith in turn had sprung from Shí'ah Islám, which
believed in the forthcoming return of the 12th *imam* (successor of
Muhammad), who would renew religion and guide the faithful. This
messianic view was the basis of the teachings of the Shaykhí sect, so
named after Shaykh Aḥmad-i-Aḥsá'í. Shaykh Aḥmad and his successor, Siyyid Kázim-i-Rashtí, abandoned traditional literalism and gave
allegorical interpretations to doctrines such as resurrection, the Last
Judgment, and the return of the 12th *imam.* They and their followers expected the appearance of the Qá'im (He Who Arises, the 12th
imam) in the immediate future.

On May 22, 1844, in Shiraz, Persia, a young descendant of
Muhammad, Mírzá 'Alí Muhammad, proclaimed to a learned Shaykhí
divine, Mullá Ḥusayn-i-Bushrú'í, that he was the expected Qá'im,
whereupon Mullá Ḥusayn became the first disciple of Mírzá 'Alí
Muhammad, who assumed the title of the Báb ("gate," or channel
of grace from someone still veiled from the sight of men).

Soon the teachings of the Báb, the principal of which was the
tidings of the coming of "Him Whom God Shall Make Manifest,"

This essay on the Bahá'í Faith is reprinted with permission from
Encyclopædia Britannica, 15th edition, © 1983 by Encyclopædia Britannica, Inc. House style for the transliteration of Persian and Arabic words has
been used.

spread throughout Persia, provoking strong opposition on the part of the clergy and the government. The Báb was arrested and, after several years of incarceration, condemned to death. In 1850 he was brought to Tabriz, where he was suspended by ropes against a wall in a public square. A regiment of several hundred soldiers fired a volley. When the smoke cleared, the large crowd that had gathered at the place of execution saw ropes cut by bullets, but the Báb had disappeared. He was found unhurt in an adjacent building, calmly conversing with a disciple. The execution was repeated, this time effectively. There followed large-scale persecutions of the Bábís in which ultimately more than 20,000 people lost their lives.

History and Extent

BAHÁ'U'LLÁH, who had been an early disciple of the Báb, was arrested in connection with an unsuccessful attempt on the life of the *shah* of Persia, Násiri'd-Dín, made in August 1852 by two Bábís intent upon avenging their master. Though Bahá'u'lláh had not known of the plot, he was thrown into the Black Pit, a notorious jail in Tehran, where he became aware of his mission as a messenger of God. He was released in January 1853 and exiled to Baghdad. There Bahá'u'lláh's leadership revived the Bábí community, and an alarmed Persian government urged the Ottoman government to move both Bahá'u'lláh and the growing number of his followers farther away from Persia's borders. Before being transferred to Constantinople, Bahá'u'lláh spent 12 days in a garden on the outskirts of Baghdad, where in April 1863 he declared to a small number of Bábís that he was the messenger of God whose advent had been prophesied by the Báb. From Constantinople, where Bahá'u'lláh spent some four months, he was transferred to Adrianople. There he made a public proclamation of his mission in letters ("tablets") addressed to the rulers of Persia, Turkey, Russia, Prussia, Austria, and Britain, to the pope, and to the Christian and Muslim clergy collectively.

An overwhelming majority of the Bábís acknowledged Bahá'u'lláh's claim and thenceforth became known as Bahá'ís. A small minority followed Bahá'u'lláh's half brother, Mírzá Yaḥyá Ṣubḥ-i-Azal, creating a temporary breach within the ranks of the Bábís. Embittered by his failure to win more than a handful of adherents,

Mírzá Yaḥyá, assisted by his supporters, provoked the Turkish government into exiling Bahá'u'lláh to Akka ('Akko, Acre), Palestine. He became, however, a victim of his own intrigues and was himself exiled to Cyprus.

For almost two years Bahá'u'lláh, his family, and a number of disciples were confined in army barracks converted into a jail. One of his sons and several companions died. When the severity of the incarceration abated, Bahá'u'lláh was permitted to reside within the walls of Akka and later in a mansion near the town. Before his life ended in 1892, Bahá'u'lláh saw his religion spread beyond Persia and the Ottoman Empire to the Caucasus, Turkistan, India, Burma, Egypt, and the Sudan.

Bahá'u'lláh appointed his eldest son, 'Abdu'l-Bahá ("Servant of the Glory," 1844–1921), as the leader of the Bahá'í community and the authorized interpreter of his teachings. 'Abdu'l-Bahá not only administered the affairs of the movement from Palestine but also actively engaged in spreading the faith, travelling in Africa, Europe, and America from 1910 to 1913. 'Abdu'l-Bahá appointed his eldest grandson, Shoghi Effendi Rabbaní (1897–1957), as his successor, Guardian of the Cause, and authorized interpreter of the teachings of Bahá'u'lláh, thus assuring the continued unity of the believers.

During 'Abdu'l-Bahá's ministry, Bahá'í groups were established in North Africa, the Far East, Australia, and the United States. Since then the movement has spread to virtually every country in the world, with particularly large and vigorous communities in Africa, Iran, India, the United States, and certain areas of Southeast Asia and the Pacific. . . . Since the 1960s the Bahá'í faith has undergone a period of rapid expansion.* By 1985 there were 4,341,000 Bahá'ís residing in more than 115,900 localities throughout the world, with 148 national spiritual assemblies (national governing bodies) and 29,664 local spiritual assemblies. Bahá'í literature has been translated into 739 languages.

---

*The remainder of this paragraph has been revised to reflect current membership statistics.—ED.

Sacred Literature

BAHÁ'Í sacred literature consists of the total corpus of the writings of Bahá'u'lláh and their interpretation and amplification in the writings of 'Abdu'l-Bahá and Shoghi Effendi. Bahá'u'lláh's literary legacy of more than 100 works includes the *Kitáb-i-Aqdas* ("The Most Holy Book"), the repository of his laws; the *Kitáb-i-Íqán (The Book of Certitude)*, an exposition of essential teachings on the nature of God and religion; *The Hidden Words,* a collection of brief utterances aimed at the edification of men's "souls and the rectification of their conduct"; *The Seven Valleys,* a mystic treatise that "describes the seven stages which the soul of the seeker must needs traverse ere it can attain the object of its existence"; *Epistle to the Son of the Wolf,* his last major work; as well as innumerable prayers, meditations, exhortations, and epistles. The Bahá'ís believe that the writings of Bahá'u'lláh are inspired and constitute God's revelation for this age.

Religious and Social Tenets

BAHÁ'U'LLÁH teaches that God is unknowable and "beyond every human attribute, such as corporeal existence, ascent and descent, egress and regress." "No tie of direct intercourse can possibly bind Him to His creatures. . . . No sign can indicate His presence or His absence. . . ." Human inability to grasp the divine essence does not lead to agnosticism, since God has chosen to reveal himself through his messengers, among them Abraham, Moses, Zoroaster, Buddha, Jesus, Muḥammad, and the Báb, who "are one and all the Exponents on earth of Him Who is the central Orb of the universe. . . ." The messengers, or, in Bahá'í terminology, "manifestations," are viewed as occupying two "stations," or occurring in two aspects. The first "is the station of pure abstraction and essential unity," in which one may speak of the oneness of the messengers of God because all are manifestations of his will and exponents of his word. This does not constitute syncretism since "the other station is the station of distinction. . . . In this respect, each manifestation of God hath a distinct individuality, a definitely prescribed mission. . . ." Thus, while the essence of all religions is one, each has specific features that correspond to the needs of a given time and place and to the level of civilization in which a manifestation appears. Since religious truth is considered relative and revelation progressive and continuing, the Bahá'ís maintain that other manifestations will appear in the future, though not, according to Bahá'u'lláh, before the expiration of a full thousand years from his own revelation.

In Bahá'í teachings God is, and has always been, the Creator. There was, therefore, never a time when the cosmos did not exist. Man was created through God's love: "Veiled in My immemorial being and in the ancient eternity of My essence, I knew My love for thee; therefore I created thee." The purpose of man's existence as taught by Bahá'u'lláh is to know and to worship God and "to carry forward an ever-advancing civilization. . . ." Man, whom Bahá'u'lláh calls "the noblest and most perfect of all created things," is endowed with an immortal soul, which, after separation from the body, enters a new form of existence. Heaven and hell are symbolic of the soul's relationship to God. Nearness to God results in good deeds and gives infinite joy, while remoteness from him leads to evil and suffering. To fulfill his high purpose, man must recognize the messenger of God within whose dispensation he lives and "observe every ordinance of him who is the desire of the world. These twin duties are inseparable. Neither is acceptable without the other."

Civilization, Bahá'u'lláh teaches, has evolved to the point where unity of mankind has become the paramount necessity. The Bahá'í faith, in the words of Shoghi Effendi,

> proclaims the necessity and the inevitability of the unification of mankind, asserts that it is gradually approaching, and claims that nothing short of the transmuting spirit of God, working through His chosen Mouthpiece in this day, can ultimately succeed in bringing it about. It, moreover, enjoins upon its followers the primary duty of an unfettered search after truth, condemns all manner of prejudice and superstition, declares the purpose of religion to be the promotion of amity and concord, proclaims its essential harmony with science, and recognizes it as the foremost agency for the pacification and the orderly progress of human society. It unequivocally maintains the principle of equal rights, opportunities and privileges for men and women, insists on compulsory education, eliminates extremes of poverty and wealth, abolishes the institution of priesthood, prohibits slavery, asceticism, mendicancy, and monasticism, prescribes monog-

amy, discourages divorce, emphasizes the necessity of strict obedience to one's government, extols any work performed in the spirit of
service to the level of worship, urges either the creation or the selection of an auxiliary international language, and delineates the outlines of those institutions that must establish and perpetuate the
general peace of mankind.

Practices

MEMBERSHIP in the Bahá'í community is open to all who profess
faith in Bahá'u'lláh and accept his teachings. There are no initiation
ceremonies, no sacraments, and no clergy. Every Bahá'í, however, is
under the spiritual obligation to pray daily; to fast 19 days a year,
going without food or drink from sunrise to sunset; to abstain totally
from narcotics, alcohol, or any substances that affect the mind; to
practice monogamy; to obtain the consent of parents to marriage;
and to attend the Nineteen Day Feast on the first day of each month
of the Bahá'í calendar. The Nineteen Day Feast, originally instituted
by the Báb, brings together the Bahá'ís of a given locality for prayer,
the reading of scriptures, the discussion of community activities,
and the enjoyment of one another's company. The feasts are designed to ensure universal participation in the affairs of the community and the cultivation of the spirit of brotherhood and fellowship. Eventually, Bahá'ís in every locality plan to erect a house of
worship around which will be grouped such institutions as a home
for the aged, an orphanage, a school, and a hospital. By the early
1980s there were houses of worship in Wilmette, Illinois; Frankfurt
am Main, West Germany; Kampala, Uganda; Sydney, Australia; and
Panama City, Panama. Houses of worship were under construction
in New Delhi, India, and in Apia, Western Samoa.* In the temples
there is no preaching; services consist of recitation of the scriptures
of all religions.

The Bahá'ís use a calendar established by the Báb and con-

---

*The House of Worship in Western Samoa was dedicated in 1984; the
House of Worship in India is to be dedicated sometime between December
1986 and February 1987.—ED.

firmed by Bahá'u'lláh, in which the year is divided into 19 months of 19 days each, with the addition of four intercalary days (five in leap years). The year begins on the first day of spring, March 21, which is a holy day. Other holy days on which work is suspended are the days commemorating the declaration of Bahá'u'lláh's mission (April 21, April 29, and May 2), the declaration of the mission of the Báb (May 23), the birth of Bahá'u'lláh (November 12), the birth of the Báb (October 20), the passing of Bahá'u'lláh (May 29), and the martyrdom of the Báb (July 9).

Organization and Administration

THE Bahá'í community is governed according to general principles proclaimed by Bahá'u'lláh and through institutions created by him that were elaborated and expanded by 'Abdu'l-Bahá. These principles and institutions constitute the Bahá'í administrative order, which the followers of the faith believe to be a blueprint of a future world order. The governance of the Bahá'í community begins on the local level with the election of a local spiritual assembly. The electoral process excludes parties or factions, nominations, and campaigning for office. The local spiritual assembly has jurisdiction over all local affairs of the Bahá'í community. Each year Bahá'ís elect delegates to a national convention that elects a national spiritual assembly with jurisdiction over the entire country. All national spiritual assemblies of the world periodically constitute themselves an international convention and elect the supreme governing body known as the Universal House of Justice. In accordance with Bahá'u'lláh's writings, the Universal House of Justice functions as the supreme administrative, legislative, and judicial body of the Bahá'í commonwealth. It applies the laws promulgated by Bahá'u'lláh and legislates on matters not covered in the sacred texts. The seat of the Universal House of Justice is in Haifa, Israel, in the immediate vicinity of the shrines of the Báb and 'Abdu'l-Bahá, and near the shrine of Bahá'u'lláh at Bahjí near Akka.

There also exist in the Bahá'í faith appointive institutions, such as the Hands of the Cause of God and the continental counselors. The former were created by Bahá'u'lláh and later assigned by 'Abdu'l-Bahá the functions of propagating the faith and protecting the community. The Hands of the Cause appointed by Shoghi Effendi in his lifetime now serve under the direction of the Universal House of Justice. The continental counsellors perform the same functions as the Hands of the Cause but are appointed by the Universal House of Justice. Assisting the counsellors in advising, inspiring, and encouraging Bahá'í institutions and individuals are auxiliary boards appointed by the counsellors and serving under their direction.

Bibliography

THE classic introduction to the Bahá'í faith, giving a general view of its history and teachings, is J. E. ESSLEMONT, *Bahá'u'lláh and the New Era*, 4th rev. ed. (1980). The most recent survey of the Bahá'í faith is WILLIAM S. HATCHER and J. DOUGLAS MARTIN, *The Bahá'í Faith: The Emerging Global Religion*, 1st ed. (1984). GEORGE TOWNSHEND, *The Promise of All Ages*, 3rd rev. ed. (1973), approaches the Bahá'í faith from a background of Christianity. The history of the Bahá'í faith has been studied by many scholars, but the most detailed and poetic account is *The Dawn-Breakers* by MUHAMMAD-I-ZARANDÍ, surnamed Nabíl, trans. and ed. by SHOGHI EFFENDI (1932, reprinted 1974; 2nd ed., 1953); the latter's *God Passes By* (1944, reprinted 1974), recounts to the end of the first Bahá'í century. The most important source for the study of the Bahá'í faith is the writings of Bahá'u'lláh and their interpretation and application by 'Abdu'l-Bahá and Shoghi Effendi. Several of Bahá'u'lláh's major works are available in excellent English translations. The *Kitáb-i-Íqán* (1950, reprinted 1981) is indispensable for understanding Bahá'í views of God, progressive revelation, and the nature of religion. *The Hidden Words* (1954, reprinted 1980) and *The Seven Valleys and the Four Valleys*, 3rd rev. ed. (1978), deal with man's spiritual life and the states of the soul. *Gleanings from the Writings of Bahá'u'lláh*, 2nd ed. (1976) is a representative selection. 'Abdu'l-Bahá's *Some Answered Questions*, 5th rev. ed. (1981), is a record of table talks on various religious themes. *The Secret of Divine Civilization*, 2nd ed. (1970) uses the problem of modernization and development to set forth the spiritual prerequisites of true progress and civilization. SHOGHI EFFENDI's writings include *The World Order of Bahá'u'lláh,*

2nd rev. ed. (1974), an exposition of principles for the establishment of universal peace and world civilization; and *The Promised
Day Is Come,* 2nd ed. (1980), an examination of the effects of
manifestation upon the modern world.

Glossary

'Abdu'l-Bahá: 1844–1921. The eldest son of Bahá'u'lláh, the Center of His Covenant, and the appointed interpreter of His writings. See the appendix for details on His life.

Báb, the: 1819–50. The Prophet-Herald of Bahá'u'lláh. See the appendix for details on His life.

Bahá'í: (1) A follower of Bahá'u'lláh. (2) Of or pertaining to Bahá'u'lláh or His Faith.

Bahá'í Faith: An independent world religion that "proclaims the necessity and the inevitability of the unification of mankind. . . . It, moreover, enjoins upon its followers the primary duty of an unfettered search after truth, condemns all manner of prejudice and superstition, declares the purpose of religion to be the promotion of amity and concord, proclaims its essential harmony with science, and recognizes it as the foremost agency for the pacification and the orderly progress of human society. It unequivocally maintains the principle of equal rights, opportunities and privileges for men and women, insists on compulsory education, eliminates extremes of poverty and wealth, abolishes the institution of priesthood, prohibits slavery, asceticism, mendicancy and monasticism, prescribes monogamy, discourages divorce, emphasizes the necessity of strict obedience to one's government, exalts any work performed in the spirit of service to the level of worship, urges either the creation or the selection of an auxiliary international language, and delineates the outlines of those institutions that must establish and perpetuate the general peace of mankind." See the appendix for more information.

Bahá'u'lláh: 1817–92. The Prophet-Founder of the Bahá'í Faith. See the appendix for details on His life.

Concourse on High: The company of holy souls of the spiritual world.

Dayspring: The place where the sun rises: a symbol for the Manifestations of God.

Daystar: The sun: a symbol for the Manifestation of God or God Himself, depending on the context.

Dispensation: A period of history beginning with the appearance of a Manifestation of God and ending with the coming of the next Manifestation.

Kingdom: The Kingdom of God.

Lesser Peace: The first of two major stages in which Bahá'ís believe peace will be established. The Lesser Peace will come about through a binding treaty among the nations for the political unification of the world. It will involve the boundaries of every nation's being clearly fixed, the size of their armaments strictly limited, the principles underlying the relations of governments toward one another definitely laid down, and all international agreements and obligations ascertained. See also "Most Great Peace" below.

Manifestation (of God): A Messenger of God through Whom God's perfections and attributes are expressed. Examples of such Manifestations are Abraham, Moses, Zoroaster, Buddha, Jesus Christ, Muhammad, the Báb, and Bahá'u'lláh.

Most Great Peace: The second of two major stages in which Bahá'ís believe peace will be established. The Most Great Peace will be the practical consequence of the spiritualization of the world and the fusion of all its races, creeds, classes, and nations. Such a peace will rest on the foundation of, and be preserved by, the ordinances of God. See also "Lesser Peace" above.

Pen of Glory: Bahá'u'lláh, the revealer of the Word of God for this Dispensation.

Pen of the Most High: See "Pen of Glory."

Qur'án (Koran): The holy book of Islám, revealed by Muhammad.

Shoghi Effendi: 1897–1957. The eldest great-grandson of Bahá'u'lláh and the Guardian of the Bahá'í Faith, a position to which he was appointed by the Will and Testament of 'Abdu'l-Bahá.

Sun of Truth: God, or His Manifestation, depending upon the context.

Supreme Concourse: The company of holy souls of the spiritual world.

Universal House of Justice: The supreme governing and legislative body of the Bahá'í Faith. Elected quinquennially at an international convention, the Universal House of Justice gives spiritual guidance to and directs the administrative activities of the worldwide Bahá'í community.

References

Abbreviations Used

ABC	*'Abdu'l-Bahá in Canada*
ABL	*'Abdu'l-Bahá in London*
ADJ	*The Advent of Divine Justice*
BA	*Bahá'í Administration*
BE	*Bahá'í Education*
BNE	*Bahá'u'lláh and the New Era*
BPUK	*Bahá'í Prayers*, U.K. edition
BPUS	*Bahá'í Prayers*, U.S. edition
CC	*Consultation: A Compilation*
ESW	*Epistle to the Son of the Wolf*
FWU	*Foundations of World Unity*
GWB	*Gleanings from the Writings of Bahá'u'lláh*
HWA	*The Hidden Words of Bahá'u'lláh* (Arabic)
HWP	*The Hidden Words of Bahá'u'lláh* (Persian)
KI	*Kitáb-i-Íqán: The Book of Certitude*
MUHJ	*Messages from The Universal House of Justice*
NT	New translation provided by the Universal House of Justice
PB	*The Proclamation of Bahá'u'lláh to the Kings and Leaders of the World*
PC	"Peace" (Unpublished compilation, August 1985)
PDIC	*The Promised Day Is Come*
PM	*Prayers and Meditations*
PT	*Paris Talks*
PUP	*The Promulgation of Universal Peace*
PWP	*The Promise of World Peace*
SAQ	*Some Answered Questions*
SCKA	*A Synopsis and Codification of the Kitáb-i-Aqdas*
SDC	*The Secret of Divine Civilization*
SF	*Spiritual Foundations*
SV	*The Seven Valleys and the Four Valleys*
SW	*Star of the West*
SWAB	*Selections from the Writings of 'Abdu'l-Bahá*

SWB   *Selections from the Writings of the Báb*
TAB   *Tablets of Abdul-Baha Abbas*
TB   *Tablets of Bahá'u'lláh Revealed after the Kitáb-i-Aqdas*
TDP   *Tablets of the Divine Plan*
WC   "Women" (Unpublished compilation, January 1986)
WOB   *The World Order of Bahá'u'lláh*
WP   *Waging Peace*
WT   *Will and Testament of 'Abdu'l-Bahá*

PART ONE: A FRAMEWORK FOR PEACE
1 The Promise of World Peace

1 PWP 13–38

PART TWO: THE PROMISE AND THE
CHALLENGE
2 From Adolescence to Adulthood: Civilization
Comes of Age

1 TB 163–64	17 PUP 11	33 PDIC 117
2 SWAB 318	18 PUP 12	34 GWB 7
3 SWAB 2	19 SWAB 283–84	35 GWB 6
4 SWAB 293	20 SF 14	36 GWB 340
5 PT 28–29	21 WOB 190	37 PUP 229
6 PUP 102–03	22 WOB 193–94	38 PUP 228–29
7 WOB 190	23 PUP 19	39 SWAB 285–86
8 WOB 36	24 PT 60	40 PDIC 118–19
9 GWB 216–17	25 TB 176–77	41 SWAB 31–32
10 SWB 129	26 PUP 294–95	42 PDIC 122–23
11 PUP 123–24	27 SWAB 287–88	43 PDIC 116
12 SW 18:345	28 SAQ 235–36	44 PDIC 117–18
13 GWB 342–43	29 SDC 67	45 BA 146–47
14 TB 69	30 PUP 451–52	46 PUP 125–26
15 PUP 102	31 SDC 3–4	47 TB 220
16 PUP 109	32 TB 174	

3 The Spiritual Roots of Peace

1 GWB 194	5 SDC 2–3	9 PUP 302–03
2 PUP 262–63	6 TB 72	10 PUP 178
3 PT 41–43	7 GWB 158–59	11 PT 72
4 PUP 49, 50, 51	8 SV 35	12 PUP 186

13 PUP 90–91
14 PUP 149
15 HWA 11
16 TB 156
17 GWB 174
18 GWB 50
19 GWB 47–48
20 PUP 173–74
21 SWAB 50
22 TB 161
23 GWB 79–81
24 GWB 67
25 GWB 299
26 SAQ 236
27 KI 34
28 GWB 68
29 PUP 278
30 PUP 59
31 GWB 331
32 PUP 361
33 GWB 289
34 SDC 71–72, 73–74
35 PUP 400–01
36 PUP 465–66
37 SDC 97–99
38 PUP 12
39 SWAB 174
40 PDIC 113
41 TB 64

42 PDIC 112–13
43 SWAB 302–03
44 PT 97–98
45 PT 31, 32–33
46 PUP 221
47 PUP 184
48 PUP 161
49 WOB 187
50 WOB 186
51 PDIC 113–15
52 PT 115–16
53 TB 125
54 TB 166
55 KI 15
56 GWB 83
57 KI 82
58 KI 165–66
59 PT 45–46
60 PUP 158
61 PUP 32
62 PUP 231
63 PT 141–44
64 PUP 231
65 PUP 374
66 PT 144–45
67 PUP 107
68 PUP 374
69 SAQ 137
70 PT 146

71 GWB 82
72 GWB 72
73 GWB 26–27
74 GWB 82–83
75 ESW 12
76 PUP 337–40
77 PUP 144
78 KI 53
79 TB 86
80 GWB 52
81 GWB 78–79
82 GWB 52, 53
83 SWAB 51–52
84 SWAB 59
85 PUP 403–05
86 PUP 197
87 PUP 115
88 PUP 95–96
89 TB 58
90 KI 91
91 GWB 203–05
92 KI 3–4
93 PUP 293
94 PUP 291
95 PUP 180
96 PUP 279–80
97 PUP 151–52
98 PUP 379–80

4 Preparing the Path to World Order

1 GWB 149
2 GWB 250
3 PUP 121
4 SAQ 248, 250
5 PT 79–80
6 PT 16–17
7 PT 80–81
8 SDC 66–67
9 PT 87
10 ADJ 37
11 ADJ 37
12 ADJ 37
13 ADJ 37

14 ADJ 37
15 ADJ 37
16 PUP 299
17 ADJ 37–38
18 PUP 427
19 NT
20 ADJ 38
21 ADJ 38
22 ADJ 38
23 PUP 113
24 PT 53
25 ADJ 38–39
26 NT TAB 124–25

27 ADJ 39
28 ADJ 39
29 ADJ 39
30 ADJ 40–41
31 PWP 25
32 SWAB 113
33 PUP 57
34 TB 64
35 HWA 57
36 SDC 24–25
37 PT 131–32
38 PT 151
39 PT 153–54

40 PUP 107
41 SAQ 273–76
42 PWP 25
43 HWP 54
44 TB 71
45 GWB 314–15
46 SWAB 115
47 PUP 238–39
48 PUP 132
49 FWU 42–43
50 TB 67–68
51 TB 167
52 PUP 299
53 SWAB 300
54 SWAB 300–01
55 PUP 354–55
56 PUP 118
57 WOB 41–42
58 PWP 25–26
59 GWB 217
60 SCKA 25
61 GWB 95
62 GWB 287–88
63 PUP 298
64 PUP 265–66
65 PUP 393
66 PUP 151
67 PT 119–22, 123
68 PT 129
69 PUP 152
70 PDIC 107–08
71 PWP 26
72 PUP 391
73 GWB 217
74 WC 16
75 WC 1
76 SWAB 79–80
77 PUP 133

78 PT 182–83
79 PT 162
80 PUP 223
81 PUP 76–77
82 PUP 76, 77
83 PUP 134
84 PUP 375
85 PUP 300
86 PUP 136–37
87 PUP 281
88 PUP 133–34
89 ABL 102–03
90 PUP 174, 175
91 PUP 108
92 PUP 134–35
93 BNE 149
94 PUP 283–84
95 PWP 11–12
96 PT 162, 163
97 PUP 284
98 WC 1
99 TB 161–62
100 BE 5
101 BE 5
102 TB 51–52
103 TB 168–69
104 SDC 39
105 SDC 18
106 SDC 109, 111–12
107 SAQ 214
108 SAQ 7–8
109 PUP 300
110 TB 90
111 SWAB 129
112 SWAB 126–27
113 SWAB 130–31
114 SWAB 129
115 SWAB 136–37

116 SWAB 135–36
117 PUP 53–54
118 PWP 27
119 SWAB 69
120 SDC 103
121 TB 127
122 GWB 173
123 TB 165–66
124 PT 155–56
125 PUP 232–33
126 PUP 60–61
127 PWP 27
128 PUP 300
129 ADJ 24–25
130 GWB 206
131 KI 120
132 PUP 60
133 SDC 60–62
134 TDP 42
135 SWAB 286–87
136 SWAB 84
137 PUP 169
138 PUP 294
139 PUP 233
140 SWAB 285
141 GWB 93–94
142 TB 36
143 TB 57
144 ADJ 23
145 GWB 317
146 TB 171
147 HWA 8
148 SWAB 206
149 SDC 59–60
150 SDC 23–24
151 SWAB 282
152 ADJ 31
153 HWA 33

5   Constructing a Peaceful and Global Civilization

1 GWB 214
2 ESW 55–56
3 HWP 48
4 PUP 297

5 SWAB 248
6 PUP 66
7 PUP 129
8 PUP 266–67

9 PUP 305
10 SWAB 36
11 WOB 42–43
12 HWA 68

13 PUP 469
14 PUP 322
15 NT
16 PUP 297–98
17 SWAB 299
18 SWAB 289
19 SWAB 247
20 SWAB 248
21 PT 147–51
22 PUP 468
23 PUP 316
24 SWAB 249, 250
25 TB 23
26 GWB 253–54
27 PUP 156–57
28 SDC 70–71
29 WP 43–44
30 SW 5:115–17
31 ABC 50–51
32 TB 165
33 ESW 31
34 ESW 30–31
35 SW 7:136
36 PUP 98–99
37 SWAB 279–80

38 SDC 64–66
39 PDIC 121–22
40 PUP 376
41 TB 127
42 TB 164
43 ADJ 28
44 TB 166–67
45 TB 36–37
46 ADJ 28
47 TB 126
48 PT 157–58
49 SDC 39
50 PT 159–60
51 PT 154
52 PT 155
53 SDC 70
54 TB 164–65
55 TB 66–67
56 TB 151
57 PB 8–9
58 PB 34
59 SDC 23
60 NT TAB 403–04
61 SDC 23
62 SDC 107–08

63 PB 67
64 TB 92–93
65 CC 3
66 CC 3
67 CC 8
68 CC 8–9
69 PUP 72–73
70 SWAB 87
71 SWAB 88
72 SWAB 87
73 CC 8
74 MUHJ 51
75 TB 168
76 CC 3
77 GWB 207
78 FWU 43
79 PUP 389
80 PUP 301
81 SWAB 249
82 NT SWAB 306–07
83 PT 155
84 WOB 40–41
85 WOB 202–04
86 PC 10
87 WOB 41

6 Securing the Basis of Human Happiness

1   GWB 215
2   GWB 286
3   TB 162
4   PUP 164
5   PUP 320–21
6   SWAB 278
7   SWAB 290–92
8   PUP 170
9   NT TAB 691
10 PUP 191
11 TB 164
12 TB 138
13 GWB 140
14 TB 36
15 SWAB 103–04
16 SWAB 1–2
17 PUP 93

18 PT 29–30
19 GWB 288
20 TB 94
21 ESW 135
22 TB 132
23 GWB 315–16
24 GWB 242
25 GWB 270–71
26 GWB 305
27 PT 80
28 SWAB 229–30
29 WT 13–14
30 SWAB 24
31 PUP 453
32 SWAB 280
33 GWB 333–34
34 ESW 122–23

35 PUP 156
36 PUP 379
37 PUP 208–09
38 SWAB 292–93
39 WOB 197–98
40 WOB 155
41 PUP 336–37
42 PUP 209
43 HWA 3
44 GWB 65
45 KI 101
46 SWAB 140
47 SAQ 195–96
48 SDC 1
49 HWP 72
50 GWB 70
51 HWA 4

52	GWB 65	71	PDIC 40–41
53	GWB 77–78	72	GWB 90–91
54	SAQ 300–01	73	PM 184
55	SAQ 79–80	74	GWB 5
56	PUP 335	75	WOB 167
57	PUP 166	76	GWB 45
58	GWB 326–27	77	GWB 10–11
59	GWB 215	78	GWB 12–13
60	GWB 290	79	ESW 144–45
61	TB 37	80	PDIC 32
62	GWB 196	81	PDIC 31
63	PUP 267	82	PUP 220–21
64	PT 113	83	PUP 153
65	PUP 325–26	84	SCKA 16
66	PUP 378	85	ESW 32–34
67	PUP 109–10	86	ESW 76–77
68	PUP 302	87	GWB 99–100
69	PUP 206	88	TB 219–20
70	PUP 115–16	89	SWAB 262–63

90	SWAB 257–58
91	PUP 120
92	SWAB 73
93	TB 243–44
94	GWB 7
95	TB 87
96	GWB 136
97	TB 84
98	SWAB 1
99	SWAB 252–53
100	WOB 169
101	WOB 205
102	WOB 19
103	WOB 206
104	PUP 370
105	SWAB 246
106	SWAB 19–20
107	PB v

PART THREE: PRAYERS FOR ACHIEVING
PEACE

7 Prayers for Peace

1	BPUK 62	5	BPUS 101	9	PUP 276
2	BPUK 60–61	6	BPUS 101–02	10	PUP 275
3	BPUS 204	7	BPUS 204–05	11	BPUS 102–03
4	SWB 176	8	BPUS 115		

Bibliography

'Abdu'l-Bahá. *'Abdu'l-Bahá in London: Addresses and Notes of Conversations.* London: Bahá'í Publishing Trust, 1982.

_____. *Foundations of World Unity: Compiled from Addresses and Tablets of 'Abdu'l-Bahá.* Wilmette, Ill.: Bahá'í Publishing Trust, 1972.

_____. *Paris Talks: Addresses Given by 'Abdu'l-Bahá in Paris in 1911.* 11th ed. London: Bahá'í Publishing Trust, 1969.

_____. *The Promulgation of Universal Peace: Talks Delivered by 'Abdu'l-Bahá during His Visit to the United States and Canada in 1912.* Compiled by Howard MacNutt. 2d ed. Wilmette, Ill.: Bahá'í Publishing Trust, 1982.

_____. *The Secret of Divine Civilization.* 3d ed. Translated by Marzieh Gail and Ali-Kuli Khan. Wilmette, Ill.: Bahá'í Publishing Trust, 1975.

_____. *Selections from the Writings of 'Abdu'l-Bahá.* Compiled by the Research Department of the Universal House of Justice. Translated by a Committee at the Bahá'í World Centre and Marzieh Gail. Haifa: Bahá'í World Centre, 1978.

_____. *Some Answered Questions.* Compiled and translated by Laura Clifford Barney. 5th ed. Wilmette, Ill.: Bahá'í Publishing Trust, 1981.

_____. *Tablets of Abdul-Baha Abbas.* 3 vols. New York: Bahai Publishing Society, 1909–16.

_____. *Tablets of the Divine Plan: Revealed by 'Abdu'l-Bahá to the North American Bahá'ís.* Rev. ed. Wilmette, Ill.: Bahá'í Publishing Trust, 1977.

_____. "Universal Peace." *Star of the West,* 5 (1 Aug. 1914), 115–18.

_____. "The Voice of Universal Peace." *Star of the West,* 18 (Feb. 1928), 343–46.

_____. *Will and Testament of 'Abdu'l-Bahá.* Wilmette, Ill.: Bahá'í Publishing Trust, 1944.

'Abdu'l-Bahá in Canada. N.p.: National Spiritual Assembly of the Bahá'ís of Canada, 1962.

285

The Báb. *Selections from the Writings of the Báb.* Compiled by the Research Department of the Universal House of Justice. Translated by Habib Taherzadeh et al. Haifa: Bahá'í World Centre, 1976.

Bahá'u'lláh. *Epistle to the Son of the Wolf.* New ed. Translated by Shoghi Effendi. Wilmette, Ill.: Bahá'í Publishing Trust, 1953.

_____. *Gleanings from the Writings of Bahá'u'lláh.* 2d ed. Translated by Shoghi Effendi. Wilmette, Ill.: Bahá'í Publishing Trust, 1976.

_____. *The Hidden Words of Bahá'u'lláh.* Translated by Shoghi Effendi. Wilmette, Ill.: Bahá'í Publishing Trust, 1939.

_____. *Kitáb-i-Íqán: The Book of Certitude.* 2d ed. Translated by Shoghi Effendi. Wilmette, Ill.: Bahá'í Publishing Trust, 1950.

_____. *Prayers and Meditations.* Translated by Shoghi Effendi. Wilmette, Ill.: Bahá'í Publishing Trust, 1938.

_____. *The Proclamation of Bahá'u'lláh to the Kings and Leaders of the World.* Haifa: Bahá'í World Centre, 1967.

_____. *The Seven Valleys and the Four Valleys.* 3d ed. Translated by Ali-Kuli Khan and Marzieh Gail. Wilmette, Ill.: Bahá'í Publishing Trust, 1978.

_____. *A Synopsis and Codification of the Kitáb-i-Aqdas: The Most Holy Book of Bahá'u'lláh.* [Compiled by the Universal House of Justice.] Haifa: Bahá'í World Centre, 1973.

_____. *Tablets of Bahá'u'lláh Revealed after the Kitáb-i-Aqdas.* Compiled by the Research Department of the Universal House of Justice. Translated by Habib Taherzadeh et al. Haifa: Bahá'í World Centre, 1978.

Bahá'u'lláh and 'Abdu'l-Bahá. "The Social Teachings of the Bahai Movement." Compiled by George O. Latimer. *Star of the West,* 7 (12 Dec. 1916), 133–39, 145–48.

Bahá'u'lláh, 'Abdu'l-Bahá, and Shoghi Effendi. *Bahá'í Education: A Compilation.* Compiled by the Research Department of the Universal House of Justice. Wilmette, Ill.: Bahá'í Publishing Trust, 1977.

_____. *Spiritual Foundations: Prayer, Meditation, and the Devotional Attitude: Extracts from the Writings of Bahá'u'lláh, 'Abdu'l-Bahá, and Shoghi Effendi.* Compiled by the Research Department of the Universal House of Justice. Wilmette, Ill.: Bahá'í Publishing Trust, 1980.

_____. *Waging Peace: Selections from the Bahá'í Writings on Universal Peace.* [Compiled by Anthony A. Lee.] Los Angeles: Kalimát, 1984.

Bahá'u'lláh, 'Abdu'l-Bahá, Shoghi Effendi, and the Universal House of Justice. *Consultation: A Compilation: Extracts from the Writings and*

Utterances of Bahá'u'lláh, 'Abdu'l-Bahá, Shoghi Effendi, and The Universal House of Justice. Compiled by the Research Department of the Universal House of Justice. Thornhill, Ontario: Bahá'í Community of Canada, 1980.

_____. "Peace." Unpublished compilation by the Research Department of the Universal House of Justice, August 1985.

_____. "Women." Unpublished compilation by the Research Department of the Universal House of Justice, January 1986.

[Bahá'u'lláh, the Báb, and 'Abdu'l-Bahá.] *Bahá'í Prayers: A Selection.* Rev. ed. London: Bahá'í Publishing Trust, 1975.

Bahá'u'lláh, the Báb, and 'Abdu'l-Bahá. *Bahá'í Prayers: A Selection of Prayers Revealed by Bahá'u'lláh, the Báb, and 'Abdu'l-Bahá.* New ed. Wilmette, Ill.: Bahá'í Publishing Trust, 1985.

Esslemont, J.E. *Bahá'u'lláh and the New Era: An Introduction to the Bahá'í Faith.* 4th rev. ed. Wilmette, Ill.: Bahá'í Publishing Trust, 1980.

Shoghi Effendi. *The Advent of Divine Justice.* Wilmette, Ill.: Bahá'í Publishing Trust, 1984.

_____. *Bahá'í Administration: Selected Messages 1922–1932.* 7th rev. ed. Wilmette, Ill.: Bahá'í Publishing Trust, 1974.

_____. *The Promised Day Is Come.* 3d ed. Wilmette, Ill.: Bahá'í Publishing Trust, 1980.

_____. *The World Order of Bahá'u'lláh: Selected Letters.* 2d ed. Wilmette, Ill.: Bahá'í Publishing Trust, 1974.

The Universal House of Justice. *Messages from The Universal House of Justice: 1968–1973.* Wilmette, Ill.: Bahá'í Publishing Trust, 1976.

_____. *The Promise of World Peace: To the Peoples of the World.* Wilmette, Ill.: Bahá'í Publishing Trust, 1985.

Index

'Abdu'l-Bahá, xi, xii, 18, 179, 250, 275
  Bahá'í groups established during ministry of, 267
  eldest son of Bahá'u'lláh, 18, 267, 275
  interpreter of teachings of Bahá'u'lláh, 18, 267, 268, 271, 272
  leader of Bahá'í community, 267
  shrine of, 271
  writings of, 272
Abraham, 32, 90, 91–92, 268
Acts. *See* Character and conduct; Deeds
Adam, 88, 103, 118, 120, 125, 148, 171
Adolescence of mankind, 5, 44, 46–47, 203
Aggression, 5, 11. *See also* Hate; War
Agriculture, 96, 109, 112, 144
Akka, 239–40, 240n, 245, 245n
Altruism. *See also* Deeds; Kindness; Philanthropy
  advantage of part of society best served by promoting advantage of whole, 122
  atrophied soul prevents, 68, 69, 100, 147, 164
  charity regarded as prince of deeds, 114–15
  cooperation and reciprocity foster, 83, 96–97, 169, 181–83
  love of world's peoples does not exclude love of own country, 122
  man has capacity to forget own interests, 18, 117, 118, 147, 217–18, 260
  man should become source of social good, 54, 109, 147–48, 215, 217, 220–22
  manifested through deeds, 99–101, 151
  mutual advancement, 100, 106
  prayers for fostering, 259–60
  Prophets of God promote, 61–62, 162–63, 217, 222
  religion inspires and is cause of, 63, 83, 164–65, 219–26
  understanding increases, 52
  will to act necessary for, 18
America, 48, 48n
  birth of nations of West, 47–48
  racism and race unity in, 108–09
Animals
  contentment of, 154–55
  justice and equality of, 104, 112, 119, 154–55
  man distinguished from, 37, 55–56, 104–05, 112, 143, 227, 232
  man is like, unless he forgets his own interests, 65, 117, 154, 234
  savagery of, 27–28, 119–20, 155
  warfare makes man more ferocious than, 127–28
Armaments. *See* War, weapons of
Arts, the, 31, 110, 145, 227
  actions cause development of, 101
  children should study arts that ensure progress, 141, 145
  crudeness of, in past, 96
  emanations of human mind, 53–54
  impossible for artist not to love own production, 164
  reflect Divine Image, 227
  reformation of, in this century, 85, 96, 249

Arts, the *(continued)*
    source of, 54
    wealth praiseworthy if acquired
        by, 109–10
    widen scope of, 141
    widespread, 212
    women must become proficient
        in, 138
Atom, 162, 227
Attachment. *See* Detachment

Báb, the, 128, 275
    Bahá'u'lláh early disciple of, 266
    declaration of, 271
    descendent of Muḥammad, 265
    established Bahá'í calendar, 270
    Founder of Bábí Faith, 265
    harbinger of Bahá'u'lláh, 265
    martyrdom of, 266, 271
    opposition of clergy and govern-
        ment to, 265–66
    Prophet of God, 91, 268
Babel, 148
Bábí community, 266–67
Backbiting. *See* Character and con-
    duct
Bahá'í community, x
    ideal characteristics of, 221–26
    offered as a model for study, 21,
        216–21
    single social organism, 21
Bahá'í Faith, 218, 218n, 265–73, 275
    accepts all Prophets of God, 129
    calendar of, 270–71
    growth of, 267
    history of, 265–67
    independent world religion, 275
    organization and administration
        of, 271–72
    elections in, 199n, 271
    institutions of, vitality of,
        225–26
    Spiritual Assemblies, 199,
        199n, 271
    practices of, 270–71
    recognizes oneness of mankind,
        15–16
    sacred literature of, 268
    tenets of, 268–70, 275
    terminology of, 268
    view of world affairs, 5–6

Bahá'ís, 275
    citizenship of, is kingdom of
        Bahá'u'lláh, 225
    conduct of, 215–26
    goal of, 225
    love among, 226
    love of, for fellowman, 225
    persecution of, 22, 246, 246n, 266
    purpose of, 217–18
    unity of, 21, 221, 222–25, 226
        offers hope to world, 21
Bahá'u'lláh, x, xi, 91, 265, 266–67,
    275
    Ancient Beauty, 218, 242, 245
    awakening of, spiritual, 237–38,
        237n
    Blessed Beauty, 214
    divine physician, 72
    education of, 237
    Founder of Bahá'í Faith, 4, 275
    Kingdom of, 225
    law of, 121, 250, 268
    Most Great Name, 214, 214n
    one of Prophets of God, 91,
        128–29
    persecutions and sufferings of,
        242–49, 266–67
    arrest in Mazindaran, 243
    banishments and exiles,
        244–45, 245n, 266–67
    imprisonment in Akka, 239,
        240, 240n, 245, 245n, 267
    imprisonment in Síyáh-Chál
        (Black Pit), 237, 237n,
        266–67
    purpose of, 243–47
    Prince of Peace, 251
    prophetic judgment of, 4
    revelation of. *See* Bahá'u'lláh,
        revelation of
    teachings of, 46, 184–85, 212,
        224–25, 249, 250, 268–70.
        See also Arts, the;
        Bahá'u'lláh, revelation of;
        Character and conduct; Con-
        sultation; Economics; Educa-
        tion; God; Government; Im-
        mortality; Independent in-
        vestigation of truth; Justice;
        Knowledge; Language; Love;
        Manifestations of God; Man-

kind; Morality; Oneness of
mankind; Peace; Prayer; Prejudice; Religion; Science;
Unity; War; Wealth; Women;
World civilization
consultation, 18
Most Great Peace, 212, 250
oneness of mankind, 29, 162,
163–64, 166, 214, 222
proposals for establishing
world peace, 16, 19–20, 22,
200, 201
race relations, 102–03
relationship to God, 269
unity of religions, 91, 129, 268
universal language, 149–51
voluntary sharing, 115
women, 131–32
world assemblage, 17–18
will of, 238
words of, sweetness of, 242
world order of, 225
writings of, 268
Wronged One, 31, 242, 243, 244,
245
Bahá'u'lláh, revelation of, 45, 216,
237, 237n, 238–40
advent of
clouds overshadow, 240
consummates past Dispensations, 238–39
heralded in all sacred scriptures, 238
manifest in human temple,
240
Prince of Peace, 251
springtime, 241–42, 250
cycle of, 250
is not final revelation, 129
Day of, 41, 49, 239, 247
laws and principles of, 250,
268–70
are ensign of Most Great Peace,
212
conflict and dissension forbidden, 216, 219
oneness and unity of mankind,
166, 222
oneness of God, 222
teachings must be spread, 249
worldwide, 121

Manifestations all recognized in,
128–29
Most Great Guidance, 156
personified by maiden, 237
power of, 184, 212
force of divine authority, 22
force of utterance, 243
no one can keep back revelation, 238
penetrative, 224
world cannot alarm Him, 247
world's equilibrium upset
through, 248
Prince of Peace, 251
Promised One, 239, 241
promises and prophecies about,
238, 241
fulfilled, 239, 240
Promised Day is come, 247
proofs of, 239
purpose of, 130, 242–48
recognition of, 242, 249
rejection of
beware of disputing, 240–41
consequences of failure to recognize, 45
religious truths recognized by,
128–29
Supreme, 216
transforming effects of, 22, 248,
249, 250
unites diverse peoples,
221–25
worldwide regeneration,
248–49
unparalleled, 239
world order envisioned in, 17,
203–05, 225, 225n, 248,
250–51. See also Peace;
World civilization
foundations of, laid by international consultation, 17–19
Most Great Peace. See Most
Great Peace; Peace
Bible, 91, 241
Birth, second, 236
Buddha, 91, 241, 268. See also Manifestations of God

Capitalism, 9. See also Ideologies,
man-made

Catastrophes. *See* Civilization, chaotic condition of; War
Century, this (twentieth), 45, 48–49, 85, 138, 173, 236, 241–42, 250, 259. *See also* Day
  age of universal reformation, 85
  century of light, 45
  century of radiance, 85, 96, 138
  new thoughts and remedies required for, 85
  peace established in, 45, 48–49, 179, 181, 236–37, 241–42
  progress in, 235, 241
  realities of things revealed in, 138
  religions unified in, 250
  sciences and arts molded anew in, 85
  unity, achievement of, in
    drive toward, 21
    most important task is, 42
    of nations, 4
Character and conduct, 37–40, 145, 151, 157–60, 212–16, 217–21, 233–37. *See also* Altruism; Deeds
  backbiting, 220
    do not look at shortcomings, 215
  be a Bahá'í, 220
  deliver man from darkness and prejudice, 174
  enemies and foes, treatment of, 155, 164, 214, 219, 220
  good, 157
    man has choice of, or evil, 36–37
  of government officials. *See* Government
  judge not others, 171
  material and spiritual natures of man reflected in, 37–39, 68–69
  moderation, 159
  morality. *See* Morality
  obedience, 62
  passions, control of, 68–69, 157, 158–59
  peace, promoting, 29, 40, 101–02, 158–59
  power of human endeavor, 101
  religion affects, 7, 65–66

  self-renunciation, 158
    result of, 38, 60
  spiritual perfections and virtues, 36, 54–57, 60, 65, 66, 220, 231, 233. *See also* Altruism; Deeds; Detachment; Equity; Forbearance; Humility; Independent investigation of truth; Justice; Kindness; Love; Morality; Philanthropy; Selflessness; Trustworthiness; Truthfulness; Unity; Will
    appear through power of God, 231
    atrophy of, 68
    attributes and characteristics of God, 90, 227–28
    basis of, is opposing passions, 158–59
    be not careless of virtues, 233–34
    development of, 39–49, 156, 232, 235–36
    education releases man's potentials, 139–40, 142–43
    effect of, on world, 165
    God sees, 157
    happiness is attainment of, 36, 56, 232
    heart can be cultivated, 156
    imperfect soul is self-centered, 147
    importance of, 234
    man alone has, 56
    Manifestations develop, 65
    material qualities should be stripped away, 39–40
    material side held in subjection, 68–69
    power of potentialities of pure souls, 157
    prayers for, 256, 258–60
    strive to manifest, 219–20
    virtues that befit human dignity, 22, 37
  strangers, see no, 219–26
  thoughts, 215
  translate, into action, 98–101
  vices can be discontinued, 56
  well-wisher of all mankind, 147
Charity. *See* Altruism; Philanthropy

Chastity, 72, 220
Children. *See* Education
Christ, 64, 90, 91–92, 127, 128, 185, 268. *See also* Manifestations of God
   divine reality promulgated by, 32
   "father is in the son," 58
   followers of, dissension among, 222
   rejection of, 74
   Pharisees disputed, 241
   revelation of, symbolized by Dove, 237n
Civilization, 152–53. *See also* Earth; Government; Mankind; Peace; World civilization
   chaotic conditions of, 4, 25–29, 35–36, 45–47, 161
   age of transition, 46–47
   common disaster threatens all, 28
   manifold ills, 60
   orientation lost, 35
   paralysis, 7, 11, 36
   planet seemingly abandoned by Providence, 28
   prevailing order defective, 4, 29
   tumult marks coming of age, 5
   chaotic conditions of, causes of
   culture unsupported by morality, 152–53
   extremes of wealth and poverty, 12, 112, 114, 116
   failure to recognize Revelation, 45
   ideologies, man-made, 8–10
   imitation, 95
   nationalism, 118–21
   racism, 12, 107–08
   religion, decline and corruption of, 7, 67–73, 85–86
   spirituality, lack of, 35
   world leaders, 29
   excess of, 31
   material, 31–35, 235. *See also* Materialism
   energy of man absorbed by, 35
   material comforts necessary, 232

   material ideals alone not sufficient, 8–10
   spiritual and, uniting of, 32–35, 156, 235–36
   progress of, 235–36
   based on religion, 6
   depends on education, 143
   ever-advancing, 21, 233, 269
   material and spiritual balance needed for, 32–35, 156, 211, 232, 235–36
   material things changed to suit, 95–96
   reconstruction of, 165, 166–67
   change conception of society, 46
   cleanse, fuse, and unify planet, 46
   convulsive changes will release human potential, 6
   divine illumination inspires change, 164–65
   new social form, 116
   new virtues and perceptions required for, 95–96
   prayers for, 259–61
   reconstruction of unified nations of West is like, 47–48
   regeneration, 248–49, 255
   remold institutions, 121
   suffering required for, 35–36, 46
   sweep away outworn doctrines and thoughts, 10, 85, 96–97
   thoughts must be translated into action for, 98–101
   unity and concord conducive to, 213
   weapons, converted, used for, 174, 181
   religion is basis of, 62–63, 66–67
Commerce, 112, 141. *See also* Economics
Consultation, 2, 10, 18, 194–99. *See also* Peace, routes to

David, song of, 239
Day, 41, 49, 239, 247
   of God, 41
   prayer for, 256
   promised, 247

Day *(continued)*
  of Promised One, 239, 241
Deeds, 101, 151, 157, 160, 215–16.
    See also Altruism; Character
    and conduct; Philanthropy
  boasting about, 100
  light of spirit apparent in, 102
  must distinguish Bahá'ís, 218
  perfection reached through vol-
    untary, 115
  power of human endeavor, 101
  progress of humanity caused by,
    218
  rulers must see consequences of,
    after death, 188–89
  translate thoughts into action,
    98–101
  volition manifests, 98
  words and, must not differ, 218
  world helped by, 101, 237
Demilitarization, 15, 167. *See also*
    Disarmament; War, abolition
    of; War, weapons of
Detachment, 102, 160, 217, 242
  renounce self, 158
  required for true understanding,
    94
  rid self of attachment to world,
    154, 161, 232
Disarmament, 10, 174–75, 177,
    178–79, 181, 184. *See also*
    Demilitarization; War, aboli-
    tion of; War, weapons of
Discovery, power of. *See* Mankind,
    faculties and powers of
Dispensation, 276. *See also*
    Bahá'u'lláh, revelation of;
    Bahá'u'lláh, teachings of;
    Manifestations of God; Pro-
    gressive revelation; Reli-
    gion(s)
Disunity. *See* Unity; War
Diversity. *See* Unity, in diversity

Earth, 151. *See also* Civilization;
    Mankind; Nature; Peace;
    World civilization
  contamination of, could prove le-
    thal, 31
  interdependency of all areas of,
    13, 44

man's tomb, 26, 119, 120–21
  one country, one homeland, 13,
    45, 155, 173, 221
  planetization of mankind, 3
  in state of pregnancy, 41
  will mirror world of God, 165–66,
    221
  world citizenship. *See* World citi-
    zenship
East (Orient) and West (Occident),
    uniting of, 53, 165, 181
  auxiliary language helpful to, 151
  cement together, 185, 212
  through love of God, 230
  one household, 155
Economics. *See also* Wealth
  currency, international, 204
  economic barriers demolished in
    world system of, 202
  interdependence of capital and
    labor, 202
  spiritual principles of, 114–16
  unity of, in world, 45
  wages and profit sharing, 113–14
  of world civilization, 17, 202, 204
Education, 14, 52, 139–48. *See also*
    Arts, the; Knowledge;
    Science
  bend minds to, 221
  of children, 144–47
  essential elements of
    auxiliary language, 148
    morals and conduct, 146
    oneness of mankind, 15
    sciences which benefit man-
      kind, 140, 141
    world citizenship, 14, 147
  financing, 144
  influence of, is universal, 143
  of human race, through word of
    God, 247–48
  lack of, 141–42, 146
    causes prejudice, 147
    causes wrongdoing, 145
  Manifestations give, 59, 64, 65
  necessity of, 14
    acquire arts and sciences, 227
    acquisition of knowledge is in-
      cumbent, 140
    for civilization, 143
    compulsory, 142, 144

educate masses, 141
ignorant must be taught, 148,
    163, 171
to obtain justice, 141–42
to release man's potential, 140,
    142–43, 145
schools, 145–46
source of, 140
    God is Educator, 255
    is knowledge of God, 57
    Manifestations give education,
        59, 64, 65
    Word of God, 247–48
types of
    material, human, and spiritual,
        143
    useful, 140–41
universal influence of, 143
use of, to benefit others, 52
of women and girls, 14, 135–36
Enemies
    regard no one as enemy, 214
    treatment of, 155, 164, 171, 219,
        220
England, 172
Equality of men and women. *See*
    Women, equality of men and
Equity, 93. *See also* Justice
Evil, choice of good or, 36–37
Evolution, 43–44. *See also* Civiliza-
    tion; Earth; Mankind
Existence. *See* Mankind, purpose
    and responsibilities of
Eye, inner and outer, 233

Fairness, 217
Family relationship, bond of, 208
Fanaticism, 8, 83
Fidelity, 217
Forbearance, 22, 60, 161, 217, 233.
    See also Selfishness
Forgiveness, 215, 220
France, 172, 196
Free will. *See* Will
Freedom, unity in, 45
Future, penetrate mysteries of, 53.
    See also Peace, routes to;
    World civilization

God
    chastisement of, 71

compassion of, 220
Creator, 269
Day of. *See* Day
Educator, 255
fear of, 244
justice of, 46
knowledge of, 162, 230, 236
    God is unknowable, 268
    Manifestations give, 57–59,
        89–90, 268
    purpose of creating man is, 21
    purpose of creation is, 229
    self-knowledge is same as, 232
    source of all learning is, 57
    war prevented through, 72
laws of. *See* Law(s)
love of. *See* Love
man is mystery of, 227
mercy of, 126, 163–64
names of, reflected in creation,
    227–28
omniscience of, 162
oneness of, 32, 75, 90, 92, 93, 126
people of, 217
politics, Divine, 173
reliance on, 233
Shepherd, 109, 165, 251
trust of, 59, 60
university of, 165
will of, 229, 233. *See also*
    Bahá'u'lláh, revelation of
Word of, 34
world of, 40
wrath of, 71
Golden Age, 46
Golden Rule
    choose for neighbor, 109
    desire for others, 189
    prefer others' good, 171
    regard others as self, 29
    treat others as self wishes to be
        treated, 7
Government, 186–94. *See also*
    World civilization
    actions of, should be tempered by
        spiritual consequences, 188
    body politic, unity of, 181–83
    consultation in. *See* Consultation
    despotic, 188
    elections and elected representa-
        tives, 192, 193

Government *(continued)*
  employees of, behavior of, 193,
      194
  evolution of, 193–94
  God, laws and knowledge of, in,
      111, 188, 191–92
  justice in, 34, 186–91
  king
      blessed, if convokes meeting
          for peace, 180
      duty of, is peace, 180–81
  militarism of, 175. *See also* War,
      weapons of
  obedience to, 199
  politics, 193–94
      Divine, 173
  statesmanship, qualities neces-
      sary in, 186–87, 191–94
  wisdom in, 190, 191

Happiness, 34, 40, 152, 232, 236
  contingent on giving, 116, 117
  depends on spiritual perfections,
      36, 56, 232
  lies in harmony, unity, and love,
      154
  material and divine civilization
      must agree for, 211, 232, 236
  nearness to God brings, 269
  obedience to laws brings, 62
  obstacles to, 173
  religion is basis of, 66
Hate, 25, 221
  importance of being free of, 219
  lack of religious unity causes, 125
  quench fire of, 217, 221
  replace thoughts of, with love,
      215
Heart, 54
Holy Spirit, 55, 67, 126, 130, 164,
      209, 211, 236
Honesty, 157
  of government employees, 193
  trustworthiness, 22, 39, 216, 233
  truthfulness, 39, 217, 233
Human nature. *See* Mankind, nature
      (reality) of
Humanity. *See* Mankind
Humility, 109, 171
  avoid boasting, 100
  pride not self in glory, 161

Ideologies, man-made, 8–9, 71. *See
  also* Materialism; National-
      ism; Religion(s)
  capitalism, 9
  communism, 71
  failure of, 9–10
  gods of idle fancies, 86
Ignorance, 14. *See also* Knowledge
  blind imitation of past causes,
      170
  dispel darkness of, 168
  leads to bad behavior, 157
  prejudices cause, 96
  some souls suffer through, 127
  teach the ignorant, 148, 171
Immorality. *See* Morality
Immortality
  goal of earthly life, 225
  man is endowed with immortal
      soul, 269
  rulers must see consequences of
      actions after death, 188–89
Income. *See* Wealth
Independent investigation of truth,
      93–97, 128. *See also* Man-
      kind, faculties and qualities
      of
  barriers to, are prejudice and
      imagination, 128
  cleanse self of earthly things for,
      94
  consultation, basis of, is, 196–97
  investigating essentials of reli-
      gion, 85
  justice necessary to see with own
      eyes, 187
  man given faculties for, 94–95
      investigate religion with sci-
          ence and reason, 78–80
Industry, 109, 110, 112, 249
Investigation. *See* Independent in-
      vestigation of truth; Man-
      kind, faculties and qualities
      of
Iran. *See* Persia
Irreligion. *See* Religion, decline of
Islam. *See* Muḥammad; Muslims

Jacob, 91, 243
Jerusalem, 239
Jesus. *See* Christ

Jews, 124, 222
  persecution of, 124
Job, 243
Judas Iscariot, 171
Justice, 39, 109, 186–91. *See also*
    Golden Rule
  equal, to all, 111
  equity, 93
  flames of, 46
  force made servant of, 205
  impartiality of, 190
  increase in, by understanding
    spiritual consequences of ac-
    tions, 188–89
  peace underlies, 75
  power of, to transform world, 190
  purpose of, is unity, 191
  reward and punishment, 186
  true station of man attained
    through, 194
  work for, 101

Kindness, 22, 99, 171, 215, 219, 222,
    233
Kings. *See* Government; Peace,
    routes to
Knowledge, 80–81, 140–41, 230.
    See also Education; Wisdom
  atom contains, 227
  clouds of, 239
  divine, reveals spiritual life, 152
  of God. *See* God, knowledge of
  most glorious gift of man, 80
  promotion of humanity's, 40. *See
    also* Education
  of self, 232–33

Labor, capital and, interdepend-
    ence of, 17, 202
Language(s)
  conveys thought and purpose,
    150
  diversity of
    arose in Babel, 148
    originally unknown, 148
  international auxiliary, 14, 45,
    148–51, 204
    consultation about, 148, 149
  key to heart is, 150
Law(s). *See also* Bahá'u'lláh, law of;
    Government; Justice; Mani-

    festations of God, laws and
    teachings revealed by
  Bahá'u'lláh's worldwide, 121
  effects of religion on, 188
  of God, 34, 98, 208
    breaking of, 98, 188–89
    justice is, 111, 186–91
    medicine for sick society is,
      59–60, 89
    morality based on, 62
    must be considered when hav-
      ing plans for ruling mankind,
      111, 188
    obedience to, 62, 188–89
    order in world maintained
      through, 62
    spiritual and material aspects
      of, 77, 84, 89–91
    Zion, law has gone forth from,
      239
  international, need for single
    code of, 17
  result of lofty ideals and sound
    minds, 33–34
  of Torah, 91
League of Nations, 3, 16, 201, 202
Lesser Peace, 180, 276
Life
  brief earthly, 225
  after death. *See* Immortality
  eternal or everlasting, 50, 62, 154,
    234, 236
    through Manifestations, 59, 61
  limitations of earthly, 219
  true, is life of spirit, 152
Love, 155
  among Bahá'ís, 226
  basis for true liberty and peace,
    208
  creation is expression of, 30
  God's love, 126, 164
    fundamental to peace, 155–56,
      226
  for man, 21, 43, 50, 126, 165,
    226, 230–31, 232, 234, 269
    prayer for, 255
  of humanity, 13, 220, 234
    love creatures for sake of God,
      215, 225
  is greater than peace, 155
  religion is channel of, 165

Love *(continued)*
  for strangers and enemies, 155
  true consultation needs, 197

Manifestations of God, 57–62,
    86–93, 125–26, 128–29,
    268–69, 276. *See also* Abra-
    ham; Adam; Báb, the;
    Bahá'u'lláh; Buddha; Christ;
    Muḥammad; Noah; Oneness
    of mankind; Peace; Reli-
    gion(s); Zoroaster
  acceptance and recognition of,
    94, 269
  adore Sun in any mirror, 92
  through meditation on their
    lives, 86
  appearance of
    cyclic and successive, 61,
      88–89, 241
    Messianic cycle prophesied by
      Moses, 92
    scriptures announce, 241
    sent forth by God, 162
  everlasting life of humankind de-
    pends on, 59
  God reflected in glory of, 58–59
  laws and teachings revealed by,
    34, 76–77, 89–91, 162
    are medicine, 59–60, 89
    food laws, 90–91
    material, are modified, 76–77,
      84, 89, 90–91
    oneness of God, 75
    oneness of mankind, 67, 75
    peace, 59, 75
    spiritual, are never changing,
      77, 84, 89–91, 125
  power of
    is from God, 58
    unites malevolent peoples,
      63–64
  purpose and effects of, 57–62
    education, 59, 64, 65
    ensure peace and tranquillity,
      59, 75
    give knowledge of God, 57–59,
      82–83, 89–90
    physicians for society, 59–60,
      89

promote unity and fellowship,
    63–65, 83, 125–26, 130
  race unity, 108
  renewal of everything, 61
  summon man to God, 57–58,
    59, 125
promises of, 241
  announcement of successor,
    84, 91–92, 125
  fulfilled, 238–39, 240
rejection of, 81–83
  "clouds" of blind imitation, 82,
    240
  divines and clerics misguided
    people, 73–75
  literal interpretations of Word
    of God led to, 74
revelations of
  differ according to require-
    ments of age, 59, 87–88, 130,
    268–69
  each has specific mission and
    book, 88
  fundamental sameness of, 32,
    87–88, 92, 125, 129
  none is final, 129
  symbols of divine summons,
    237n
sacrifice of, 73, 127, 242–47
unity of, 32, 86–93, 125, 128–29
  "agents of one civilizing pro-
    cess," 8
  Bahá'u'lláh verifies, 129
  each is return of former, 86–87
  in spite of individual character-
    istics, 87–88
  "succession of spiritual lumi-
    naries," 6
  successor announced and pred-
    ecessor confirmed by each,
    84, 91–92, 125
Mankind. *See also* Character and
    conduct; Civilization; Im-
    mortality; Life; Oneness of
    mankind; Soul; Unity
  creation of, 57, 60, 161–62, 221,
    229, 269
  to carry forward an ever-ad-
    vancing civilization, 21, 233,
    269

made in image of God, 50, 55, 90, 226, 227
equality of, before God, 220
evolutionary stages and progress of, 5, 20, 41–49, 61–62, 164–65, 167, 203, 235
  adolescence, 5, 44, 46–47, 203
  depend on balance of material and spiritual, 32–35, 156, 211, 232, 235–36
  depend on love and amity, 154
  ethical development depends on religion, 84, 90
  gifts and bestowals suited to, 44
  Manifestations responsible for, 59–67
  man's destiny is to manifest potentialities, 41
  maturity of mankind, 5, 19, 44, 46–47, 203, 235, 250
  unity is goal of, 20, 43, 203
faculties and qualities of, 39, 50–57, 231. See also Character and conduct; Soul; Will
  atrophy of, 68
  intellect, 50–54, 228
  latent potentialities, 41, 49, 156, 157
  mind, 6, 78–79, 162, 229, 235–36
  power of investigation and discovery, 55–56, 94–95
  use of, for welfare of humanity, 39, 52, 233–36
happiness of. See Happiness
nature (reality) of, 6, 36–39, 55, 227–30
  convulsive changes will release potentialities of, 6
  created in image of God, 50, 55, 59, 60, 226, 227
  ferocity of, 26–27, 37
  imperfections in, 38–39, 162
  man can become heavenly being, 38
  material or lower, 36–39, 152, 232
  perfections in, 39, 219
  selfish and aggressive, seen as, 5, 11
  spiritual or higher, 36–37, 56, 152, 232
purpose and responsibilities of, 40, 54, 55, 154, 232
  carry forward ever-advancing civilization, 21, 233, 269
  increase love and amity, 164, 217, 221, 234
  know, love, and worship God, 21, 229, 269
  know self, 232–33
  promote peace, 40, 154, 168
rebirth of, 40, 49, 50
station of, 41, 49, 50, 157, 233
  lofty, can be attained, 151–52
  true, attained through justice, 194
Material world, 39, 55–56. See also Nature
Materialism, 8–10. See also Ideologies, man-made
  causes of
    decline of religion, 69–70
    desire and passion for worldly affairs, 69, 158–59, 213–14
    degradation of civilization, 69–70
  failure of, 9
  material civilization, 31–35
    combining of, with spiritual civilization, 32–35, 156, 211, 232, 235–36
    insufficiency of, 8–10, 232
  material comforts necessary, 232
  material nature of man, 36–39, 152, 232
Meetings, blessed when interracial, 106
Mercy, 22, 109, 224
  of God, 126, 163–64
Moderation, 31, 159
Money. See Economics; Wealth
Morality. See also Character and conduct; Deeds
  changes in, necessary, 85, 235
  decline in, 67–73
  importance of training children in, 146

Morality *(continued)*
  one code of, taught by Manifestations, 76
  religion is source of, 62, 65–66, 69, 84, 90
Moses, 64, 88, 90, 91–92, 222, 268
  Burning Bush appears to, 237n
Most Great Name, 214, 214n, 221
Most Great Peace, 276
  accomplished only through divine power, 67
  ensign of, is teachings of Bahá'u'lláh, 212
  life of body of human world, 36
  man's greatest glory is to serve cause of, 29
  shall come, 22, 251
Muḥammad, 64–65, 74, 91
  Angel Gabriel appears to, 237n
Muslims, 123, 222

Náṣiri'd-Dín Sháh (of Persia), 194n
Nationalism, 13, 47, 71, 118–22. *See also* Nations; Patriotism
  boundaries created by man, not God, 118, 119, 120
  concept of, created by selfish souls, 118, 119
  must yield to love of all humanity, 13, 118, 121–22, 184, 203. *See also* World citizenship
  result of, is war, 169–70
Nations. *See also* Government; World civilization
  boundaries of
    must be fixed, 18–19, 178, 183
    not created by God, 118, 119, 120
  cooperation among, 3–4, 11, 13, 20–21
  evanescence of, 56
  knowledge is pride of, 54
  nation building completed, 3, 20, 203
  oneness and interdependence of, 13, 45, 118–22, 185, 251
    earth is one country, 13, 118, 119, 121, 173, 206, 221
    people must love world, not country, 13, 118, 121–22, 184

  subordination of national interests to those of world, 16–17, 121, 185, 203
  world citizenship. *See* World citizenship
  unified nations of West, birth of, 47–48
  unity of, to be established in this century, 45, 48–49, 179, 181, 236–37, 241–42
Nature, 39, 55–56
  captives of world of, 214
  defects of, 37
  immersion in. *See* Materialism
  law of, binds all but man, 51
Negotiation. *See* Consultation
Noah, 90
Nuclear weapons. *See* War, weapons of

Obedience
  to government, 199
  to laws of God, 62, 171–72, 188
Oneness of mankind, 15–16, 102–09, 120–21, 161–68, 218–19. *See also* Nations, oneness and interdependence of; Racism; Unity
  Adam is father of all, 103, 120, 171
  in America, 106, 107–09
  Bahá'u'lláh proclaimed, 29, 163, 166, 167, 218
  black people are as pupil of eye, 103
  concept of
    beauty in varied colors, 102, 105, 106, 210
    created from one tree, 29
    created from same dust, 161, 167
    divine purpose in varied forms, 105
    drops from one ocean, 221
    equality of all, 103
    fingers of one hand, 213
    fruit, leaves of one tree, 29, 118, 163, 168, 206, 212, 214, 221
    God loves all without making distinctions, 103, 162, 164

herbs from same garden, 221
indivisible, 46
members of one body, 213
pearls from one shell, 218, 221
race, one original, 103, 120,
    161, 171
servants of one God, 163, 234
sheep of God, 162, 165, 168
single-hued pavilion, 183
stars of same sky, 218
students of one Educator, 234
upholders of one order, 221
waves of one sea, 163, 218
in West, 106
differences among men, real, are
    faithfulness and obedience,
    171–72
implications of, 15–16, 163,
    166–67
diversity should be cause of
    love, 106
friendship with every race, 215
heart, not color, important,
    103–04, 108
interracial friendship, fellow-
    ship, and meetings, 106, 107,
    108, 163, 168
offending another offends God,
    173
organic change in society, 166
Satan, no people are of, 163
strive to increase love and ami-
    ty, 164, 217, 221, 234
world citizenship. See World
    citizenship
racial differences, origin of, 104
recognition of
    blind imitation hinders, 95
    divine power necessary for, 67
    implement, with legal meas-
        ures, 12, 108, 203
    leaders have failed in, 29
religion teaches, 75, 108

Patriotism, 16, 121–22, 185. See also
    Nationalism
Bahá'u'lláh's law does not stifle
    sane, 185, 224
insufficiency of, 185, 208
larger sense of, includes all races
    and lands, 120

prejudice of, 118, 119, 120
Paul, Saint, 171
Peace, 29–30. See also Century, this;
    Civilization; War; World civi-
    lization
Bahá'u'lláh bore sufferings to es-
    tablish, 242–46
barriers to, 4–5, 11, 175
    extremes of wealth and pover-
        ty, 12, 112–14
    inability to articulate desire for
        peace, 11
    incorrect view of human na-
        ture, 5, 11
    inequality of sexes, 13–14,
        130–39
    materialism. See Materialism
    militarism, 175
    nationalism. See Nationalism
    paralysis of will, 11, 36
    prejudice of all kinds, 168–73
    racism, 12, 107–08
    religious strife, 13, 122–30
    weapons, new, 153
bases for
    inner state supported by spiri-
        tual attitudes, 14
    oneness of mankind. See One-
        ness of mankind
    righteousness and justice, 205.
        See also Justice
    spiritual principles, 14–15
elements conducive to establish-
    ing, 12–15
    auxiliary language, 14, 148–51
    awakening man to harm of war,
        156
    demilitarization, 174–79
    education, 14. See also Educa-
        tion
    eliminating extremes of wealth
        and poverty, 12–13, 111
    equality of men and women,
        13–14, 130–39
    international activities, in-
        crease in, 13
    love of humanity, 13, 220, 234.
        See also Love
    obsolete doctrines, sweeping
        away, 10, 13, 129–30. See also
        Religion(s), unity of

Peace *(continued)*
    opposing thoughts of war with
      thoughts of peace, 215
    prejudices, abandonment of,
      12, 15, 168–74
    race unity, 107–09
    religious differences, submerg-
      ing, 13, 129–30
    sharing, voluntary, 115
    unity of mankind. *See* Unity
  hopeful signs of, 3–4
    Bahá'í community offers, 21
    ecumenism, 21
    international cooperation, 3–4,
      11–12, 20–21
  kings, duty of, is to establish,
    180–81
  Lesser, 180, 276
  Most Great. *See* Most Great Peace
  panacea of every disease is,
    175–76
  possibility and promises of, 3,
    5–6, 46–49, 67, 101–02,
    205–06, 251. *See also* Centu-
    ry, this; Day
    Bahá'u'lláh promises, 22, 46,
      251
    divinely intended, 48
    Golden Age, 46
    imminent, 22
    soon will present order be
      rolled up, 41
    stormy sea shall be calmed, 102
    time is ripe, 185
    time of the end, 47
    this generation, 19
    wars shall pass away, 22
  prayers for, 255–61
  Prince of, 251
  promotion of, man called to, 154,
    158, 159–60, 168, 205
  religion's role in establishing,
    6–8, 13
    channel of love, 165
    promotion of unity and cooper-
      ation, 75, 83, 84, 207, 208
  routes to, 175–79, 182–83
    adopt binding treaty or frame-
      work, 11, 18–19, 67, 176–78,
      183–84
    adversities and horrors, 3, 35

    armistice, initial, 20
    businessmen, financiers, and
      soldiers must arise, 178
    consultation, 2, 10, 18
    convoke world meeting, 17–18,
      180–81, 183–84
    determination and commit-
      ment required, 101
    disarmament, 177–79
    educate public, 175, 176–77,
      177–78
    inculcate peaceful ideals in in-
      stitutions, 177
    political agreements alone not
      enough, 14
    raise context to level of princi-
      ple, 14
    reverses and setbacks in, 48
    spiritual principles, use of,
      14–15
    translate words and thoughts
      into action, 98–100, 101
    United Nations could arise, 19
    United States will realize world
      peace, 48, 48n
  stages of, 19–20. *See also* Lesser
    Peace; Most Great Peace
Persia (Iran), 194, 223, 246–47n
Peter, Saint, 240
Philanthropy, 109–10, 111, 114–17.
    See also Altruism; Deeds
  eternal happiness contingent on
    giving, 116, 117
Philosophy, failure of, 211
Piety, 216
Planetization of mankind, 3
Politics. *See* Government
Poor, the, 114, 115, 116–17. *See also*
    Wealth
Poverty. *See* Wealth
Prayer, purity of heart while en-
    gaged in, 233
Prayers for
  Day of God, 256
  love of God, 255
  peace, 259–61
  reformation of world, 258–59
  spiritual development, 256, 258,
    259–60
  unity, 255–56, 257–58, 259–60
Prejudice, 71, 72, 74–75. *See also*

Nationalism; Racism; Reli-
gion(s), prejudice and
strife in
abandonment of all, 168–74
effects of
deprivation and ignorance, 96
discord and bloodshed, 168
obstacle to human happiness,
173
war, 168–73
political and patriotic, 13, 47, 71,
118–22. *See also* Nationalism
racial, 12, 71, 107–08, 120. *See
also* Racism
religious. *See* Religion(s), prejudice and strife in
Press, the, 204
Pride, 109. *See also* Humility
Prince of Peace, 251
Progressive revelation, 88–89,
128–29, 225. *See also* Reli-
gion(s), unity of
Prophets. *See* Manifestations of God
Punishment. *See* Reward and punishment
Purity, 233

Qu'rán, 241, 276
people of, 246
quotations from, 63, 115, 153,
162, 193, 246

Race unity. *See* Oneness of mankind
Races of man
one original race, 103, 120, 161,
171
origins of, 104
Racism, 12, 71, 107–08, 120. *See
also* Prejudice
abandonment of, 251
in America, 107–09
is illusion, 171
racial distinction has no basis,
103, 120, 161, 171
in West, 106
Reality
of each created thing, 227
investigation of. *See* Independent
investigation of truth
of man. *See* Mankind, nature
(reality) of

oneness of, 90, 95, 126
Reason. *See* Science
Religion(s), 6–8, 62–67. *See also*
God; Ideologies, man-made;
Manifestations of God; Word
of God
civilizations based on, 62, 63
consort with all, 122
corruption of, 7–8, 71–72
attachment to outward forms,
79
false gods, 71
fanaticism and bigotry, 8, 83
imitation of old forms, 75, 77,
92, 125
religious leaders cause, 73–75
superstition. *See* Superstition
worshiping product of own
imaginations, 79
cyclic nature of, 88–89, 128–29
decline of, 67–73, 164
because dogma disagrees with
science, 80
precedes rebirth of religion,
241, 248–49
results of, are perversion and
degradation, 69–70
differences among, due to requirements of age, 123, 130
investigation of. *See* Independent
investigation of truth
laws and teachings of, 75, 76–77.
See also Golden Rule; Law(s)
of God
material, changed as necessary,
76–77, 84, 89–91
medicine for sick society,
59–60
obedience to, 62, 188–89
order maintained in world
through, 62
spiritual, are eternal, 76, 77, 78,
89–91
merits of, cannot be judged by
acts of followers, 63
prejudice and strife in, 83–86,
123–26, 170–71
abolished by Bahá'u'lláh's revelation 122
absence of religion preferable
to, 123, 127

Religion(s) *(continued)*
  blind imitation causes, 84, 95,
    170
  causes war and conflict, 13, 129
  Crusades, 123–24
  dogmatic observances cause,
    84, 126
  fanaticism, 8, 83
  misunderstanding causes, 63,
    128
  religious leaders cause, 7,
    74–75, 170
  progressive nature of, 88–89,
    128–29, 225
  purpose of, 75, 128
    build character, 7, 65–67. *See
      also* Character and conduct
    establish love and unity, 6–8,
      13, 62–65, 75, 83, 84, 165,
      207, 208
    inculcate morality, 62, 65–66,
      68
    link humanity with God, 6
    prevent crime, 68
    protect welfare of humanity, 68,
      73, 207
  relativity of truth of, 129. *See also*
    Progressive revelation
  science and. *See* Science
  unity of, 8, 83, 92–93, 122–23,
    125, 127, 130, 241
    allegiance to one revelation,
      205
    become one in Faith, 251
    century for, 250. *See also* Cen-
      tury, this
    divine reality is one, 32, 90, 92,
      126
    fourth candle of unity is, 45
    fundamentals are one, 75
    one source, 93, 123
    religious leaders asked to sub-
      merge differences, 13,
      129–30
    search for truth will bring, 128
    strife will be stilled, 17
Resignation to God's decree, 233
Revelation of Bahá'u'lláh. *See*
  Bahá'u'lláh, revelation of
Reward and punishment, 186, 188.
  See also Justice

Rich, the. *See* Wealth

Satan and satanic qualities, 37. *See
  also* Mankind, nature (reali-
    ty) of
  no people are of Satan, 163
  warfare is satanic, 156
Science, 31, 52–54
  actions will help progress of, 101
  advances in, in this century, 4, 13,
    85, 249
  can solve practical problems of
    humanity, 4
  contract world into single
    neighborhood, 13, 121
  creates both progress and barbar-
    ism, 34
  discoverer of all things, 52
  insufficiency of attainment of, of
    past, 96
  international undertakings in
    field of, 4
  is a bestowal of God, 52
  likened to a mirror, 53
  origin of, 52, 54
  reflection of Divine Image, 227
  religion and, 76–81
    artificial barriers between, 7, 76
    pronounced at variance with,
      76, 77–80
    reconciliation of, 204
    two wings of progress are, 77
    weigh religion with balance of
      science, 78–80
  universal reformation of, 85, 249
  use of
    benefit mankind, 52, 53, 54,
      140, 141
    discover verities of universe, 52
    end war, 52
    find pathway to God, 52
    solve problems and administer
      united world, 4
  widespread, 212
  women must become proficient
    in, 138
Selfishness, 147
Selflessness
  renounce self, 158
  well-wisher of mankind, 147
Shepherd, 109, 165

God is, 109, 165, 251
Manifestations are Shepherds, 125
true, 251
Shoghi Effendi Rabbani, xi, xii, 16, 20, 267, 276
Sincerity, 217
Society. *See* Civilization
Soul, 54, 162, 232
immortal, man is endowed with, 269
spiritual qualities of, can atrophy, 68
Spiritual perfections. *See* Character and conduct; Mankind, nature (reality) of
Statesmanship. *See* Government
Submission. *See* Obedience
Superstition, 93, 125. *See also* Ideologies, man-made
free Sun from darkness of, 92
gods of idle fancies, 86
gods of vain imaginings, 130
people delight in, 93
priest-prompted, 129
racial distinction is, 103
religion without science is, 76, 79, 80
shatter idols of, 93
superstitious practices of present religion, 77, 125
worship products of own imaginations, 79

Taqíy-i-Najafí, Shaykh Muhammad, 242n
Technology. *See* Science
Tomb, earth is man's, 26, 119, 121
Torah, 227, 241
laws of, 91
Trustworthiness, 22, 216, 233
Truth. *See also* Independent investigation of truth; Reality
acceptance of, 96
in consultation, 196–97, 198
is one, 81, 126, 128
relation of, to peace, 30
religious, is relative, 129
sea of, 166
search for, 93–97
weigh religion with balance of science to find, 78–80

Truthfulness, 217, 233
Twentieth century. *See* Century, this

United Nations, 3, 11–12, 16, 19, 20
United States. *See* America
Unity, 20–21, 42–45, 122, 130, 181–83, 203. *See also* Oneness of mankind; Peace; Religion(s); World civilization
of Bahá'ís. *See* Bahá'ís
bases of
love of God, 230–31
religion and religious unity, 63–65, 83, 92–93, 207
spiritual, 165, 207–12
teachings of Bahá'u'lláh, 207, 211–12
Words of God, 102, 207, 211
candles of, seven, 45
disunity, 20, 123–29, 209. *See also* War
in diversity, 15–16, 121, 209–11
diversity should be cause of love, 106
interracial meetings blessed, 106
love of God brings, 230–31
spiritual basis of, 208
establishment of, 20–21, 44–45, 203–05, 209
century for, 42–43, 168. *See also* Century, this
goal of, excels every other goal, 216
goal of humanity is, 20, 203
Holy Spirit, role of, in, 130, 209, 211
"Kingdom shall be God's" stamped on every heart, 207
mankind's well-being depends on, 20, 207
not possible in earlier centuries, 44
not possible through material, patriotic, or political means, 67, 208–09
root out source of contention, 122
science and religion will reconcile to bring, 81
stages in, 203

Unity *(continued)*
    thoughts, importance of, in,
        98–101, 215
    increase in, strive to create, 102,
        106, 234
    practice of, 212–16
    dissension forbidden, 216, 219
    ideal communication, 165
    interracial friendship and meet-
        ings, 106, 107–08, 168
    prayers for, 255–60
    results of, 182–83, 212
    world citizenship. *See* World citi-
        zenship
Universal House of Justice, ix, xii, 4,
    199 n, 271, 277

Victoria, Queen (of England), 192,
    192 n
Virtues. *See* Character and conduct,
    spiritual perfections and vir-
    tues

War, 25–28, 29–30, 42, 156, 169–70,
    185. *See also* Peace
    abolition of, 14, 31, 176–79
    agree on united attack against
        aggressor, 19
    Bahá'u'lláh bore sufferings for
        sake of, 246
    complex task, 14
    conflict and dissension forbid-
        den, 216, 219
    divine power necessary for,
        67
    fear of nuclear holocaust will
        force armistice, 20
    movements call for end to, 4
    quench fires of war, 165
    societal systems have failed in,
        28
    United Nations could arise for,
        19
    unlearn science of war, 42
    wars shall pass away, 22, 251
    weapons, new, cannot bring,
        153
    women will bring, 137, 139
    causes of, 27, 169, 170
    ambition, 26–27

banning weapons will not re-
    move, 10–11
commercial expansion, 27
disparity between rich and
    poor, 12, 114
governmental glorification of
    war, 175
nationalism, 27, 120, 121, 169,
    170
political, 169, 170
prejudices, 168–73
racial distinctions, 27, 121, 169,
    170
religious dogma and imitation,
    13, 27, 75, 95, 129, 169, 170
territorial conquest, 27
thoughts of war bring destruc-
    tion, 215
Crusades, 123–24
futility of, 172–73
    men fight for tombs, 26, 119,
        121
    no victory worth consequent
        evils, 172
glorification of, 27
    by governments, 175
    immaturity of human race ex-
        pressed by, 5
    is satanic, 156
Italo-Turkish, 176, 176 n
justification for, 175
religious, history of, 123–24
results of, 169–70, 172–73
    blood has stained earth, 127
    consumption of men and
        wealth, 159
    destructive, 182
    thoughts of, 215
weapons of, 10, 31–32, 34
    battleships transformed to mer-
        chant vessels, 179
    burden of expense of, 153, 174,
        175
    contamination of earth by, 31
    convert, into instruments of re-
        construction, 174, 181
    current, compared with an-
        cient, 30, 31–32
    demilitarization, 15, 167
    disarmament, 10, 174–75, 177,
        178–79, 181, 184

new, lead to deadlier ones, 153
Wealth. *See also* Economics; Philanthropy; Poor
absolute equality impossible, 112–13, 117
eternal happiness contingent on giving, 116
is praiseworthy, 109
problems of poverty and, 8–9, 12–13, 109–17
   combine spiritual, moral, and practical approaches to solve, 12, 114
   education of masses to increase wealth, 141
   involve those affected in solving, 114
   love will solve, 116
   moderation, 110, 112, 113
   necessities for everyone, 110, 111
   remedy, with legislation, 111, 113, 116
   spiritual verities of, 12, 114, 116
   twentieth century will solve, 117
   voluntary sharing, 109, 111, 115, 116
station of man unrelated to, 159
use of, to benefit mankind, 109–10
wages and profit sharing, 113–14
Weapons. *See* War, weapons of
Weights and measures, international, 204
West. *See* East (Orient) and West (Occident), uniting of
Will
consultative, 3, 18
determination required for peace, 14, 101
free, 51, 55, 98–100
   choice of good or evil, 98–99
induced by spiritual principles, 15
paralysis of, 11, 36
Wisdom, 157, 187, 189, 191, 227. *See also* Knowledge
Women, 130–39
aptitude and capability of, must be proven, 138

acquire spiritual powers, 139
increase wisdom and holiness, 139
created for men, 131
education of, 14, 135, 136
   necessity of, 14
same as man, 134, 136
equality of men and, 13–14, 130–39
   century for, 131–32
   declaration of, inspires hope, 133
   lack of opportunity and education have prevented, 132, 134, 135, 136
   necessary for human progress, 133, 134
   necessary for peace, 13
   servants and handmaidens regarded on same plane, 131
   two hands, 134
   two wings of bird, 134
first educators of mankind are, 136
greater importance of, to race, 136
qualities of, 137
   able to govern in danger and crisis, 136
   moral courage, 136
   will permeate civilization, 137–38
   wisdom and holiness, 139
war will be ended by, 137, 139
Word of God, 34. *See also* Bahá'u'lláh, revelation of; Bahá'u'lláh, teachings of; Bible; God; Qu'rán
literal interpretation of, 74
Work. *See also* Wealth
labor and capital interdependent, 17
wages and profit sharing, 113–14
World. *See* Earth
World citizenship, 13, 17, 45, 121, 185. *See also* Nations, oneness and interdependence of
of Bahá'ís, 225
importance of teaching, 14, 147
transmute nationalism into consciousness of, 203

World civilization, 15–17, 46–47,
    165–67, 250. *See also* Civili-
    zation; Day; Government;
    Peace; Unity
  bases of
    Bahá'u'lláh's revelation, 121,
      250
    force made servant of justice,
      205
    justice, 186, 188, 205
    material progress combined
      with spiritual, 32–35, 156,
      211, 232, 235–36
    reward and punishment, 186,
      188
    spiritual principles, 14–15
    spiritual virtues, 165. *See also*
      Character and conduct
    unity and concord, 213. *See
      also* Peace; Unity
    unity of world of man with
      God, 36
  descriptions of ultimate, 41, 167,
    183, 202–05, 250–51. *See also*
    Most Great Peace
    Abhá Paradise, 166, 166n
    future is radiant, 46
    Golden Age, 46
    Great Age, 47
    masculine and feminine ele-
      ments in balance, 137–38
    mirror world of God, 165
    new social form, 116
    time of the end, 47
  establishment of
    binding treaty or framework,
      11, 18–19, 176, 177, 178,
      183–84
    convoke meeting for, 17–18,
      180–81, 183
    fiery ordeal will bring, 47
    inevitable, 167
    through power of God, 167

  present-day order rolled up and
    new one spread, 41
  reverses and setbacks in, 48
  struggle for, like birth of uni-
    fied nations of West, 47–48
  suffering required for, 35, 46
  translate thoughts into action,
    98–101
  religion in, 32, 205
  structure and administration of,
    16, 17, 183–84, 200–05
    armaments limited, 184
    commonwealth, union, or su-
      perstate, 17, 18, 36, 205
    economics, 17, 202, 204–05
    excessive centralization avoid-
      ed, 16, 121
    intercommunications will link,
      204
    national boundaries marked,
      18–19, 178, 183
    national interests subordinated
      to international, 16–17, 121,
      185, 202
    oneness of mankind embodied
      in, 15–16
    police or executive force, 17,
      184, 204
    resources controlled, 205
    scientific advances make possi-
      ble, 4
    single code of law, 17, 202–03
    Supreme Tribunal or World
      Council, 17, 183, 200–02, 204
    united attack against aggressor,
      180, 181, 184, 201
    unified yet diverse, 121, 167
    world metropolis, 204

Zend-Avesta, 241
Zion, 239
Zoroaster, 91
  Sacred Fire of, 237n